In the secular polity that we know as India, there is one religion that has always reigned supreme—Cricket. From its fledgling days in the Thirties, through the decades till the present time, cricket has captured the imagination and heart of millions of Indians, more so than any other sport. From outstanding batsmen to sensational bowlers and fielders, Indian cricket has seen them all.

Exceptional batsmen like C.K. Nayudu, Lala Amarnath, Vijay Merchant, Vijay Hazare, Syed Mushtaq Ali, Polly Umrigar, Vijay Manjrekar and the Nawab of Pataudi defied the odds and came up with great performances that attracted attention all over the cricketing world. Indian cricket has come far from the days of its infancy, as the batsmen of the Seventies, Eighties and Nineties have become the cynosure wherever the game is played. And after all these years we now have a player who is widely acknowledged as the world's best batsman.

This book captures the exploits of twenty of the greatest Indian batsmen—from Nayudu, the trendsetter in the Thirties to the explosive batting skills of Sehwag in the new millennium. Little known facts, interesting anecdotes, and a faithful retelling of their great deeds mark the book that is virtually a panorama on Indian batsmanship over the last seventy-five years.

A sports journalist for thirty-seven years, Partab Ramchand has specialised in cricket writing. He has worked for the *Indian Express*, *Sportsworld* magazine, Clickcricket.com and Cricinfo. He has covered the World Cup in February-March 1996 in Sri Lanka as also the Singer Cup tournament in Colombo in August-September 1996, both for the *Indian Express*, and the inaugural Test match between India and Bangladesh at Dhaka in 2000 for Cricinfo.

Besides authoring several books on cricket, he has compered sports progra
programmes

# GREAT
# INDIAN BATSMEN

Partab Ramchand

*Rupa & Co*

Copyright © Partab Ramchand 2005

Published 2005 by
Rupa . Co
7/16, Ansari Road, Daryaganj,
New Delhi 110 002

*Sales Centres:*

Allahabad Bangalore Chandigarh
Chennai Hyderabad Jaipur Kathmandu
Kolkata Mumbai Pune

The Publishers would like to thank Kamal Julka
for providing some of the photographs used in the book.

Typeset in 12 pt. Garamond by
Nikita Overseas Pvt Ltd
1410 Chiranjiv Tower,
43 Nehru Place
New Delhi 110 019

Printed in India by
Saurabh Printers Pvt Ltd,
A-16, Sector-IV,
Noida 201 301

# CONTENTS

# PREFACE

I find that I have almost always been swimming upstream in my projects over the last thirty years. This going against the tide started with my second book *Great Moments in Indian Cricket* published in 1976 where I had to choose the ten greatest Test matches among the 144 played till then. In my next venture *Great Indian Cricketers* published in 1979 I had to pick 21 out of 143 players who had represented the country till then. In 1984 came *Great Feats of Indian Cricket* and I had to restrict myself to nine out of numerous exceptional performances. Recently for a project that was translated into Tamil my publishers wanted me to select 15 of the most memorable Tests India had been involved in – out of over 380 matches! And for this book I had to keep the figure down to 20.

Given the fact that India has produced a number of outstanding batsmen it wasn't an easy task. Of course, while most picked themselves it was the last three or four borderline cases that presented me with the most difficulty. I can now honestly admit that while 17 selected themselves, I was in a quandary as to who to include among Lala Amarnath, Chandu Borde, Navjot Sidhu and Dilip Sardesai. Most reluctantly I had to leave out Sardesai. How I wish the figure agreed upon could be the odd figure of 21 instead of the even figure of 20! Believe me it was a most difficult decision. And having decided to include only Test players Prof D.B. Deodhar was another who had to be excluded. His career would otherwise have constituted the first chapter of the book.

A disturbing trend I have noticed is that today's generation of cricket lovers seem content to know about contemporary players. Certainly their knowledge of the past greats is very limited. This is borne out through my interaction with several hardcore cricket enthusiasts as also by a number of polls conducted by various publications. The questions pertaining to the greatest Indian team, greatest batsmen, greatest bowlers, greatest all rounders and so on invariably have only cricketers stretching back at most to the Seventies. Today's generation of cricket lovers have been brought up on television and DVD's, and because there is so little footage of cricket played from the Thirties to the Sixties the younger followers of the game are quite ignorant of the great feats performed by C.K. Nayudu and Lala Amarnath, Vijay Merchant and Mushtaq Ali, Vijay Hazare and Vijay Manjrekar, Polly Umrigar and the Nawab of Pataudi. I am only mentioning batsmen since this is a book on great Indian batsmen but their ignorance of Mohammed Nissar, Amar Singh, Vinoo Mankad, Ghulam Ahmed and Subash Gupte is as appalling.

Reading, unfortunately, is a vanishing habit. In my youth in the Fifties and Sixties we were brought up on books from where we got to know about the exploits of great cricketers of previous years. I remember avidly reading about Trumper and Hobbs, Hammond and Hutton, O'Reilly and Grimmett, Nayudu and Merchant and going through books written by Neville Cardus, Ray Robinson, R.C. Robertson Glasgow, A.A. Thomson and Berry Sarbhadhikari. Little wonder then there is this tendency by today's generation of cricket lovers to belittle or dismiss the facts, figures and statistics associated with cricketers of a bygone era.

I think it is here that writers and historians closely associated with the game over an extended period have a role to play in educating today's cricket followers about the stand out performances that the heroes of yore notched up and I can only hope that this book achieves the objective. While on the subject I may mention that the Phoenix XI – the greatest ever Indian team selected in 2002 by a panel of 20 professional cricket writers, young and old had a balanced look where every outstanding player from the Thirties to the Nineties was represented.

It's easy for the followers of the game today – particularly the young and the uninitiated – to point out that the Test average of Nayudu was

25 and Mushtaq Ali 32 while Tendulkar and Dravid average well over 55. These enthusiasts should be informed that it is never easy to represent a country in its formative years. The dice is frequently loaded against them and more often than not the players – both batsmen and bowlers I must add – are fighting a losing battle against far more experienced sides who also have better players. I have always had a high regard for the older cricketers who had to swim upstream and epitomise courage in adversity while, of course, I retain my admiration for today's cricketers. From the Thirties to the Sixties when Indian teams suffered one setback after another, went from one defeat to another with very few victories to show for all their efforts, the country was fortunate to have players like C.K. Nayudu, Lala Amarnath, Vijay Merchant, Vijay Hazare, Mushtaq Ali, Polly Umrigar, Vijay Manjrekar and the Nawab of Pataudi who defied the odds and came up with great performances that attracted attention all over the cricketing world.

Then came the major turning point in Indian cricket – the India Rubber Year of 1971 when the team won contests in West Indies and England for the first time, and a certain Sunil Manohar Gavaskar made his presence in no uncertain terms. Since then Indian cricket has gone from strength to strength and the batsmen of the Seventies, Eighties and Nineties have been the cynosure wherever the game has been played. They have displayed the skill and artistry traditionally associated with batsmen from the subcontinent as also technical excellence, an ideal temperament and the important qualities of courage, dedication, determination and concentration. And after all these years we now have a player who is widely acknowledged as the world's best batsman. It's about time! But the deeds of Sachin Tendulkar and company should not in any way dim the lustre surrounding the feats of Nayudu and his contemporaries. To cite just one example – though it is certainly not an isolated one – Vijay Hazare's hundred in each innings in a losing cause against Lindwall and Miller at Adelaide in 1948 is as great a feat as anything notched up by Tendulkar and Dravid, Laxman and Sehwag.

A word about the approach adopted in compiling the book. I have followed the chronological order so that hopefully it will be easy for the reader to start with the Thirties and continue till the new millennium.

That way the reader can get an idea about how Indian batsmanship has evolved over the years. In general I have opted for a straightforward narrative style wherein my attempt has been to record a batsman's career from start to finish. Only while recounting the careers of Gavaskar and Tendulkar have I made an exception. This is primarily because if I had followed the same narrative pattern, the chapters on the two Greats would have far exceeded the word limit the publishers and I have tried to maintain for each chapter. Safely assuming that the reader knows more than enough about the outstanding feats notched up by these two cricketers – surely the greatest batsmen Indian cricket has produced – I have tried to give fleeting glimpses of their great moments in their epoch-making careers. It will be also noticed that I have not neglected figures. As a cricket statistician of sorts myself, I realise the importance of facts and figures to back a player's records and have made liberal use of them.

I have touched upon any other aspect of a player – his fielding, his captaincy, his personality, any controversies he might have been involved in – only fleetingly. The chief focus has been on his capabilities as a batsman, what has made him great and his immense contribution in this field to the country. I must mention here that readers who look for something sensational, gossipy or juicy will be disappointed. This is not a book for that kind of readership. I have just recounted the exploits of the batsmen in simple, straightforward style. My mind goes back to a brief telephone conversation I had with S.K. Gurunathan, then sports editor of *The Hindu*, in 1965. I was then still at school and interested in cricket writing. When I rang him up for advice, he told me in the course of that conversation that I should try and keep the language as simple and straightforward as I could for 'you must keep in mind that what you are writing might be read by the common man'. I have tried to follow that advice in all my books and have never had any cause to regret it.

Partab Ramchand
Chennai
February 2005

# 1

# Cottari Kankaiya **Nayudu**

The Pioneer, the Trendsetter, the Path-breaker

Almost as inevitably as the sun rises in the east, any book on great Indian batsmen will have to begin with Cottari Kankaiya Nayudu. He was the pioneer, the standard bearer, the man who set the trend for other Indian cricketers to follow. He remains the yardstick by which future generations of batsmen have been judged. One has only to go through the marvellous tributes that have been paid to him to realise the full impact that Nayudu has had on Indian cricket – and indeed international cricket. 'You have only to see him pick up a ball and throw it like lightning to know that he is a born cricketer,' said Jack Hobbs. C.B. Fry hailed him as 'one of the finest living cricketers, a splendid athlete, an artist and a great performer'. Neville Cardus: 'He has no style yet he is all style'. Peter Foenander of Sri Lanka: 'He is my beau ideal of a cricketer. As a stylist and fast scorer, not a mere slogger he is comparable with cricketers like Charlie McCartney and Wally Hammond.' J.M. Kilburn on Nayudu's batting for Indians against Yorkshire: 'Only when he was batting did the wizardry of Bowes' swing bowling disappear and the demon of Verity's spin vanish from our conscience.' J.W. Weigall, another critic wrote: 'He showed the crowd that Woolley was not the only who could hit.' Even the stern and taciturn Douglas Jardine was moved to say that 'at the wicket he is comparable to a right-handed Woolley. Both remain masters of every shot the game knows.' When CK died in November 1967, the Indian Cricket almanac from Madras carried a fairly long appreciation by a man who knew him personally – V. Pattabhiraman – and also carried a photograph inscribed with just two words: India's Greatest. And that's exactly what Nayudu was.

There is a certain aura, a certain halo about the Nayudu name that has not diminished one bit over the years. A dynamic personality, he had everything – elegance, charm, style – and not just in his cricket. 'Leave alone his batting,' Mushtaq Ali, his Holkar colleague and close friend for many years told me some three decades ago. 'It was a pleasure even to see him walk.' And one must remember that Mushtaq himself was a great crowd puller, who combined the aesthetic and adventurous aspects of the game in his play. But he was the first to admit that he could not be compared to Nayudu, his guru. And whenever the tall, lissome figure of Nayudu made his way to the crease you could be sure that he would carry all that grace into his play.

'CK' as he was popularly known, was THE great figure of the early days, the first Indian cricketer to receive the kind of international acclaim that seemed reserved for Englishmen and Australians. Even today some seventy-five years after his peak period and more than thirty-seven years after his death, Nayudu is one cricketer to be held in awe. Over the last six decades and more many outstanding batsmen have donned India colours and some of them have gone on to become all-time greats. But the advent of these players has not meant the displacement of Nayudu from the greatest Indian XI. Almost every such dream team – from the players' angle, the experts' angle or the fans' angle – will have Nayudu in it. When Vijay Hazare passed away towards the last days of 2004, Raj Singh Dungarpur, a former chairman of the selection committee, a former president of the Board of Control for Cricket in India, a former first-class cricketer, and above all a well informed follower of the game who has followed the nuances and the players closely over the last sixty years and more, in his tribute to Hazare said that he was one of the five greatest Indian batsmen. The other four according to Dungarpur were Nayudu, Merchant, Gavaskar and Tendulkar. It is a choice that few discerning cricket fans will argue with. Indeed, even the younger generation, brought upon Gavaskar and Tendulkar, never tire of reading about Nayudu or hearing about his outstanding deeds.

Nayudu was born in Nagpur on October 31, 1895. Astonishingly, for those who know Nayudu as the attacking genius and a sixer-hitter, it may come as a surprise to know that when he started out in the game, he was a plodder, a bore to watch. The big change came about when Ranji, who happened to be a friend of Nayudu's father from their undergraduate days at Cambridge, was amazed that a boy with such obvious gifts – height, reach, quickfootedness – should be so lacking in enterprise in his batting approach. He wondered why the young CK would not hit the ball, whereupon under the elder Nayudu's guidance CK transformed himself into an attacking cricketer.

Not only did he change his approach to the game, Nayudu, a natural athlete, now took to a strenuous regime of physical fitness. And by 1916 he was good enough to be invited to play for the Hindus in the Quadrangular tournament at Bombay. From then on every year whether the Hindus won or not, Nayudu was usually the top scorer. More important, he was developing into a crowd puller, the like of which had not been seen in the game in this country. Spectators came to see him batting and little else. The tall, erect player with the graceful walk, military bearing and steely wrists had the crowds anticipating a big score – with plenty of big hits thrown in – every time. And Nayudu, more often than not, did not disappoint. Opposition bowlers knew they had to get Nayudu out if they wanted to beat the Hindus, and applied all the pressure and tried all their tricks. But Nayudu had an answer to everything they could throw up.

In the Twenties Nayudu's pyrotechnic batting skills meant that he was the most talked about cricketer in the land. He had in fact ceased to be a great Hindu batsman. Before him, there was the great Parsee batsman and the great Muslim bowler. Nayudu was by now established as the first great Indian cricketer with a rapport with the crowd that was second to none. His was a household name, known through the length and breadth of the country. And thanks to one innings played in the closing days of 1926, he was soon to become a name outside the country too. In scoring 153 in 116 minutes for the Hindu XI against Arthur Gilligan's MCC side at Bombay in 1926-27 Nayudu hit 11 sixes. And the attack included Maurice Tate and George Geary. A break up of the remarkable innings showed that he took 16 scoring strokes to reach his first 50 with four sixes and five fours; 17 strokes to reach his second 50 with three sixes and five fours; and 16 strokes for his final

50 with four sixes and four fours. Totally, there were 49 scoring strokes with 11 sixes and 14 fours which provided him 122 of the 153 runs. Nayudu had established a world record for most number of sixes in an innings – a figure unsurpassed till John Reid hit 15 sixes in an innings of 296 for Wellington in 1962-63. Even today, nearly eighty years later, it still remains one of the most talked about batting feats in Indian cricket.

In a way, it does seem ironic to mention so many statistics while discussing that unforgettable knock because Nayudu never really did care for facts and figures. Writing in the inaugural issue of the Indian cricket almanac in 1947, he summed up his approach to the game succinctly when he noted: 'Our age is an age of business and cricket has not escaped the fatal touch of commercialism. There is a tendency to regard statistics as the best indication of a player's ability. This has led to the emergence of a school of stonewallers. Cricket must be played in harmony with its inherent genius with wild and free abandon. Let our players attack the bowlers and provide spectators with a feast of strokeplay. If cricket, like life is full of uncertainties, why make it a dull affair?'

Nayudu's reputation as a cricketer and entertainer, following that glorious knock, now skyrocketed. Moreover, by example he had shown that Indian cricketers were refreshingly different. As Nayudu proved, they had to innovate strokes, not go by the textbook alone. He himself observed once: 'India can ill afford to neglect this style of batting since her Oriental genius is noted for being venturesome and having a greater repertoire of shots than are mentioned in the textbooks. Indians can never regard themselves as cricketers if they are not brilliant.' One of his first pupils was the young Mushtaq Ali, and of course since then there have been many others directly descended from the Nayudu school of batting. But Nayudu, as I said, has remained the pioneer, the trendsetter and the path-breaker.

In 1930, the Maharajkumar of Vizianagaram persuaded Jack Hobbs and Herbert Sutcliffe to visit India. The two were very keen on seeing Nayudu, of whom they had by now heard so much. Nayudu played alongside the two legends of world cricket for Vizzy's team, and Hobbs and Sutcliffe were duly impressed by Nayudu's style and approach. 'You have only to see him pick up a ball and throw it like lightning to know that he is a born cricketer,' said Hobbs.

When Nayudu went to England in 1932 as a member of the first official Indian team, he found himself being hailed as the 'Indian Bradman' thanks to his exploits back home. He did not let the seamy atmosphere associated with the tour – groupism and parochialism – affect his batting. His performances on the tour were so striking that Wisden chose him as one of the five cricketers of the year in 1933. Even under extreme stress, Nayudu's batting was free and fearless. Not once did it act as an impediment to his natural attacking style, and by the end of the tour there was little doubt that he had enhanced his lofty reputation. He remained the leading Indian personality. His batting attracted considerable attention and led the greats of the game pay him sincere and handsome tributes. He easily headed the first-class figures with 1618 runs at an average of 40.45 with five centuries.

Moreover, as a batsman, Nayudu was one of the great entertainers of the day. When he was batting, very rarely was there the dull thud that generally accompanies the defensive shot. For him, the ball was there to be hit – and to be hit hard, high and far. He specialised in hitting sixes, and in this he was a gay cavalier in the swashbuckling tradition of a Jessop or a Constantine. On the 1932 tour, Nayudu hit 36 sixes which was just behind Constantine's 37 sixes struck on the first West Indian tour of England in 1928 as the most number of sixes struck in an English season by a touring batsman. An English critic described one particular hit as 'the ball was last seen sailing in an easterly direction'. For all his big hitting, Nayudu was no slogger as such. His dizzy rate of scoring did not mean that he was going to abandon the scientific aspects of cricket, upon which his game was built anyway. Each stroke was made with artistry, each was properly chosen for the ball it had to meet. Nayudu turned the art of big hitting into an exact science. No batsman in Indian cricket is more associated with big hits and sixes.

Nayudu's greatness also lay in his adaptability to situations. Being a naturally attacking batsman it was thought it would be difficult for Nayudu to alter his approach when it came to saving a match through defensive batting. But he displayed this facet of his batsmanship against

England at Calcutta in 1933-34. India were forced to follow on 156 runs behind and the batsmen were given clear orders to dig in. Setting the perfect example was the captain himself. The Eden Gardens crowd watched a totally new Nayudu in 'action'. It must have been difficult for a player of his natural ability to avoid strokes. But he unselfishly eschewed all risks for the sake of the side and played each ball dutifully at his feet. Coming in at 58 for two, Nayudu batted two and three quarter hours for 38 and by the time he was sixth out at 149, India were well on their way to staving off defeat – which they did.

Courage was one quality that Nayudu had in abundance. Aware of his reputation as the outstanding player for a team that was 'the babes of international cricket', he knew he had to lead by example and never shirked his responsibility. The apotheosis of this was seen in the final Test at the Oval in 1936 when he was in his forty-first year. In fact almost everything else, during his long and illustrious career, pales into insignificance when placed alongside this knock. It proved to be his last Test innings and Nayudu, probably sensing it, made it a memorable one.

India were following on, 249 runs behind. Nayudu entered after four wickets had gone down for 159 to join the obdurate Dilawar Hussain. Gubby Allen, the England captain was having a great series. He could be awkwardly quick on his day and tested Nayudu with a few bouncers. Undaunted, Nayudu hooked a couple of them to the fence, determined to take on Allen and Voce headlong. Allen then hurtled down an ultra-fast short delivery, which caught Nayudu unawares. He was hit in the region of the heart with a sickening thud that could be heard all round the ground. Dropping his bat, Nayudu held his chest and walked around a bit. He was obviously in great pain. Even as Dilawar and some of the fieldsmen converged upon him anxiously, he bent over in agony, seemingly unable to breathe. Then suddenly, he stood erect, waved them all away and motioned for play to continue. He refused to leave the crease and prepared to face the next ball. Allen sent down another short delivery that must have scarcely been slower than the previous one. Nayudu promptly hooked it to the ropes!

That was a typical Nayudu retort. He continued to bat with grace and power. Thrilling pulls, daring hooks and handsome drives flowed from his bat in gay profusion. He got to his 50 and saw his team avert the innings defeat. Nayudu was finally seventh out at 295 after making 81 in about two and a half hours. His innings was the apotheosis of courage, a fitting swan song to one of the most dynamic cricketers of his era. In an otherwise gloomy tour, his bravery at the Oval shone brightly. Mushtaq Ali paid the ultimate tribute to his mentor when he wrote in *Cricket Delightful* that 'My association with C.K. Nayudu goes back to 1926. I have seen him play many a grand innings but to me his 81 in the Oval Test following his injury was by far the most spectacular and courageous. One great feature of Nayudu's temperament was that whenever he was injured badly he batted more heroically defying all medical advice.' This was so much in keeping with the man's image and approach.

By the Forties his international career was over but there was no way Nayudu could give up cricket completely. And thanks to the formation of the Holkar Cricket Association, he was about to start his second innings in the game, which was no less illustrious than the first. Moreover, he was out to prove that he was still agile enough to have a long and glorious first-class career, that age was no barrier for a fit sportsperson. He was now a father figure in Indian cricket, and spent the remaining phase of his career in helping Holkar to repeated triumphs in the Ranji Trophy and passing on the benefits of his vast experience to younger players who would go on to play for the country. He also continued to score hundreds and in the 1945-46 final against a strong Baroda side, Nayudu, just past his own half century, summoned up the skill and stamina to hit a double century! His 200 compiled in six and a half hours, included 20 hits to the ropes. He followed this up with 50 in the second innings. Preceding this, Nayudu had hit 101 against Mysore in the semifinal. Has India produced a fitter cricketer, one really wonders?

In 1953, Nayudu retired from the services of His Highness Maharajah of Holkar, but that did not mean an end to his cricketing career. After all he was not even sixty yet! He switched over to Uttar Pradesh and in 1956-57 at the age of sixty-one led them in the national championship. In the match against Rajasthan that season he scored 84 and in the process, lifted Mankad, then at the peak of his powers and twenty-two years his junior, for sixes off successive balls before he was run out. Then in the quarterfinal against Bombay, who were champions that year, he scored 52 in the second innings when his side was facing an innings defeat. Dicky Rutnagar was moved to write: 'Nayudu gave the younger members of his team another lesson in how to face accurate bowling. His runs were made in so superb a manner that but for his grey hair, a slightly receded forehead and the missing moustache, one could never have told the CK of 1957 from the batsman we knew in the Thirties. That old cocksureness, the panther like leap to the pitch of the ball – they were still all there.'

But then Nayudu was as doughty as he was daring. In the Ranji Trophy final in 1951-52 against Bombay, Nayudu in his fifty-seventh year was taking on the pace of Dattu Phadkar with a degree of comfort. Phadkar, then twenty-six and very much the spearhead of the Indian attack unleashed a short one that struck Nayudu in the mouth. Two front teeth were broken and he was bleeding profusely. But he simply refused all suggestions for medical assistance. He just brushed aside the broken pieces of his teeth lying on the pitch in front of him and prepared to face the next ball. Phadkar, perhaps more shaken by the incident than Nayudu, then sent down a delivery that was considerably slower. Nayudu, sensing the situation, told Madhav Mantri, the Bombay skipper, 'Tell Dattu not to let up. I am perfectly okay.' He continued his innings till Mankad bowled him for 66.

The 1956-57 season was his last in the Ranji Trophy. One thought at sixty-one, Nayudu's first-class career was finally over. But he had to have one last fling – at the age of sixty-eight! In 1963 there were a series of National Defence Fund matches in the wake of the Chinese aggression. Nayudu willingly played in one of them in his hometown of Nagpur, scoring ten not out and one. Playing along with him in the match were Ramakant Desai, Budhi Kunderan, Polly Umrigar, Nawab of Pataudi (Jr), Chandu Borde, Abbas Ali Baig, Ajit Wadekar and the Mankads, Vinoo and Ashok. Nayudu had more than bridged the generation gap! With that, the curtain finally came down on Nayudu's illustrious career. He had played first-class cricket in six decades – probably the only cricketer to do so.

Nayudu was the recipient of the Padma Bhushan in 1955. His services to the cause of Indian cricket have never been equalled. They probably never will be. Even young cricket followers, whose grandfathers were contemporaries of Nayudu and who were born after the great man breathed his last, have no hesitation in naming Nayudu as one of their first choices in an all-time Indian XI. That is perhaps the ultimate tribute to Cottari Kankaiya Nayudu.

# 2

# Nanik Bharadwaj **Amarnath**

### 'The Byron of Indian Cricket'

If C.K. Nayudu is one cricketer who should not be judged on statistics alone, the same argument could be advanced to underscore the greatness of Lala Amarnath as a batsman. As a splendid all-rounder, shrewd captain and multi-faceted personality, Nanik Bharadwaj Amarnath later titled as the more familiarly known Lala takes his place among the outstanding Indian cricketers of all time. Colourful and controversial, he possessed a touch of flair in whatever he did. After all, did not Don Bradman write in *Farewell to Cricket* that 'I look back on the season with Amarnath as my opposite number as one of my most pleasant cricket years. Amarnath was such a pleasant ambassador and throughout the tour I found him absolutely charming in every respect.'

But the fact remains that Amarnath also takes his place firmly in the top Indian batsmen on the basis of his dare devilry, attacking skills and breathless stroke play. As veteran journalist P.N. Sundaresan, cricket correspondent for *The Hindu* in the Sixties and Seventies, wrote in his introduction to his book *Not so Unofficial* that dealt with the unofficial Test matches that India played: 'For cricket lovers of my generation, our great hero was Amarnath.' Sundaresan was just a few years younger than Amarnath. But there is little doubt that over the years Amarnath bridged the generation gap many times over and was a hero to a much younger generation of cricket followers. Such was the personal charisma, the dynamic personality of the man. As a batsman, he was once described as 'a pure romantic, the Byron of Indian cricket'. I feel that among all descriptions, this says it best. Amarnath was a true product of the Nayudu school, for he too eschewed defence as far as possible and preferred carrying the fight to the enemy camp as it were, sometimes darting yards out to take the bowler on the full and dispatch the ball to the untenanted parts of the ground. At times, in fact, he overdid the bravado and his confidence had a touch of arrogance. All the same for the sheer razzle dazzle of his batting Amarnath had few equals.

Though Amarnath in anyone's book would be classified as a genuine all-rounder, by the same yardstick there is little doubt that he achieved outstanding feats more with the bat than with the ball. Born in Lahore in 1911, Amarnath played for the Hindus in the Quadrangular and made his mark early as befitting a player of his talent, skill and temperament. After seeing Amarnath making a scintillating 109 for Southern Punjab against Douglas Jardine's MCC squad in 1933-34, Alec Hosie, one of the selectors, hailed Amarnath as the 'Bradman of India'.

Not unexpectedly, when the team for the first Test at Bombay was announced, Amarnath was a popular inclusion. And he wasted little time in making his mark on the international scene by achieving a double distinction. He was the first Indian to get a Test century and the first to get one on his debut. A modest 38 – top score it might be added – in the first innings was just the prelude to a colourful display of pyrotechnics in the second. As Mushtaq Ali, who was one of the reserves in the match recalls: 'In daring and audacity, it was incomparable with any other innings I have seen him play. It was indeed one of the grandest Test hundreds I have seen by anyone anywhere.'

Amarnath went in at number three and faced a deficit of 219 runs, India having lost both the openers to 'Nobby' Clark for 21 runs. Despite the dire situation that his side was in, Amarnath straightaway went for the bowling. It was an approach typical of the man. He batted in such daring fashion that Jardine soon dispensed with his close-set field and spread them around the outfield like a man opening his umbrella in the face of a sudden shower. And on the Bombay Gymkhana ground that memorable December day, there were a shower of runs flowing in gay profusion from Amarnath's bat. Even the great C.K. Nayudu, no slouch when it came to attacking batsmanship, just seemed to stand by and watch from the other end as the hot-blooded youth made Clark,

Morris Nichols, Hedley Verity and James Langridge look no better than the club bowlers he faced in local Punjab cricket. From various close-in positions, Jardine could only watch the fireworks in awe.

The story goes that Nayudu on joining Amarnath whispered something in his ear. It was always Nayudu's contention that Indian batsmen should go for their strokes, should be naturally attacking players. Evidently he saw in Amarnath a kindred spirit who was destined to achieve greatness. In any event Amarnath playing brilliantly all round the wicket simply tore the attack apart and raced to 83 in just 78 minutes. It was a new experience for Nayudu to play a secondary role. But he was held spellbound almost as much as the spectators, who were beside themselves with joy as they witnessed Amarnath's bold and effervescent stroke play. The prospect of a historic hundred sobered Amarnath down, but only just. He still got to his century in 117 minutes, encouraged no doubt by Nayudu's timely bit of advice to go a bit easy as he neared his hundred. By stumps Amarnath was 102 and Nayudu 44 and the Indian fightback was well and truly on. As the two batsmen came back to the pavilion, amazing scenes were witnessed. The spectators swarmed on to the pitch. Amarnath was engulfed, garlanded and congratulated even as women tore off their jewellery to present it to him. The Maharajas gave Amarnath money and other expensive gifts and the nation proclaimed a cricketing hero.

Nayudu and Amarnath resumed on the final morning with India having a fighting chance of saving the game. The two presented an interesting contrast, for at thirty-eight Nayudu was very much the big name of the day while Amarnath at twenty-two was the fast rising young star. They added 186 runs for the third wicket before Nayudu was out for 67. A run later Amarnath played a full-blooded hook shot off Clark but Nichols brought off a splendid catch. For his 118 Amarnath batted three and a half hours. A high proportion of his runs – 84 – came from boundary hits and symbolised his aggressive approach.

It became immediately obvious that Amarnath was one of the batting rocks around which the Indian batting of the future would be built. Indeed, the jaunty young man with the toothy grin and an engaging personality seemed to symbolise the bright future of Indian cricket, and the experts wrote in glowing terms of his dazzling batsmanship. E.H.D. Sewell who had watched all the cricketing nations of the Empire over the past few years, said of Amarnath: 'I class him above the Nawab of Pataudi and the equal of Duleep at the beginning of their first-class careers.' Indeed, Amarnath in some circles was already being compared to the other prodigiously gifted young batsman in international cricket – George Headley of the West Indies. He was the subject of heady praise, but somehow it was felt that Amarnath would not let all this – as well as the early success – go to his head.

And yet after a cursory glance at his final Test figures one is tempted to have serious doubts as to whether Amarnath's record entitles him to join the pantheons of the Greats. On the face of it such a modest statistical record hardly measures up to all the rhetoric praise showered on Amarnath at the start of his career. But one must analyse Amarnath's career closely to get a true picture. In the first place it must not be forgotten that Amarnath was a genuine all-rounder capable of picking up 45 wickets at 32.91 apiece. Secondly, he lost ten years because of the Second World War and this was the period when he was at his peak, proof of this being his scintillating batting against Jack Ryder's Australian team in 1935-36 and against Lord Tennyson's English team two years later. Third, his brushes with authority – thanks to his outspoken nature – meant that he missed quite a few matches, including two full rubbers against the two Commonwealth sides in 1949-50 and in the following year.

Most crucial, however, was the treatment meted out to Amarnath on the tour of England in 1936. At twenty-four, he was confidence personified as he embarked on the trip. And in the first five weeks of the tour he lived up to his reputation as one of India's brightest young stars, scoring 613 runs including three hundreds – two of them in the same match against Essex and picking up 32 wickets. And then, as everyone associated with Indian cricket history is aware, his triumphant run was suddenly halted. Amarnath was sent back home as a disciplinary measure for reasons that need no re-telling here. A crestfallen Amarnath, during the long and lonely journey back to India, said he would never play cricket again and would take to tennis. Of course, no one took him at his word. The Beaumont committee of inquiry into the sordid events of the 1936 tour exonerated Amarnath terming the decision to send him back 'stern', and he was back in the Indian side that played against Lord Tennyson's team scoring a scintillating 123 to boot in the third 'Test' at Calcutta.

Throughout the War years, Amarnath put up a sterling show in the Pentangular and Ranji Trophy tournaments. By 1945, when it was time for the resumption of international cricket, Amarnath was not only one of the leading players in the land, he was an outstanding personality. He was always news. On and off the field he unwittingly or otherwise made sure that he was always in the public eye. He made brilliant centuries, bowled like no one else in his time, fielded in a facile manner that belied his build and led his teams as shrewdly and wisely as only he could. This was all on the field. Off it, he was involved in countless scraps with officialdom, fighting for more freedom, better facilities and bulkier pay packets. He was the most outspoken player of his time – this was later seen in his comments in newspapers or on radio and TV – and cared 'two hoots' for administrators. Oh yes, Lala was a character. You liked him because he was open and candid. Or you disliked him because he was blunt and rude. But one thing was sure: you could never ignore him. Amarnath wouldn't have liked that!

When India toured England in 1946, there was a perceptible change in the team composition and this had a profound effect on Amarnath's future. The batting manned by the likes of Vijay Merchant, Mushtaq Ali, Rusi Modi, Vijay Hazare and Vinoo Mankad was in capable hands though Amarnath frequently came good with the bat when it mattered. But in the absence of the old firm of Mohammed Nissar and Amar Singh, the bowling wore a rather emaciated look. Mankad had quickly established himself as the leading left arm spin bowler in the world. But there was really no support, and Amarnath from playing a secondary role in the pre-War years was now suddenly a frontline bowler. Indeed, Mankad and Amarnath were India's outstanding bowlers in the three match series against England, and his lone batting success was a rumbustious 50 in the first Test at Lord's. Coming in at number eight he made merry against the bowling of Alec Bedser and Doug Wright, getting his runs out of 78 scored while he was at the crease.

One did not associate Amarnath with big scores, given his electrifying approach to batting. But during the 1946-47 season he made his highest first-class score – 262 for India-in-England against Rest of India at Calcutta, clear proof that he had the twin powers of determination and concentration to play a long innings, even if he was basically an attacking batsman. In the process, he shared a 410-run stand for the third wicket with Modi, an Indian record for any wicket at the time.

It was thus with a degree of confidence that he embarked on the tour of Australia in 1947-48. But circumstances again militated his contribution with the bat. The withdrawal of Merchant, Modi and Mushtaq Ali from the team due to various reasons meant that he had to shoulder a lot of responsibility. In addition, he and Mankad remained the two frontline bowlers and Merchant's withdrawal had elevated Amarnath to the captaincy. Outside the Tests he was simply amazing, reeling off centuries in the State games. In the Tests, however, he was restricted to just 140 runs from ten innings – figures not at all in keeping with his reputation. As Bradman observed in *Farewell to Cricket* when analysing Amarnath's failure: 'Perhaps the responsibility of being captain weighed heavily on Amarnath's shoulders. Whether it did or not one must be accurate and point out that Amarnath trusted his eyesight and natural ability to such an extent that he allowed himself the discretion of hitting against the break and otherwise taking unnecessary risks. This brought about his downfall on numerous occasions.' But then, of course, this was typical of Amarnath who did show brief glimpses of his power and artistry when he belted Ray Lindwall and Keith Miller to all parts of the ground in the fourth Test at Adelaide. Coming in at six for two he hammered his way to 46 out of 63.

Amarnath's inability to produce the form he was capable of in the Tests was particularly puzzling when placed against some of his knocks in the first-class games. Here he was the Amarnath the cricketing world knew and admired. His driving and cutting were particularly delightful, and spectators who only the previous season had seen the genius of Denis Compton were again treated to attacking batsmanship that was based on a keen eye and twinkling footwork. In the second match of the tour against South Australia, Amarnath made 144 in three hours. In the second innings, the Indians were set a target of 287 runs in 180 minutes. They lost half the side for 60 but Vinoo Mankad (116) and Amarnath (94) added 175 runs for the unbroken sixth wicket in well under two hours to bring the touring team to within, in racing parlance, 'a short head' of victory. Amarnath himself just failed to beat the clock for his second century of the match.

In the next match against Victoria, Amarnath proceeded to play one of the greatest innings ever seen at the Melbourne Cricket Ground. Bounding Bill Johnston's destructive left arm saw Mankad, Rangnekar and Hazare all snick matches behind without a run still on the board. Amarnath came in at this ticklish moment. His daring, thrilling strokeplay soon removed the gloom from the Indian camp. His footwork, reflexes and eyesight saw him make strokes that were beyond the reach of most other batsmen. When the innings terminated at 403, Amarnath was unbeaten with 228. Even old timers ranked it as among the most sensational double centuries in MCG's long history.

After failing in one match Amarnath thundered back, and on the eve of the first Test, scored a superb 172 not out against Queensland. Later on the tour he had scores of 171 and 135, and when one considers that he had to share the burden of the bowling with Mankad, the true value of his batting gets magnified several times over. With 1162 runs at an average of 58.10 Amarnath easily headed the tour figures, and this record somewhat camouflaged his dismal run in the Test matches. But, of course, this had to be just a passing phase and in the next season against the West Indies at home, Amarnath was back to somewhere near his best in scoring 294 runs at 36.75 with two half centuries.

In keeping with his bustling nature Amarnath could never say no to a challenge. In the Adelaide Test he had promoted himself in the batting order when India were six for two and led the counter-attack in the face of an Aussie total of 674. A year later, at Bombay, he did pretty much the same thing. Requiring 361 for victory, India were nine for two. Again Amarnath promoted himself and with dazzling strokes on both sides of the wicket retrieved India's hopes. He put the much younger and in-form Modi in the shade, and out of a third wicket partnership of 72 got 39. It was a mini masterpiece, and as an inspiring innings ranks very high for India almost pulled off an unexpected victory finishing with 355 for eight. But then rising to the occasion and accepting a challenge headlong was very much in keeping with the Amarnath image.

Little could anyone have known it then but that little gem at Bombay was Amarnath's last notable innings. Well entrenched as India's captain and still acknowledged as one of the leading players in the country, Amarnath in 1949 was at the height of his power and popularity. Life seemed to be rosy for him, particularly as he had just become the proud father of newborn son Surinder. All of a sudden, there was a loud thunder over the Indian cricket horizon in the form of a serious quarrel between Amarnath and the president of the Indian Cricket Board Anthony de Mello. The undisputed monarch of Indian cricket, de Mello had always thought Amarnath to be 'too independent'. Known to favour Merchant, de Mello was perhaps waiting for a chance to hit back at Amarnath. He got it when Amarnath, in the course of a press interview at Lucknow, made some characteristically pungent remarks against the Board, accusing it, among other things, of 'power politics'.

De Mello was furious. At an extraordinary general meeting of the Board in April, he pushed through a resolution that Amarnath be 'suspended from domestic and representative cricket in India for continuous misbehaviour and breach of discipline'. To substantiate his accusations, de Mello produced a list of some two-dozen acts of indiscipline. Amarnath, never one to be cowed down, hit back and for months the Indian cricket horizon had a seamy outlook. There were threats, damage suits, hand-outs, press conferences, statements, counter-statements, the lot − as only to be expected when the 'warring' parties happen to be the Board president and the Indian captain. An uneasy compromise was reached and the ripples were felt for long, but it is worth recalling that noted cricket writer Berry Sarbhadhikary, who probably knew the inside stories of Indian cricket more accurately than most, came to the conclusion that de Mello was 'rather misguided in denouncing the national captain on grounds which could not hold much water'.

Amarnath was never really the same cricketer after this unhappy episode. First, the captaincy was taken away from him. Secondly, he was not selected to play against both the first Commonwealth team in 1949-50 and the second Commonwealth team the next season. Only after de Mello was ousted from the post in 1951 could Amarnath come back. By the time he was forty and though he still had it in him to make sizeable contributions as a captain and bowler, his batting had seen better days. His last fling with the bat was to make 61 not out in a losing cause against Pakistan at Lucknow in 1952, a month past his forty-first birthday. Coming in at 77 for five with India on their way to an innings defeat, Amarnath in typically belligerent manner did pretty much what he liked with the bowling to remain unconquered.

If his final figures are not in keeping with Amarnath's skill and class, the reasons behind this have already been examined. Amarnath's reputation as one of the great entertainers in the Indian batting hierarchy is secure and unchallenged. The tributes paid to him when he passed away in New Delhi in August 2000 were handsome and sincere. They came from all over the world and were headed by Bradman himself.

# 3

# Vijay Madhavji **Merchant**

Next only to the Don

There are innumerable striking aspects about Vijay Madhavji Merchant's batting, so let's get the most impressive statistic first up. Only Don Bradman with figures of 95.14 has a better career average than Vijay Merchant's 71.22 in first-class cricket. That fact alone should be enough for Merchant to take his place among the all-time Greats.

Unlike C.K. Nayudu and Lala Amarnath who should not be judged on figures alone, Merchant's statistics are an accurate assessment as to why he remains one of half a dozen outstanding Indian batsmen of all time. Figures meant a lot to him – befittingly as he was from both the business community and the Bombay school of batting. In the latter school, of course, he was the pioneer and departed from the crease only after he had completed his course from the Merchant book of cricket. And what did the school – and the book – teach? Let's hear it from Merchant himself: 'Batting is built around a specific science. The secret is timing and patience. For example, you do not play the hook shot till you are seeing the ball as big as a football. Eschew all risks. Get behind the line of every ball and play it on merit. If you stay at the crease, the runs will come.'

Merchant followed these commandments like the Holy Gospel. And the result was there for the cricketing world to gape in wonder. Merchant had a record of scoring a century every fifth innings in first-class cricket. In Test cricket he hit a hundred every six innings despite the fact that in his prime he missed out on ten years of Test cricket because of the Second World War. Merchant, who always looked fragile, had another obstacle to conquer – ill health. After the War he suffered a series of physical setbacks and it seemed fated that Merchant should never lead India in an official Test though, of course, he did captain the country in unofficial 'Tests'. He was in fact named captain of the Indian team to Australia in 1947-48 and again for the series at home against West Indies the following season. But on both occasions Merchant had to withdraw because of failing health. But philosopher-gentleman that he was he took all this in his stride as one of those 'downs' in life, and was always polished in his behaviour and impeccable in his manners.

His batting too was polished and his record pretty immaculate. Merchant had the critics raving about his batting. Despite the advent of Sunil Gavaskar and Sachin Tendulkar, in the eyes of many, Merchant remains India's greatest ever all round batsman. On good wickets or bad, against pace or swing, cut or spin, in good light or dim, he was simply the master. When one saw the short, capped, neatly dressed figure of Merchant walking out to bat, one was sure to witness a most technically sound innings – an innings straight out of 'How to play cricket'. Merchant's stance at the crease was perfect, the most balanced and composed stance any student of the game could hope to see. The moment he went in to bat, to the next three, four or five hours – quite often it was more – the 22 yards between the stumps was his 'home'.

The statistics associated with Merchant's career are mind-boggling and eye-rubbing. In a first-class career that stretched from 1929 to 1952, Merchant amassed 13,248 runs with 44 hundreds with a highest score of 359 not out. Playing for Bombay in the Ranji Trophy, Merchant had a tally of 3639 runs at an unbelievable average of 98.75 including 16 hundreds in just 47 innings. In the Pentangular tournament, his tally was 1457 runs from only 12 innings at the Bradmanesque average of 162.12. These are the kind of figures that have been beyond other relentless run machines of the game, past masters who were known for their dedication, determination, concentration, an insatiable appetite for runs and a penchant for big scores. That is what gives Merchant the unique status he has enjoyed for years – and will continue to enjoy for as long as the game is played.

Merchant made his first-class debut playing for the Hindus in the Quadrangular. He represented the Hindus in the tournament from 1929 to 1946. A series of consistent scores made him out to be uncommonly gifted, and very soon it was obvious that here was a long-term prospect worth persevering with. He had perfect footwork and a good eye. His cutting, both square and late, was masterly and he played the fastest of bowlers with ease. He had a leg glance that was in the tradition of the patron saint Ranji. Most of all, he impressed everyone with his technique and temperament. He was a careful builder of an innings and had an almost gluttonous appetite for runs. His was the kind of sure approach that Indian cricket could do with in those formative years of international cricket. He carried these same qualities into the Ranji Trophy tournament that was inaugurated in 1934-35 and was Bombay's batting bulwark for over a decade and a half.

Bowlers on the international stage had a taste of the Merchant school of batting from 1933 when he made his Test debut against Douglas Jardine's MCC team. There were no big scores in his six innings – his lowest was 17 and his highest 54 – but he had served enough notice and at the end of the tour, Jardine hailed Merchant as 'the soundest batsman in India'. To any other young man, this kind of heady praise could have had disastrous results. For the levelheaded Merchant, it only spurred him on to greater efforts.

It was on the 1936 tour of England that Merchant really touched the heights of batting. He arrived with the reputation of being among the three best batsmen in the side, the others being Nayudu and Amarnath. But well before the end of the tour, Merchant had proved beyond doubt that he was India's best batsman. It was not a happy tour for there were many seamy incidents on and off the field, the team's record in first-class matches was woeful and the three match Test series was lost rather badly. To make matters worse, it was a very wet summer and encountering the English pitches was no easy task. Amidst all this, the batting of Merchant provided about the only sunlight in an otherwise dark summer. His aggregate of 1745 runs – far ahead of the second placed Nayudu (1102) – was enough to mark him out as a batsman with certain special qualities. But what really impressed those who saw him was the manner in which he made those runs. His batting was an object lesson in getting the better of difficult conditions and different types of pitches.

In the first-class games his batting was impressive enough. But it was his performance in the Test series that caught the fancy of the English players, critics and public. In the first Test he started modestly enough. A watchful 35 in the first innings was followed by the first of his two ducks in Test cricket in the second. The now legendary opening pair of Merchant and Mushtaq Ali came together for the first time in the second Test at Manchester and they immediately produced Indian cricket's first storybook feat. Merchant led off with 33 in the first innings. And in the second, as probably every Indian cricket follower knows only too well, the two put on 203 runs, Merchant getting 114 and Mushtaq 112. The runs were compiled in only about 150 minutes. The two made a striking contrast, with Mushtaq making daring and thrilling strokes while Merchant's shots were controlled, classical and correct. As one critic wrote: 'they were as dissimilar as curry and rice and just as effective in combination'. A later generation saw something of the Merchant-Mushtaq duo in the Gavaskar-Srikkanth pairing.

Their partnership drew superlatives from the rather cynical English writers. Neville Cardus was particularly impressed by Merchant's batting and he waxed eloquent: 'Merchant is, in method, the Indians' good European. He could easily be England's opening batsman. He is a thoroughly organised player. He thinks out his strokes, does not perform them by instinct. He has brilliant thrusts all round the wicket but he is master of them all, not slave to them, selecting quickly but wisely, never a creature of impulse. Here was international quality batsmanship, good enough to lay the foundation of any innings – and lay it, not only soundly but also with method, wearing the dress of style. If Merchant were English, he would solve the selection committee's most pressing problem of finding a safe No 1 batsman for the trip to Australia, capable not only of defence, but of taking good bowling in charge.'

Indeed, so acute was the problem England faced with regard to an opening batsman that the authorities thought of sending a huge photograph of Merchant along with the team to help inspire them! Another critic wrote that Merchant's strokes were so measured that one could see, as it were, 'the foot rule peeping out of his pocket'. Merchant completed the series with two more knocks that further enhanced his reputation. Scoring 52 and 48 in the final Test, he brought his tally to 282. Merchant came back from the tour riding a crest of success, and when Wisden selected him as one of the five cricketers of the year it was an honour richly deserved.

As the Forties approached, it was clear that Merchant was now approaching his zenith as a run-making machine. Ever the perfectionist, he still practised with religious fervour. In his garden in Bombay, he built a concrete pitch and whenever Amar Singh came to the city, he stayed with Merchant and bowled to him for hours on the concrete. The Forties, in fact, have always been considered the golden age of batting in Indian cricket. Runs came in a cascade, records fell in a heap match after match and year after year, double centuries, even triple centuries – and one quadruple hundred – were notched up with regularity and it was a bad time to be a bowler. Leading this run glut was Merchant, possibly encouraged by the fact that there was now another Vijay who also revealed an insatiable appetite for runs – Hazare. Their healthy rivalry throughout the decade meant that India now had not just one, but two world-class batsmen and this could only augur well for the future.

Merchant's remarkable run in the Ranji Trophy commenced from the 1938-39 season. There were only three games for him but he scored 334 runs and with a highest score of 143 not out, his average for the season became 334. Hazare's feat the next season gave him a fresh impetus. Playing for Maharashtra against Baroda, Hazare scored 316 not out, making him the first Indian to get a triple century. That season, Hazare amassed 619 runs in five innings at an average of 154.75. For the time being, he had outscored Merchant – but not for long. This only served to make Merchant more determined and as the Forties unfolded, he was involved in a fascinating tall scoring duel with Hazare. The two Vijays matched each other – in stroke production and run production – and one big score followed another.

During the 1941-42 season, Merchant, having just turned thirty, commenced a run glut that was positively Bradmanesque. In November, he got an unbeaten 170 for Bombay against Nawanagar in the Ranji Trophy. In December, Merchant scored 243 not out against the Muslims and 221 against the Parsees in the Pentangular and followed this up with 153 not out against Sind in the Ranji Trophy. In seven innings of the two concurrent tournaments, Merchant compiled 932 runs at a staggering average of 233. This included a run of 634 runs before he was dismissed, a world record at the time. He had hit 787 runs in four successive innings and was the first batsman in first-class cricket to make four consecutive scores of 150 or more. In 1943-44, for the Hindus against the Rest, he made 250 not out. The same season in the Ranji Trophy, he finally set aside Hazare's record by compiling 359 not out for Bombay against Maharashtra. Monumental patience, spread over nine hours brought that score which remained his peak and was for some years the highest score in the Ranji Trophy. He began the 1944-45 season by scoring 221 not out for the Hindus against the Parsees in the Pentangular. He celebrated the New Year with a score of 217 for Bombay against Western India. In the final, Merchant came up with 278 against Holkar for which he batted eight hours in the March sun. During this innings, he completed 1000 runs for the season, a rare feat since the Indian first-class season was then of limited duration. He rounded off this eye-rubbing sequence by hitting 234 not out against Sind in the opening match the following season and followed it up with 171 against Baroda and 121 against Nawanagar. Twice did Merchant score four hundreds in successive innings in the Ranji Trophy.

Thus it was with an even bigger reputation that Merchant embarked on the tour of England in 1946. Great things were predicted for him – and he surpassed even these expectations! It was a bleak summer, wetter than 1936 and one of the wettest on record. But for Merchant, the sun shone as usual. Having batted during the fickle English weather and on the dicey wickets, he brought all his experience into play. The result was an astonishing tally of 2385 runs with seven hundreds and an unbelievable average of 74.53. He strode like a Colossus, his other teammates – among them such greats as Hazare, Amarnath and Mankad – having to battle for minor positions among the successes of the tour. So complete was his mastery that he scored over 1000 runs more than the second placed Hazare. And his average was 25 runs more per innings than Hazare – something unheard of for a touring side. He proved he could get big scores outside India too by notching up 242 not out against Lancashire and 205 against Sussex. No other Indian player has scored seven centuries on a tour of England and, needless to say, no batsman from the country has topped the 2000-run mark.

In the Tests too he was the leading batsman by far. In the first Test he was restricted to scores of 12 and 27. But in the second he scored 78 and nought, sharing a 124-run partnership with Mushtaq Ali for the first wicket. And in the final Test, he notched up his second hundred against England scoring 128. It was very much a typical Merchant sheet anchor innings for he was seventh out at 272. As only to be expected by now, he finished on top in the Test aggregates and averages.

With such an enviable record, Merchant could very well have been satisfied and proud. But a story during the tour vividly illustrates his single-minded dedication to the art and science of batsmanship. It was noticed that Merchant carried a movie camera with him. It transpired that he wanted films taken of his innings during the tour so that when he was out he could watch the particular mistake he made and rectify it the next time. He used to shake his head with dismay while watching the films. This was not a case of 'crying over spilt milk', for in his next outing he would take particular care to see that he did not commit that same error. He was indeed the supreme perfectionist. It is this dedication, determination and concentration that has earned for Merchant the respect with which he is regarded today, more than seventeen years after his death.

In 1947 Merchant was still very much at his peak. Unfortunately though the last few years of his career were rather melancholic thanks to various bouts with ill health. Disheartened, Merchant contemplated retirement in 1950 but was persuaded to stay on by Board President Anthony de Mello, a fervent Merchant admirer. Merchant finally took his rightful place as captain for the series against the second Commonwealth team in 1950-51. He did not disappoint with the bat. In the only 'Test' he batted against the first Commonwealth team the previous season when he led the Indian team in the first two games before he became ill, he scored 78 and 94. Against the second Commonwealth team he tallied 407 runs with a century and two fifties.

His batting was still good enough but it was quite obvious that this was not the Merchant of old, the run-amasser, who would never surrender his wicket at all, let alone cheaply, who loved to occupy the crease for hours and hours and score centuries and double centuries. And yet Merchant had to bow out of international cricket on a royal note. Nothing less would do for a batsman of his calibre and stature. And fittingly, in what turned out to be his last Test innings, he got a century.

This came about in the first Test against England at New Delhi in 1951-52. With de Mello being ousted as president in 1951, Merchant lost the captaincy that went to Hazare. Ever the gentleman, Merchant was among the first to congratulate Hazare and declared his willingness to play under the younger man. He also partnered him in a big stand. Replying to England's 203, India lost two wickets for 64 on the second morning when Hazare joined Merchant. The two, while not exactly dominating the bowling, did enough to suggest that a long association was very much on the cards. This was the first time in Tests that Merchant and Hazare, the two great run-amassers of the previous decade, were batting together for any length of time and to many it seemed that they were batting against each other, not for India. On a good wicket the two masters should have been murdering the bowlers, it was argued. Instead, in a full day only 186 runs were scored for the loss of two wickets and just 39 runs came in the last 90 minutes. On the third day, when Merchant and Hazare continued to bat for quite a while, the situation was only slightly better – 232 runs were scored for the loss of four wickets in five and a half hours. The pair added 211 runs, an Indian record for any wicket, before Brian Statham bowled Merchant for 154. This was the highest score made by an Indian in Test cricket, surpassing Hazare's 145 against Australia four years before. Merchant had batted seven and a half hours and hit 20 fours. Shortly before close of play, Hazare regained the record score and reached 164 before the innings was declared first thing on the fourth morning.

In the second innings, Merchant while making a desperate dive in an attempt to take a catch injured his shoulder. At forty, he reckoned he could not go on for too long and soon afterwards announced his retirement. It was premature, for Merchant still had a lot of cricket left in him as evidenced by the last hundred. His experience would have been priceless on the tour of England that followed, particularly with the repeated failings of the opening pair. But timing on and off the field had never been Merchant's problem. It was he who coined the well known cricketing phrase, 'retire when people ask why and not why not'. It was always his intention to go out when still on top and that's exactly what he did. Excellent though his final international record is, it is sometimes worth pondering as to what Merchant's final tally would have been if he had played those ten Test matches against Australia and West Indies.

To some of the modern generation, his big scores may give the impression that Merchant was a laborious, heartless, ruthless, run-getting machine. This is not exactly so. He had all the strokes – both pretty and powerful. His cut was felicitous. Especially superb was his late cut. It was at times executed so late that it seemed to race to the boundary off the wicketkeeper's gloves. He could hook with relish, though he avoided the stroke until it was absolutely necessary. Quick footwork and a keen eye saw him judge a ball and get to the pitch of it sooner than most batsmen. Suppleness of wrist saw him execute the cut and glance delicately. On occasions, his glance was played in so fine a fashion that even the umpire was hard pressed to decide whether it was made off the bat or pad. There was actually no particular bowling that he relished most – all came alike to him! However, his approach was never based on violence. He was always 'a gentle executioner'. His batting, in the final analysis, was a blend of Bradman and England's Herbert Sutcliffe – scoring runs with methodical efficiency and at the same time always looking solid and safe as the Red Fort, never giving the impression of getting out. That's the enduring image of Merchant who passed away in Bombay in October 1987.

# 4

## Syed Mushtaq **Ali**

Entertainer par Excellence

Watching him bat was like seeing a trapeze artist at work. Every time you watch the latter, you feel that at any time, he will fall from the rope, strung high above the ground. You watch in amazement and wonder. But deep down there is still a lurking doubt. You wait for the imminent disaster – which never comes. The trapeze artist finishes his feat smoothly, as well as effortlessly, displaying a wonderful sense of balance. And when at last everything is over, with the tension gone, you cheer loud and long.

It was the same with Syed Mushtaq Ali. When you saw him dancing yards down the wicket – to a bowler of considerable pace – or when you saw his famous 'waft' for which he pulled the ball from outside the off stump and banished it to the mid wicket boundary, you were left gazing in disbelief. You wondered how long it would last. Again you waited for the stumps to be shattered any moment. But they never were. At least, not until he had made a substantial score – which hardly looked possible when you saw him bat for the first few minutes.

Neville Cardus once wrote an essay entitled 'When Art Triumphs over Science'. In it he underscored the point that the scientific aspect of cricket was fine, it was correct and had to be obeyed. But one could not make an absolute rule of it. There were exceptions. And players of immense talent and prodigious gifts could get away with strokes that are not in any coaching manual. This observation fits in with the age-old story of the coach and the little boy. The latter made a cross batted swipe with such timing that the ball raced to the boundary. The coach angrily pulled up the boy. 'Look at the position of your legs. They are all wrong.' The boy innocently retorted: 'But sir, look where the ball has gone.' Mushtaq belonged to this gifted category. He was an original. In his time, there was no one like him. And as a swashbuckler, as a buccaneering batsman and as an entertainer par excellence who enjoyed a spontaneous rapport with the spectators, he remains supreme.

On paper, Mushtaq's figures in first-class cricket and Test matches are such as to rate him below the level of greatness. Partly this was due to the fact that in his unorthodox and daring batting, which enthralled spectators, there was always an element of risk. But that is only part of the story. Mushtaq was one of the most shabbily treated cricketers in the history of the game in this country. For a born genius like him, he should have played many more Tests than the mere 11 he did. If there is one cricketer who has received a raw deal from the selectors and the administrators, it is Mushtaq. Somehow or the other, he was not selected for many international games. India played Tests with many players who were not fit to don Mushtaq's gloves or pads while 'the Indian conjurer', as one critic so charmed by his batting had called him, sat aimlessly on the sidelines. Every time he was belatedly called back, spectators would ask, 'His batting is so fantastic, why hasn't he been played in the other matches?' Came another season and Mushtaq would promptly find his name missing again from the Indian team. This went on season after season until even Mushtaq, made of a stern temperament, could stand it no longer. So although fit and with much good cricket still left in him, Mushtaq sadly retired prematurely.

All the same Mushtaq enjoyed a first-class career that lasted thirty-four years. Not many flamboyant batsmen have had such an extended career. Swashbucklers generally entertain for a short while and then make their exit. But Mushtaq stayed the course because of several reasons. The foremost among them must be fitness. I first met Mushtaq some thirty years back when he came to Madras on a coaching assignment and could hardly believe when I was told he was almost sixty. There he was walking as gracefully as ever. He stood tall and erect, and still cut a handsome figure. There was not an extra ounce of flesh around his body. When he talked of cricketers of the day lacking grace he was justified. Photographs taken during his young days give the image of an Adonis. It was much the same twenty-five years after I had met him. My young journalist colleagues who met him in Indore had a hard time in keeping up with Mushtaq, who at eighty-five was outpacing them during a walk. He was still alert, could remember a lot about the events of his day, and remained engaging company.

Another important reason behind Mushtaq's long career is the basic fact that he enjoyed the game – just as the spectators enjoyed his unique style of batting. Anyone who has read his autobiography *Cricket Delightful* will understand this aspect. He had to endure so many setbacks in his cricketing career and personal life but all this never affected his batting. He continued to play in his inimitable uninhibited manner, but never forgot that cricket is a gentleman's game, a noble game, a graceful game. To Mushtaq, cricket epitomised the delights of life, and he played the game all through to transmit that delight to all around him. And Mushtaq was elegant in his approach, careful never to do anything that would sully the image of cricket.

During the conversation I had with him during his visit to Madras long ago he pointed out, more in anguish than anger, that players of the later day had no rapport with the crowd. Again he was justified. Few cricketers had the special kind of relationship with the paying spectators that Mushtaq has had. Little wonder then that he wrote in his dedication to his autobiography: 'I had been wondering whether I could in some way repay the kindness and love bestowed upon me by thousands of my beloved fans throughout my cricket career, spanning a period of about thirty years. To them, as a token of humble gratitude, this book is affectionately dedicated.' It was a truly touching gesture from an entertainer par excellence.

Mushtaq who was born in Indore in 1914 took to the game as naturally as a child picks up a toy. He soon caught the eye of C.K. Nayudu, who became his guru. In 1930-31 he made a lasting impression on Jack Hobbs and Herbert Sutcliffe, who had come to India on Vizzy's invitation. Making his debut for the Muslims in the Quadrangular tournament, Mushtaq made rapid strides but more as a left arm spinner than as a batsman. In fact he earned his first Test cap against Jardine's MCC team in 1933-34 as a bowler who could bat a bit. There was no dream debut for the teenager at Calcutta's Eden Gardens however.

He scored nine and 18 and picked up the wicket of Jardine. But one significant happening was the fact that in the second innings he opened the innings and put on 57 runs with Naoomal Jeoomal. In the next Test at Madras, he again opened in the second innings. So Nayudu and the selectors had seen some possibilities in him. On the face of it, he did not have a very successful series but as with so many talented youngsters, one had only to see a little bit of Mushtaq to firmly conclude that he was a long-term prospect.

The tour of England in 1936 had a major influence on Mushtaq as it made him a more complete batsman. He had left for the tour with certain misgivings as to how he would fare in English conditions. But a natural like him should never have worried. He came back from the tour a vastly improved player and with his reputation enhanced. He topped the 1000-run mark hitting four centuries, and impressed even such erudite critics like Jack Hobbs with his unorthodox, though elegant style.

Midway through the tour it was obvious that his bowling would now take a backseat and he was being looked upon as a frontline batsman – and even as an opener.

In the second Test at Manchester, Merchant and Mushtaq were paired for the first time and over the years, the pair attained legendary status. The unlikely duo was associated in Indian cricket's first storybook feat. They opened on the second afternoon with India facing a deficit of 368 runs. The rest, as the cliché goes, is history. The two put on 203 runs in 150 minutes for one of the great match saving stands in history. Mushtaq was the first to get his hundred – incidentally the first Test century by an Indian batsman in England. Critics fell over each other in trying to find words to describe the batting of two very different batsmen who were so very effective as a combo. Describing a stroke made by Mushtaq off Gover, a writer said 'he sent the ball over the grass so swiftly, it might have been a ray of light'. He took 15 runs in one over of Gubby Allen, the England captain, and raced towards his hundred. As he himself says, 'the faster Allen bowled outside the off stump, the harder I pulled him to leg for a string of fours'. So very much in keeping with the Mushtaq approach! With Merchant being the steadying influence at the other end, Mushtaq curbed his impetuosity and reached the nineties. Walter Hammond, while taking his position at slip between overs, told Mushtaq, 'My boy, be steady, get your hundred first.' The hundred duly came up amidst thunderous cheers. Mushtaq describes the scene in his autobiography thus: 'It was the day of days, my whole life compressed into a single as it were. In scoring a Test century in England I had not only fulfilled my cherished ambition but had given Indian cricket a tremendous shot in the arm and I cannot help violating the cannons of modesty by asserting that the innings is still spoken of in England by those who have seen the world's best players in top form time and again.'

A still dazed Mushtaq who at stumps was 106 not out in a total of 190 for no loss, was cheered all the way to the pavilion. Among the personages who came to the dressing room to congratulate him were Jack Hobbs, Douglas Jardine, C.B. Fry and Sir Pelham Warner. 'Ranji would have been the happiest man to witness your innings,' said Fry. Hobbs said that the best present he could offer was his genuine appreciation. Mushtaq received many congratulatory cables while his captain Vizzy presented him with a gold wristwatch. But perhaps the happiest man was C.K. Nayudu whose smile conveyed the following message: 'I knew you could do it.' Describing Mushtaq's innings, Cardus wrote: 'His cricket at times was touched with genius and imagination. There was suppleness and a loose, easy grace which concealed power, as the feline silkiness conceals the strength of some jungle beauty of gleaming eyes and sharp fangs.'

Next morning, the two became the first overseas pair to put up a double century opening stand against England in England. Mushtaq was finally out for 112, giving Robbins a return catch while attempting a full-blooded straight drive. Merchant also got his hundred and India were able to save the match honourably. In the final Test at the Oval, the two were now firmly entrenched as the opening pair and they had partnerships of 81 and 64. Mushtaq rounded off the series with scores of 52 and 17 and had an impressive tally of 202 runs for the three Tests. 'He won't make good as an opening batsman. He takes too many risks,' said the critics. If that was so, how does one explain Mushtaq's consistency?

On his second tour of England in 1946 Mushtaq was less successful, scoring just under 700 runs and without a single century. But amidst all this, he somehow found the ability to rise to the big occasion as always. Due to uncertain form, he himself opted out of the first Test at Lord's. But he came back to play the second Test at Old Trafford. The venue must have brought back pleasant memories of that memorable day, ten years before. And Merchant and Mushtaq, inspired by these thoughts, put on a stand of 124 runs in almost even time, with Merchant getting 78 and Mushtaq 46. For once, being on a lean trot, Mushtaq did not take as many risks he was normally used to taking and was content playing a supporting role to Merchant. In the final Test at the Oval, the two were again concerned in a fruitful stand, but this time Mushtaq was back in his swashbuckling role. Play on the first day was restricted to the last 90 minutes because of rain. In the murky light, Merchant and Mushtaq, showing perfect understanding, maintained a good run rate. Mushtaq, in characteristic fashion, hit out at everything. When stumps were drawn, India were 79 for no loss with Mushtaq 48 to his partner's 30. He continued to bat in the same cavalier manner on the second morning before he was run out for 59 in a stand of 94. This signalled a rather premature end to the Merchant-Mushtaq partnership in Tests. They had opened seven times in four Tests. There were three stands over the half-century, one over the century and one over the double century marks. In every Test they opened, they had at least a stand of 50. Totally they strung together 584 runs from seven innings at an average of 83.42. It is futile even to look for a greater Indian opening pair, for all the great deeds of Gavaskar and Chauhan in the late Seventies and early Eighties.

Mushtaq's popularity was underscored by a unique incident during the 1945-46 season. It came about during the series against the Australian Services team that came to India to play three 'Tests'. Mushtaq was an automatic choice for the first 'Test' at Bombay but being ill he could not play in it. He informed the Indian Cricket Board about his indisposition, but reports had it that after being invited Mushtaq had not turned up at Bombay. As a result, he was dropped from the team to play the second 'Test' at Calcutta. His exclusion became a talking point and then turned into a mood of resentment among the public with whom Mushtaq was always a favourite. During the match against East Zone which preceded the Calcutta 'Test' a group of angry fans gathered in front of the pavilion shouting, 'We want Mushtaq – no Mushtaq, no Test'. The crowd swelled and threatened violence, breaking into the pavilion at the Eden Gardens and surrounding Duleepsinhji, who was the chairman of the selection committee. They even manhandled him until he gave an assurance that he would try his best to have Mushtaq in the team for the 'Test'. The ultimate result of the unique protest was that Mushtaq played. Has there been a greater tribute to any cricketer anywhere? After all, the ultimate acclaim is always from the fans.

From the late Forties, however, the story of Mushtaq's career reads like a tragic film script interspersed with some happy touches. He was named in the Indian team to tour Australia in 1947-48. Merchant, who was named captain, then withdrew and Mushtaq was chosen as deputy to the new captain Amarnath. But with the death of his elder brother Iqbal Ali at this juncture, Mushtaq Ali had no option but to withdraw from the touring squad. When the mourning period was over, the team was still awaiting departure from Calcutta. With the backing of the Maharajah of Holkar, Mushtaq was encouraged to inform the Indian Cricket Board that he was now available to go with the team. Confident of making the trip, Mushtaq started packing but was stunned to receive a cable from Anthony de Mello, the all powerful Board chief, stating that there was no place for him in the team. As Mushtaq recalls in his autobiography, 'the telegram remains with me as a cruel reminder of the wrong done to me by depriving me of the chance of playing for my country at a time when there was dire need for a recognised opening batsman'.

Against West Indies at home the next season the same raw deal was handed out to Mushtaq. For no particular reason he was not included in the teams for the first two Tests. Then suddenly one fine morning Mushtaq found his name in the team for the third Test at Calcutta. Could it be because the selectors did not want another demonstration in favour of Mushtaq, who was most popular with the Calcutta crowd?

Fully aware that his Test place was uncertain and one cheap dismissal could mean the end of his Test career, Mushtaq was determined not to fail. He made a typical 54 out of 77 in the first innings. But he was at his most flamboyant in the second innings. India were set a tough target of 431 in 415 minutes. Mushtaq straightaway went for the bowling in his inimitable style and put even Rusi Modi, who was having a great series, in the shade. Prior Jones, the West Indies fast bowler just had no idea where to pitch the ball to Mushtaq. This he himself admitted at the end of the match and said that 'if ever Mushtaq came to West Indies, he would be adored and idolized'. Good length balls, short-pitched deliveries and balls pitched well up – all with the same fate as Mushtaq went on his buccaneering way. He scored 106 out of 154 in a stay of just over three hours, and when he was out the crowd rose to him for an ovation that was possibly the biggest Mushtaq had received in his career.

The story of 1948-49 was repeated the next season when the first Commonwealth team visited India. Again Mushtaq was not considered for the first two 'Tests' but he was back in the team for the Calcutta Test. It was now obvious that Mushtaq's presence was required at the Eden Gardens for drawing a big crowd. He did not disappoint, and with two brisk knocks of 40 and 45 paved the way for India's first win in the series. In the next 'Test' at Kanpur, Mushtaq played an innings that was scarcely inferior to the one played at Calcutta the year before. He made 129 out of 218 scored while he was at the crease. By his own standards, this was one of Mushtaq's most responsible knocks. Yet he batted only a little over fours hours in all.

But it was in the final 'Test' at Madras that Mushtaq was associated with a storybook incident that old timers in the city still talk about for its courage and daring. Indeed, it reads more like fiction than fact. India needed 259 for victory. In an hour on the penultimate day, they scored 50 for one. Mushtaq had made 38 of these but in the closing stages he was badly hit by a rising ball from Fitzmaurice on the fourth finger of his right hand. X-rays revealed this as a fracture and the doctor advised complete rest. This ruled him out for the last day of the Test. But India after being well on the road to victory at 216 for three suffered a middle order collapse and slid to 255 for seven. Mushtaq could not resist the temptation and instead of leaving the task to the tailenders, he decided to try and finish it off himself. He asked his colleagues to help him with the pads. Mushtaq describes the scene thus: 'I got my right hand glove ripped open and inserted the plastered finger into it to help me support the handle of the bat. I can never forget the excitement I felt when I emerged from the pavilion, still suffering excruciating pain. On my unexpected appearance at a crucial stage, the crowd gave me a grand ovation. From the point of my emergence from the pavilion down to my taking guard, I was clapped throughout. With Adhikari at the other end, I blocked a few balls from Worrell and Ray Smith. Then, stepping out to a faster one from Smith, I managed to convert it into a half volley and drove it with one hand towards mid off. The ball hit the fence and the Indian team's victory target was achieved. The spectators broke the cordon, rushed into the field and literally mobbed me. On our way to my host's place our car was stopped by a cheering crowd at many places on the road.'

The next season Mushtaq played in four of the five 'Tests' against the second Commonwealth team, and did well enough to suggest that he would be an automatic choice for the Test series against England to be played the following year. But where Mushtaq was concerned, it was perhaps wrong to be so optimistic. In the Ranji Trophy, he was really peaking and in 1950-51 notched up four hundreds in the season. As he himself noted: 'If matches in the National championship are no index of cricket form, the tournament should have been scrapped. And if that index was worth anything, my selection in any Indian team during the early and mid-Fifties was automatic.'

Mushtaq was not considered for the first four Tests of the series against England in 1951-52. Most unexpectedly he was picked for the final Test at Madras that resulted in India's historic maiden victory in Test cricket. But Mushtaq hardly played any part in the triumph scoring but 22, though in the process he put on 53 runs for the first wicket with 'new boy' Pankaj Roy. Little could anyone have known then but that was the end of Mushtaq's Test career. In fact, when he was not selected for the tours of England in 1952 and West Indies in 1953 and the Test series at home against Pakistan in 1952-53, it did seem his international career was over. But the selectors' 'yo-yo' treatment of Mushtaq had one final fling. Against the SJOC team in 1953-54 he was included in one 'Test', scored 48 and 70 not out and that was the end of his intermittent international career.

In the Sixties and Seventies Mushtaq did a lot of coaching in various parts of the country. His affable temperament made him a very popular coach and he was a big hit with the youngsters. He was also good copy for journalists who interviewed him in the last couple of decades of the 20th century for his views were forthright, honest and to the point. In 2002 he was presented with a special memento at the Wisden awards ceremony in London for being the first Indian to score a Test hundred in England. He remained remarkably fit till his last days, and when he passed away in June this year at ninety, the tributes to arguably the supreme entertainer in Indian cricket history were spontaneous and sincere.

# 5

# Vijay Samuel **Hazare**

## Courage in Adversity

He was the original 'wall' of Indian cricket and the ultimate doughty warrior. He never flinched from the fastest of bowlers on the nastiest of pitches and not only faced up to them squarely but also made fluent strokes straight out of the textbook. As a prolific run-getter he almost matched Vijay Merchant. This fact alone is perhaps enough to illustrate the greatness of Vijay Samuel Hazare. But actually Hazare was the very personification of the phrase 'courage in adversity'.

Possibly no other Indian batsman has had to face more ticklish situations during his international career. Time and again he walked into a crisis and over and over again he played the role of Horatio on the tottering bridge with a combination of glorious stroke play and sage-like concentration, based on superb technique, incomparable temperament and rock-like defence. Among all the stories surrounding Hazare's courage in adversity, I have always found the following tale most touching. It happened in Bombay in December 1948 during the second Test match against West Indies. A taxi screeched to a halt at one of the roadside teashops where some cricket fans were listening to the running commentary on the radio. The taxi driver asked them what the score was. One of them replied that India had lost two wickets cheaply. The taxi driver immediately asked, 'What about Hazare?' The listener replied that he was still batting. 'Then there is nothing to worry about, is there? Hazare will rescue us,' said the taxi driver with absolute nonchalance as he settled down to order his cup of 'chaai'.

The story symbolised the hopes the entire nation pinned on Hazare. People sensed that no matter how grim the situation, he would pull the country out of the crisis. In the late Forties and early Fifties, when Indian batsmanship was particularly brittle, it was to Hazare that the Indian cricket fan looked for salvation. And uncomplainingly and unfailingly he provided the solution to the problem – whether he was facing such varied bowlers as Ray Lindwall and Jim Laker, Keith Miller and Malcolm Hilton, Fred Trueman and Roy Tattersall, Alec Bedser and Roley Jenkins, Prior Jones and Ian Johnson or Brian Statham and Bill Johnston. Looking at that long list of outstanding bowlers he faced in his 30 Tests, one will notice that they represent every possible type of bowling conceivable in cricket. And his record is there for all to see and gaze at unbelievingly. In 52 innings, Hazare scored seven centuries and nine fifties. In three successive rubbers he scored six hundreds, two in each. For two short periods, he held the record for the highest individual score for India. It must not be forgotten that he notched up these figures while almost always battling the odds, when in a losing cause and when appearing for a team still in its formative years in international cricket.

By itself his Test record is a handsome one. What enhances the value of his feats is that, more often than not, they were accomplished under extreme stress. Hazare's normal position in the batting order was number four and he invariably used to come in after two wickets had fallen quickly. Hardly had he settled down when a couple of more batsmen would be dismissed. Once again Hazare would have to steer the sinking ship out of the 'whirlpool' of disaster. And the pressure on him was back breaking, for he batted with the full knowledge that one mistake by him and the whole team would collapse like a structure constructed with adulterated cement.

Let's consider some instances. In the first innings of the Adelaide Test in 1948, Hazare came in when three wickets had gone for 69. A little over an hour later, it was 133 for five. Hazare, joined by Phadkar, took the score to 321 before he left having made 116. The runs were made in the face of an Australian total of 674 and the attack spearheaded by Lindwall and Miller, continued with McCool, Johnson and Toshack. Came the second innings and this time India contrived to lose two wickets, both to Lindwall, without a run on the board. Hazare picked this unenviable situation to come in and he did not go till the score was 273 for eight. Out of that, his personal score was 145. The next highest was Hemu Adhikari's 51. This gave him the distinction of scoring a century in each innings, the first, and for twenty-three years the only, Indian to achieve this feat and the first to accomplish the feat on successive days. The impact of the innings was such that it is still talked about today, more than fifty-five years after the event.

From various positions in the field, Don Bradman watched Hazare closely – and he had the opportunity to do so for long! The shrewd observer of the game and players that he always was, Bradman was greatly impressed by Hazare's masterly technique. As one whose batting was also based on the soundness of technique, Bradman knew its importance and was quick to appreciate a batsman with this rare quality. He was generous in his praise of Hazare. In his autobiography *Farewell to Cricket* Bradman wrote: 'I had been very impressed by the soundness of Hazare and the correctness of his stroke production. I want to call attention to Hazare's skill and his right to be classed as a great player.' Not unexpectedly, Hazare's batting drew rave notices from the Australian press.

The scene shifts from Adelaide to Bombay. In the second Test of the 1948-49 series against West Indies, India were forced to follow on 356 runs behind. Two wickets fell for 33 runs. Hazare joined Modi late on the fourth afternoon with defeat staring India in the face. At close, the two were still together with India's score at 95. On the final morning, Modi (112) left at 189. Hazare, in the company of Amarnath, carried on and was unconquered at final draw of stumps with 134. In the third Test at Calcutta, for once there was no crisis, but scores of 59 and 58 not out confirmed his consistency. His fighting qualities were again called for in the next Test at Madras when in the second innings, while all batsmen around him were falling like twigs in the storm that Jones, Trim and Gomez were causing, Hazare alone stood firm with an innings of 52 in a total of 144.

Came the final Test at Bombay and Hazare's performance came as a fitting climax to what was a great series for him. In the first innings he entered at 37 for two and stayed to make 40, the top score. In the second innings, India chasing a formidable victory target of 361 had lost three wickets for 81 when Hazare came in. First, with Modi he added 139 runs for the fourth wicket. And then while wickets continued to fall, he stayed firm and did not depart until he saw that India were on the verge of pulling off what should have been a remarkable victory. His batting was masterly until Jones bowled him for 122. By then he had seen India advance to 303 for seven.

He was still doing the rescue act when England visited India in 1951-52. In the first Test at New Delhi, India lost two wickets for 64. Hazare joined Merchant and the two were concerned in an association that broke records as well as bowlers' hearts. They added 211 runs before Merchant was dismissed for 154. Hazare went on to overhaul that score and remained not out with 164. In the next Test he came in when India were 99 for two and went on to make a mellifluous 155, departing only when the score had reached 388 for five.

These facts are impressive, but they pale into insignificance when put alongside his gallant exploits during the Indian team's disastrous tour of England in 1952. By now Hazare had been saddled with the captaincy and there was genuine cause for concern about whether the additional responsibility would not hinder the performance of India's main batsman. On the contrary, Hazare rose to the occasion with batting of the highest order in terms of technique, courage, skill, determination and concentration. And he certainly had ample opportunities to display these manifold qualities in no small measure, with the team suffering one setback after another. The series was hardly an hour old when he was called upon to steer his side out of disaster. He went in when the scoreboard read 40 for two. Soon it became 42 for three. Vijay Manjrekar joined Hazare and the two took the total to 264 before the captain was out for 89. The 222-run fourth wicket stand was then the record Indian partnership for any wicket.

There was no respite for Hazare in the second innings. Indeed, this time he had to face a crisis no batsman before him or since has faced in international cricket. With a token deficit of 41, India lost four wickets without a run on the board. This was the time Hazare picked to enter the arena. To boot, he was to avert a hat trick and against Trueman at his most menacing. He not only prevented the hat trick but also went on to make 56 of the bravest runs he had ever made while adding 105 runs with Phadkar for the sixth wicket.

Came the next Test and for Hazare it only meant another crisis. For once he entered with the score a healthy looking 116 for two. But what was the use? This time the later batsmen just refused to take their captain's lead and stay with him. The ultimate total was a woefully inadequate 235 with Hazare left high and dry on 69 not out. It was the same story in the second innings. Roy and Adhikari had gone for 59 runs when Hazare joined Vinoo Mankad. The captain concentrated on giving support to Mankad, who was at his glorious best. The stand was worth 211 runs before Mankad was out for 184. Shortly afterwards Hazare left for 49.

In the third Test at Manchester, where India were dismissed twice in one day for 58 and 82 and lost by an innings and 207 runs, Hazare did what was expected of him. The score was an all too familiar four for two when he entered. It soon became 17 for five. In a small stand of 28 runs with Manjrekar, Hazare put up a stouthearted defence. This time he was up against something more than just good bowling – a nasty uncovered Old Trafford pitch. Trueman was at his devastating best. Like a gale he was sweeping the Indian batsmen aside as he liked. But even in these adverse conditions, Hazare stood firm. He made 16 and it took a superb delivery from Bedser to remove him, the ball coming from the leg stump to hit the off stump at a murderous pace. After his fall at 45, the innings crumbled. The second innings was like a re-run. One for seven. Two for seven. That was how the innings went. Hazare joined Adhikari and made 16, staying till the total was 55.

Came the final Test at the Oval. And in keeping with his valiant exploits, Hazare played a classic knock. This time the score was five for two when he came in to bat on a spiteful wicket again. It soon became six for five. With some support from Phadkar and Divecha, he took the score to 71 before he was seventh out for 38 – a knock which the experts hailed as a little gem. One critic wrote that 'it was superb exhibition of batting on a bad wicket'. His figures for the series – 333 runs at an average of 55.50 – deserve to be written in letters of platinum, given the circumstances under which the runs were made.

In a way it was sad that Hazare, time and again, was forced into the rescue act. Though he played the role in an exemplary fashion, it did have an effect on his batting, and he became a bit bogged down by the responsibility of carrying his side's fragile batting on his shoulders. This was a pity because Hazare was a natural stroke player. His cutting, especially square off the wicket, has not been bettered among Indian batsmen. Later generations seeing Chandu Borde, Gundappa Viswanath and Rahul Dravid play this stroke may have some idea of how Hazare executed it. He was a handsome driver of the ball. His off drive was played with a relaxed silkiness and his on drive was executed in regal fashion. He was the grandest player of cricket's grandest stroke, the cover drive. He played the more aggressive pull and hook shots vigorously but safely. Basically, Hazare's mode of batting was modelled on that of Merchant's in that he also was a run-amasser, a batsman capable of running up tall scores, with an unfulfilled appetite for runs. His concentration, dedication and determination have become legendary. A keen eye saw any change that the bowler might have made in his delivery.

Hazare, the stroke player supreme, was best seen in the two rubbers against the Commonwealth teams. There was no real crisis that plagued India in these two series and Hazare's batting was at his most glorious. In the first series in 1949-50 he hit 677 runs at an average of 96.71, including scores of 140 and 175 not out. In the second series, which was in the following season, he hit 634 runs at an average of 79.25 including scores of 144 not out, 115 and 134. From this angle, the best of Hazare was also seen in the Quadrangular and Pentangular tournaments and in the Ranji Trophy. It was here that he ran Merchant close overall, frequently outscored him and enjoyed his healthy rivalry with him during the Forties when the two were involved in a supreme duel for supremacy in aiming to be the leading batsman in the country.

Hazare who was born in 1915 first played for Central India in the Ranji Trophy and quickly making his mark, was selected to play against Lord Tennyson's team in 1937-38. He had only modest success and his first years in the Ranji Trophy too were largely uneventful. A Maharashtrian Christian, Hazare could not even play in the Quadrangular whose competing teams were Hindus, Muslims, Europeans and Parsees. It was only when the Rest team was included in 1937 and the competition became a Pentangular that Hazare could play in the tournament. His fortunes turned for the better when Deodhar got him over to Poona to play for Maharashtra in 1939. The impact was immediate. Hazare in the meantime had come under the influence of Clarrie Grimmett in India on a coaching assignment. The legendary Australian leg spinner's job ostensibly was to examine whether Hazare's promising leg breaks were of the type that could be developed further. Instead, Grimmett quickly came to the conclusion that Hazare, while being a bowler good enough to finish with 595 wickets in first-class cricket and dismiss Bradman twice in Tests, was going to be a great batsman. He encouraged him along these lines. Then in 1938, Hazare made a private visit to England and was fired up after seeing the batting of Bradman and McCabe, Hammond and Hutton. When he came under Deodhar's tutelage he was more than ready for the big stage.

In January 1940, Hazare completed a feat that attracted considerable attention countrywide. He became the first Indian to hit a triple hundred in first-class cricket. Playing for Maharashtra against Baroda he scored 316 not out at Poona. In the process he added 245 runs for the ninth wicket with Nagarwalla (98), still an Indian record. In the semifinal against Southern Punjab, he scored 155. In five innings, Hazare scored 619 runs at an average of 154.75 and served notice that here was a batsman who could challenge Merchant for the post of leading batsman in the country.

Indeed, that Poona innings triggered off the Merchant-Hazare duel for supremacy that lasted through the next decade. In both the Pentangular and the Ranji Trophy tournaments, crowds flocked to see the two in action. Centuries and double centuries were now the order of the day as far as Merchant and Hazare were concerned. And there were a couple of triple hundreds too. In 1941-42 Merchant scored 243 not out for Hindus against Muslims. A few days later, in the final against the Parsees he scored 221.

By 1943-44 the rivalry between the two was at its zenith. And Hazare picked this season to play a most remarkable knock that in certain ways has no parallel in first-class cricket anywhere. In the

Pentangular, playing for Rest, he first took 248 off the Muslims attack. This surpassed Merchant's score of 243 not out. Merchant's retort was swift. Within a week the Rest met the Hindus in the final. Shortly before tea on the second day, after batting five minutes short of seven hours, Merchant reached 250 and immediately declared the innings closed. Hazare who had sent down 51 overs during the Hindus innings, still had the skill and stamina to top score with 59 in the Rest first innings of 133. But the most unforgettable episode was still to be played out. Following on, Rest lost wickets at regular intervals but Hazare batted on and on. He looked quite secure but found no one to stay with him until his brother Vivek Hazare joined him for the sixth wicket. Vivek was a moderate batsman but this time summoned all his skill and courage to stay with his more famous brother, even if he did not contribute much. By the end of the fourth day, the two were still together with Vijay just past his hundred. Next morning, as Vivek produced the straightest of bats, Vijay continued to play his strokes freely. He passed 150, then 200 and finally 250. Having equalled Merchant's record, Hazare now aimed for 300. After the partnership had put on 300 in five and a half hours, Vivek was out for 21. The other batsmen did not stay for long and when the ninth wicket fell, Hazare was 295. With the last man at the crease, Hazare finally reached the landmark and then finally tired, he was out for 309 out of a total of 387. He had batted six hours and 40 minutes and had hit eighty percent of the side's total, something unheard of in first-class cricket. And in hitting his second triple hundred, he achieved something that was beyond even Merchant. Indeed in six innings that year, Hazare amassed 1017 runs with the string of scores reading 248, 59, 309, 101, 223 and 87 – the first Indian to score 1000 runs in a season. It was really all quite mind-boggling and eye-rubbing stuff, and somehow his name seemed appropriate for such feats as Hazare resembles 'Hazaar' (Hindi for thousand).

Hazare was not through with tall scores yet. In 1946-47, he and Gul Mohammed were associated in a world record partnership of 577 runs for the fourth wicket in the Ranji Trophy final between Baroda and Holkar – a record that still stands after almost sixty years. Hazare compiled 288 in ten and a half hours while Gul remained unbeaten with 319. This was on top of having taken six for 85 in the Holkar first innings. And so it went on season after season. Hazare had turned Maharashtra into a force to be reckoned with. Now he made Baroda a team to be feared. Between 1942-43 and 1957-58, Hazare's peak period, Baroda won the Ranji Trophy four times and were runners-up twice, despite the presence of the always strong Bombay and Holkar. By the time he had played his last Ranji game Hazare had scored 6312 runs – a record in the competition – at an average of 68.61. The tally was broken only in the early Eighties by Ashok Mankad. Hazare hit 22 hundreds, another record, which stood till the mid-Eighties when Brijesh Patel surpassed it. Both Mankad and Patel however played many more games. In first-class cricket Hazare is comfortably perched in the top ten career averages of all time. He made a hundred every six innings compared to Merchant's one in five, and in the list of Indian century makers Hazare with 60 is second to Sunil Gavaskar whose 81 hundreds have come at the rate of one in seven innings. Judged by any standards, Hazare remains a true phenomenon of Indian cricket.

After his playing career was finally over, Hazare became a selector and in 1960 succeeded Amarnath as chairman, a post he held for three years. Shy and reserved by nature, Hazare went out of the spotlight after that and for about forty years lived quietly in his Baroda home, over the years becoming the living legend of Indian cricket. Even Len Hutton, the England captain during the 1952 series, remembered Hazare during an interview in Madras eighteen years later as 'the quiet chap'. In 2003 after a very long time Hazare was seen at a public function, when he in a wheelchair piloted by his grandson Kunal was an honoured guest at the Ceat awards night in Mumbai. In a typically generous gesture Hazare donated his 1953 West Indies tour blazer to the CCI museum. When Hazare passed away in December 2004 the sincere and handsome tributes came from far and wide – in keeping with his stature as a world-class cricketer. For his gallant deeds, the name of Vijay Samuel Hazare will be enshrined in the history of Indian cricket forever in letters of platinum.

# 6

# Pehlon Ratanjee **Umrigar**

The 'Palm Tree Hitter'

He had a modest start to his international career but by the time he had retired, Pehlon Ratanjee Umrigar had all the major Indian batting records standing in his name. In fact, his tally of runs and centuries stood for more than sixteen years and were broken only by a certain Sunil Manohar Gavaskar. There was never any doubt as to his stature as the country's premier batsman in the Fifties and a noble torchbearer to the great stars who preceded him. In fact, Umrigar succeeded Merchant and Hazare as the leading Indian batsman, a prolific run-getter who was a feared opponent. However, he did not earn this reputation overnight and worked hard to get it.

Born in Sholapur in 1926, 'Polly' Umrigar made his first-class debut in 1944 for Bombay in the Ranji Trophy. It was steady, rather than startling progress for this tall, broad-shouldered, imposing young man, but an unbeaten 115 for Combined Universities against the West Indies team in 1948-49 really brought him into the national spotlight. Included in the Indian team for the second Test at Bombay, Umrigar scored 30 and in a vital stand that played its part in India drawing the match, he and Dattu Phadkar added 79 runs for the seventh wicket after six wickets had gone down for 150 in the face of a West Indian total of 629 for six declared.

Umrigar did not play again in the series, but was an automatic choice for the Indian team that took on the first Commonwealth side the next season. He played in all five 'Tests' and scores of 34 not out, 55, 67 and 59 – towards a tally of 276 runs in the series – meant that he had arrived. He did even better against the stronger second Commonwealth

team the following season. Scores of 56, 130, 93, 110, 57 and 63 –
towards a quantum leap tally of 562 runs – had proved that he had
superseded all other batsmen and was next only to Hazare in the Indian
batting hierarchy. By this time it was not just the run of scores – this
was impressive enough – that attracted attention. It was the manner of
his play. Umrigar had altered the face of Indian batsmanship. For long,
it had nestled under the Merchant-Hazare school of building an innings,
of technical excellence. Umrigar had all this and something more. The
manner in which he jumped out to the slow bowlers and lifted the ball
to the untenanted parts of the field was something that endeared him
to the crowds. In the course of his 110 in the Madras 'Test' for example,
he went from 90 to 102 with two successive sixes off Frank Worrell.
In time, Umrigar earned the sobriquet 'palm tree hitter'. Indeed, many
of his sixes landed near the trees that surrounded most of the grounds
in India at the time. Umrigar was perhaps the first batsman to uncover
the Ramadhin mystery. The confident – even rough – manner in which
he dealt with him in the series against the second Commonwealth team
was an object lesson for other batsmen. Ramadhin's spin held no puzzle
for Umrigar who darted out and lifted him with disdain. Umrigar
handled Ramadhin in the same way that Sachin Tendulkar dealt with
Shane Warne half a century later.

But his accent on attack did not mean that Umrigar was going
to neglect the basic principles of batting. His batting was built on
sound technical aspects but his uncommon gifts, his broad shoulders
and arms, his sturdy build and his considerable height saw him get
to the ball early and then treat it harshly. Umrigar was essentially a
driver. His cuts were neat dabs and his glances were little turns of the
bat and the wrist. Initially he had a bit of a crouching stance but he
changed it in 1953 to a more upright one. Consequently, he lost some
of his offside strokes. But then he developed a sounder defence and the
change in no way affected his stronger on side shots. Indeed, there was
no better player of the ball in this area for sheer power and productivity.
Umrigar never hesitated in coming yards out to the tossed up delivery,
and he was at his best against spin bowling, even if it was of the
highest class.

This is not to say that Umrigar could not play fast bowling. Too much has been made of his failures in England in 1952 – which admittedly were shocking – and too little has been written about his success there seven years later, the gradual progress he made in combating fast bowling and his excellent record against the West Indian speedsters. After his nightmarish experiences against Freddie Trueman in 1952, he faced Frank King, the leading Caribbean fast bowler of the time, with ease in the West Indies in 1953 and throughout the Fifties and early Sixties, was the one Indian who had a splendid record against Hall, Gilchrist, Stayers and Watson. He did reasonably well against Lindwall in the 1956 series against Australia. That is why there is no truth in the theory that Umrigar could not play fast bowling. In two successive rubbers, he was India's highest run-getter against Hall and Gilchrist, Stayers and Watson. After all, he did hit Hall for four boundaries in one over in the Port of Spain Test match in 1962. And he did fight back to take a century off the same Trueman in 1959. No, whichever way one looks at it, there is certainly no basis in the charge.

As I said, by 1951 Umrigar was next only to Hazare in the Indian batting rankings. And he was soon involved in a storybook incident in the series against England that winter. In his first six innings he totalled only 113 runs and was dropped for the final Test at Madras. However, an injury to Adhikari on the eve of the match saw Umrigar back in the squad. He seized the opportunity to score the first of his hundreds. Coming in early on the third morning with India 216 for five in reply to England's 266, Umrigar figured in fruitful partnerships with Phadkar and C.D. Gopinath for the sixth and seventh wickets, and remained unbeaten with 130 as India went on to take a commanding lead on their way to their historic maiden Test victory.

Umrigar thus embarked on the tour of England with confidence oozing from his muscular frame. But while it is pleasant to note his deeds in the first-class matches, it is painful to relate his pathetic exploits in the Tests. He was plainly in distress against Trueman to whom he fell four times in seven innings. A tally of 43 runs at an average of 6.14 was unbelievable. But outside the Tests he was as commanding a batsman as any to visit England since the Second World War. Never did any

Indian batsman hit the ball so consistently powerfully as Umrigar. All his big innings (he had three double hundreds and two centuries) were made in double quick time, and in the course of these the bowling never looked more helpless. These run feasts helped conceal his Test match nightmares, and he easily topped the tour aggregates with 1688 runs, more than 600 runs ahead of the second placed Hazare.

No doubt glad to be back home, Umrigar made light of the bowling in the Bombay Test against Pakistan. His 102 in 161 minutes, during which he dominated a fourth wicket partnership of 183 runs with Hazare, was the finest attacking innings he had yet played. But this was just a prelude to the greater feats to come in the Caribbean islands in early 1953. The West Indies were then a formidable side. While their chief strength lay in their batting, their bowling too was almost as strong. There was Frank King, a pace bowler of repute, the swing of Gerry Gomez and Frank Worrell and above all the twin spin threat of Ramadhin and Valentine. That India performed creditably – they lost only one match out of five – was not a little due to Umrigar's consistent batting. He started off with 130 and 69 in the first Test and followed it up with 56 and six, 61 and 67, one and 40 not out, 117 and 13. His aggregate of 560 runs equalled Rusi Modi's tally set up in the 1948-49 season against the same opponents but was a new record for a series away from home.

Back from the tour, Umrigar suddenly found himself chosen captain for the first two 'Tests' against the SJOC team. The sturdy Parsee was elevated to the top job in Indian cricket ahead of the more experienced Phadkar and Mankad. India won the first 'Test' and drew the second. Then for some inexplicable reason he was replaced as leader for the next three games. The burden of captaincy had not, however, affected his batting, which he proved by running up scores of 47, 83, 112 not out and 87. The following season on the tour of Pakistan, Umrigar maintained his reputation and headed the Test averages with a series of consistent scores including 32, 78 and 108. During the early stages of his century Umrigar was at his most commanding and the bowlers were as helpless as butterflies in a gale. Ultimately Pakistan captain A.H. Kardar resorted to ultra-defensive measures like packing the on side and instructing his bowlers to send down deliveries outside the leg stump that curbed his strike rate. Umrigar still got his 108 out of 152 scored while he was at the crease.

The Indians enjoyed a run feast at the expense of the New Zealand bowlers in 1955-56, and setting the example was Umrigar. In the first Test at Hyderabad, he became the first Indian batsman to get a double century. His 223 took him eight and a half hours to compile and he slammed 27 fours, then a record. The other batsmen took the cue, and totally there were six hundreds and three double centuries compiled in the series. Umrigar, who by this time had been restored to the captaincy, encouraged such tall scoring. Thrice in quick succession in the series did the record for the highest Indian total in Tests go overboard. Even the individual record changed hands rapidly. Umrigar's 223 was equalled by Mankad in the next Test. Mankad then scaled a new peak by scoring 231 in the final Test at Madras. Brought up in the Bombay school of batting, under the tutelage of Merchant and Modi, Umrigar reasoned that while the breezy and attractive sixties and seventies had their place, they were not enough to win matches.

Umrigar had only a modest series against Australia in 1956. He had only one knock of note in the three Tests but in compiling it, displayed a little known aspect of his batting. He was always known to be an attacking batsman but on this occasion, in the second Test at Bombay, what was needed was a back to the ball fight by India, who were 272 runs behind on the first innings. Winning was out of the question but with careful batting, the match could be saved. The fall of the first wicket at 31 put India in a spot for there was still plenty of time left on the penultimate day. Umrigar curbed his natural attacking instincts for the sake of his side, put his head down and displaying deep concentration and an unwavering defence, starred in the successful rearguard action. By the time he was dismissed just before tea on the final day – he was fourth out at 217 after batting six hours for 78 – the match had virtually been saved.

The seamy off-the-field happenings during the 1958-59 series against the West Indies affected Umrigar, who was unwittingly engulfed by the sordid misdeeds of petty-minded officials. But while it ultimately led to his resignation from the captaincy on the eve of the fourth Test, it had no palpable bearing on his batting. With scores of 55, 36, 57, 34, 44 not out and 76, Umrigar provided one of the few silver linings in a series that was lost badly. He again headed the run tally with 337 runs, and by playing Hall and Gilchrist fearlessly showed that the theory that he could not play fast bowling was just that – an unfounded theory.

Still it was with a sense of foreboding that Umrigar would have approached the Test series in England in 1959. Outside the Tests he was again the commanding batsman, getting his quota of three double centuries and two hundreds. And this time he made runs in the Tests too, exploding once and for all the myth that he was still 'scared' of fast bowling. From 43 runs in seven innings in 1952, he advanced to 230 runs from eight innings. Only Nari Contractor (233) made more runs in a series that was lost by a mile. But perhaps the happiest moment of his career came when he scored a century in the fourth Test at Manchester, hooking and pulling his old foe Trueman with utmost confidence and courage. With that 118 – the highest score for India in the Tests – he wiped out the unhappy memories of seven years ago. Outside the Tests he was up to his usual piratical deeds and tallied 1826 runs for the tour, which was over 600 runs more than the next best Pankaj Roy who played nine more innings. Umrigar had his heart set upon crossing the 2000-run mark and emulating Merchant, but he had to miss the last six matches due to a fractured finger. This, in fact, ended his run of 41 consecutive Tests when he missed the game at the Oval.

By now Umrigar was the elder statesman of Indian cricket and the youngsters looked up to him for guidance and inspiration. However, he could not provide them much help in the series against Australia back home in 1959-60. For one thing, he was out of form scoring only 52 runs in five innings – his least productive series. Secondly, a back injury sustained during the third Test meant that he could take no further part in the rubber. He, however, came back with a bang in the next series. Umrigar always relished Pakistani bowling. He had got hundreds against them both in 1952-53 and two years later. Now he proceeded to take three centuries off them in the five matches during the 1960-61 contest, becoming the first Indian to hit as many hundreds in a series. Umrigar completed what was a fabulous run for him in the next series against England in 1961-62. In his first 46 Tests, he had scored seven centuries. In the next five Tests, he accounted for four more including three in successive Tests. His run, which started in the series against Pakistan, culminated in his 147 not out against England at Kanpur.

When Umrigar left with the Indian team on the tour of the West Indies in 1962 there was no indication that this would be his last trip. Already, however, the batting responsibilities over such a long period along with his recent additional bowling duties, had taken their toll. In the last few years, Mankad, Ghulam Ahmed, Gupte, Ramchand and Phadkar had all called it a day and with the new bowlers not up to the mark, Umrigar had started to bowl more than usual. In the series against Pakistan, for example, twice he bowled in excess of 50 overs an innings – and each time followed it up with a hundred! This continued on the West Indies tour. In the first Test he sent down 35 overs; in the third Test, completely against the doctor's orders, he bowled 49 overs. And in the fourth Test he sent down 56 overs to capture five wickets for 107 runs. All this told even on his magnificent physique. But like the gallant, uncomplaining warrior, he bore the brunt and never let it affect his batting. On this tour he continued performing the heroic role. A modest beginning in the first Test was only a prelude to greater things. In the second Test he made 50 and 32. And in the fourth Test at Port of Spain with a performance that should, but for some unreasonable reason has not been put right alongside Mankad's feat at Lord's ten years before. In absolutely no way is Umrigar's feat inferior to Mankad's. But while reference is made time and again to the latter, Umrigar's is barely remembered. Could it be because Mankad's drama was enacted at Lord's?

As I said, Umrigar led off with five for 107 off 56 overs with West Indies scoring 444 for nine declared. In reply, India lost half the side for 30 runs to 'Hurricane Hall' who took all the wickets. Umrigar, aided by Pataudi and Borde, initiated a recovery and India reached 197. Umrigar top-scored with 56. In the follow on, Umrigar came in at 192 for four. When India were all out a little over four hours later, the total was 422 and Umrigar remained unconquered with 172. For its sheer savage demolition of the famed West Indian attack, which started with Hall and Stayers and continued with Sobers, Gibbs and Worrell, the knock is unparalleled. Some of the figures associated with it make for astounding reading. His 50 took him 77 minutes and included in it were five boundaries. His 100 came up in 156 minutes with 12 hits to the fence. His 150 was scored in only 203 minutes. His 172 came up out of 230 in just 248 minutes. He dominated partnerships like few batsmen have. With Borde (13), he added 42 runs for the seventh wicket. His ninth wicket stand with Nadkarni (23) yielded 93 runs. The climax to his innings – by common consent his greatest ever – came during his last wicket stand with Budhi Kunderan. The wicketkeeper batsman was no slouch with the bat but his share of their association of 51 was four!

More than the figures, it was the manner in which be handled the pacemen in particular that attracted considerable attention. His failures in England in 1952 had followed him like a dark, gloomy shadow throughout his playing days. He had, over the years, partly got out of it with his impressive record against pace. Now with this violent shake-up of the West Indian pace attack, he broke off the shackles forever. No one could say now that Umrigar could not play fast bowling. It was during this unforgettable knock that Umrigar summoned up the courage to hit Hall for four boundaries in one over. Despite having a strained back, which saw him bat down the order, Umrigar played in the final Test and scored 32 and 60 (top score) to finish this, his greatest series in a grand manner. And it somehow seemed fitting that Umrigar was the top scorer in what proved to be his last Test innings.

On his return Umrigar consulted a doctor, and after he was sure that he could not stand the strain of a five-day Test again, he announced his retirement from Test cricket. He could not have done so at a more appropriate time, having come back on a crest of success. And when the Indian team took the field in a Test next without the tall, broad-shouldered, imposing figure of Umrigar standing at first slip, it somehow looked an altogether different team. 'Even when he did not get runs, Umrigar's presence in the side was always a source of confidence and inspiration to the younger players,' wrote Dicky Rutnagur when he bowed out of Test cricket. That just about sums up Umrigar's contribution to Indian cricket as a great batsman, a great leader, and a great team man.

For all his stature as the leading Indian cricketing personality of his time, Umrigar always remained boyishly enthusiastic about even Saturday afternoon cricket. It was this enthusiasm that saw Umrigar play first-class cricket for almost twenty-five years. And by the time he retired, he held all the main Indian Test records – most matches (59), most runs (3631), and most hundreds (12) – and as I said it wasn't until Gavaskar came along that the batting records finally went overboard in the late Seventies. And it was not until thirty years later that one of his famous records – the highest score by an Indian outside India – was broken. His 252 not out against Cambridge University in 1959 was surpassed only in 1989 by Navjot Sidhu who scored 286 against Jamaica. But of course some of his records, like scoring six double centuries on two tours of England, still stand. As S.K. Gurunathan put it aptly while paying tribute to Umrigar when he retired: 'In the brief history of Test cricket in India, there is no one who has taken upon himself so much as Polly Umrigar. He has been the spine of India's batting, her spearhead in bowling, her most outstanding fieldsman and one of her shrewdest captains. It will take a long time before his feats are surpassed.'

Umrigar continued playing first-class cricket for some time after his retirement from the Test scene. And could someone like Umrigar ever give up the game altogether after his playing career was finally over? In the Seventies, he managed Indian teams to New Zealand and West Indies in 1976 and to Australia in 1977-78, bringing all his enthusiasm and expertise into another field. In 1978 he took over as chairman of the selection committee, a post he held for five successive terms before becoming executive secretary of the Indian Cricket Board. Even today, at seventy-nine, 'Polly Kaka' as he is known to a later generation, is a respected figure, still very much involved with the National Cricket Academy and sundry cricketing matters. Long may Indian cricket benefit from his pearls of wisdom!

# 7

# Vijay Laxman **Manjrekar**

An Artist and a Technician

B ooks on the game have described him as 'a very correct right hand batsman with sterling defence and a large repertoire of strokes'. The Indian Cricket annual, in its 1975 edition while featuring him in its special portrait gallery, called him 'A stylist with a solid base'. A keen student of the game would always closely follow his technically perfect batting. He was the delight of the both the artist and the technician. If they wanted to see a champagne innings, the spectators looked to him more than anyone else. Above all, his country looked to him for steering it out of disaster with one solid knock after another blending substance and style.

Vijay Laxman Manjrekar was by any standards a superb craftsman. It was this right-handed classicist, the man who was the very epitome of textbook batsmanship, who either held the Indian batting together in the Fifties when the going was rough or was in the forefront in taking complete charge when things were smooth. Given the record of Indian cricket during the time Manjrekar played for the country – from 1951 to 1965 – it was, more often, the former. And Manjrekar was not only the man for the crisis he also did the rescue act with poise and panache. He was easily the classiest batsman in the side and a direct descendent of Hazare. What Hazare was to Indian cricket in the late Forties and early Fifties, Manjrekar was to Indian cricket a decade later.

Manjrekar was certainly not an original. As I said, he was a noble torchbearer of the flame lit by another Vijay. But his influence on Indian cricket extended well beyond 1965. Both the batting giants of the Seventies – Gavaskar and Viswanath – admitted all too readily that they had been greatly influenced by his lyrical batting. Manjrekar certainly bridged the generation gap in Indian cricket, in that players of different generations openly admitted that he was the best batsman. Subash Gupte, whose career ran parallel to Manjrekar, said he was the best player of spin bowling, a view echoed by Prasanna, who came into Test cricket when Manjrekar was in the evening of his career. It was the same with pace bowling. Ramakant Desai, when asked who was the best Indian batsman he bowled to, replied without hesitation: 'Vijay Manjrekar without the faintest shadow of a doubt. He was a superb technician. What technique, what craftsmanship, what a rock-like defence.'

Indeed, if Omar Khayyam had some knowledge of cricket and had seen Manjrekar bat, he would have written volumes of rhetoric about him. His off drive and cover drive, strokes that he happily played often, were a joy to behold. They did not easily vanish from memory and one still enjoyed them long after the match was over. Manjrekar was a peerless player of the square cut. Even a forward defensive stroke by Manjrekar – normally a dull thud of bat against ball – was not to be missed for as they say 'it was straight out of the book'. Superb timing was the essence of all his strokes.

Of course, he had his critics. People who said he was slow and laborious, that he was playing for himself and not the side, that he was fat and tortoise-like in the field. While he was certainly not a Mushtaq Ali or a Srikkanth, this charge is highly exaggerated. Like Hazare, he also came to the crease at a time when, invariably, quick wickets had fallen. On other occasions, he came in when time was of greater importance than runs. During the major part of his career, he was one of the main pillars of Indian batting and he certainly could not afford to sell his wicket cheaply. Canny and watchful, Manjrekar built his innings carefully, run by run, minute by minute, brick by brick. True, he sometimes batted as if in a stupor and carried his cautious approach to extremes particularly late in his career. This did not make him any more popular with the crowd who, in the closing stage of his career, jeeringly called him 'old man'. But the end justifies the means and no one can scoff at his record.

Manjrekar was born in Bombay in 1931. Few cricketers have made a stronger impact so early and while still a schoolboy. Manjrekar was hailed as a prodigy. While still a student, he made his Ranji Trophy for Bombay in 1949. Indian selectors have generally been conservative in their approach but even they could not ignore Manjrekar's obvious class and played him in a 'Test' against the second Commonwealth team in 1950-51 while he was still a teenager. He was not an instant success but in racing parlance, he was a stayer, not a sprinter. He was one to back as a winner. Sure enough, the selectors persevered with him, and making his Test debut against England at Calcutta the next season, he made a venturesome 48. Going in after five wickets had fallen for 144 runs – in reply to England's 342 – Manjrekar showed no signs of nerves. His style immediately blossomed. Nimble footwork saw him combat the spin of Tattersall and Watkins. But he was at his best against the pace of Statham and Ridgway, hooking and cutting both of them with impunity. He put even the seasoned and aggressive Phadkar in the shade during their sixth wicket stand of 76 runs. In the next match, on a turning track he made six and 20 and was automatic choice for the tour of England that followed.

Very few players came out with credit on this otherwise disastrous tour and one of them was Manjrekar. He scored 1059 runs at an average of 39.22, finishing third in both the tour aggregates and averages. He achieved the same positions in the Tests. And among all the generally creditable performances was one achievement that would seem credible only in fiction books – except for the fact that it really happened and is there in the record books. Winning the toss in the first Test at Leeds, India soon ran into trouble and lost three wickets for 42. It was at this juncture that twenty-year-old Manjrekar, in his first Test in England, joined Hazare. The captain was holding firm but could he depend on the youngster to stay with him and help in the resurrection of the innings?

Hardly had the stand progressed a little when people were asking the question in reverse. Could Hazare stay long enough for Manjrekar to complete a total recovery? It seemed astonishing but true. For out in the middle, Manjrekar was batting in a manner that had the Headingley crowd rubbing their eyes in disbelief. They could hardly come to terms with the fact that this youngster, with just two Tests in India behind him, was now treating the pace of Trueman, the swing of Bedser and the spin of Laker, Watkins and Jenkins with equal contempt. Manjrekar was at his most glorious in the hour after lunch when with handsome drives, delectable cuts and thrilling hooks he scored 40 while his great partner accounted for nine! He continued in much the same vein in the next hour and at the tea interval, Manjrekar, who had given Hazare a ten minute start, was on 95 to his captain's 60. Displaying the patience of a veteran, Manjrekar batted carefully and took another half an hour to reach his hundred. A century in his first Test in England! It was a dream come true innings. Incidentally, it was also his maiden three-figure knock in first-class cricket. Overcome by happiness, Manjrekar now batted with gay abandon. With Hazare proving as indomitable as ever, the stand progressed till it reached the record figure of 222, the highest Indian partnership for any wicket, before the captain fell for 89. In the next over Manjrekar was brilliantly held at slip by Watkins off Trueman. His score of 133, at the time the highest by an Indian in a Test in England, included 19 boundaries.

This was almost a once-in-a-lifetime knock and it was too much to expect Manjrekar to bring off something similar again during the series. There was, however, a little gem in the third Test at Old Trafford. On a nasty wicket, he came in at 17 for five, hit Trueman for four firm boundaries and diligently built up his score to 22, the highest in a total of 58. He was out entirely due to the vagaries of the pitch, a ball from Trueman suddenly rising up to his chin. As a protective gesture, he raised his bat but as luck would have it, the ball went off the handle for a tame catch to gully.

Injuries restricted Manjrekar's Test appearances to two in the series against Pakistan, but he came into his own when India visited the Caribbean islands in 1953. After a slow start, his batting blossomed fully, culminating in a great endurance feat in the final Test at Kingston. India, 264 runs behind, had lost the first wicket at 80. Manjrekar joined Roy early on the fifth day with virtually two days remaining. His concentration never wavered. He was still there with Roy at lunch. They were still batting at tea. When it seemed like nothing would separate the two, Manjrekar made his first mistimed stroke and was caught at slip. This was about 15 minutes before stumps. For nearly four and a half hours, Manjrekar had batted with a sense of dedication that won the admiration of those present. His 118 – out of a stand of 237 – had placed India firmly on the road towards a draw. The partnership was the highest Indian stand for the second wicket. This, coming on top of his record association for the fourth wicket with Hazare a year earlier, gave Manjrekar a creditable double. Not satisfied, he was to make it a unique treble a couple of years later.

In a dull and moderate scoring series against Pakistan in 1954-55, Manjrekar's batting was one of the few plus points. An early run of three successive half centuries saw him finish second to Umrigar in both the averages and aggregates. Manjrekar's classy batting reached a peak during the series against New Zealand the following season. Six innings brought him two hundreds and a 90 towards a total of 386 runs at an average of 77.20. He started off with 118 in the first Test at Hyderabad, in the process adding 238 runs for the third wicket with Umrigar. This completed the 'unique treble' I mentioned earlier. For a long time Manjrekar was the only batsman to share in three partnership records. His ability to play a long innings was proved in the third Test at New Delhi. Facing a New Zealand total of 450 for two declared, India lost two wickets for 111 when Manjrekar walked to the wicket. When he left, nine hours later, the total was 458 for six and Manjrekar's score was 177. Even though the bowling was not particularly strong, for sheer perfection of stroke execution this remained one of his best knocks. His 90 in the next Test at Calcutta was made when India, facing a deficit of 204 runs, were fighting to stave off defeat. Manjrekar helped put India on the road to an honourable draw by adding 144 runs for the third wicket with Roy.

Manjrekar's consistency was one of the few things that are remembered from the 1956 series against Australia, which can otherwise be best forgotten by Indians. In a low scoring series, at least from the Indian point of view, Manjrekar came out with full credit. There were no big scores but no real failures too and it was a creditable record against Lindwall, Davidson and Benaud. His lowest score was 16 and the highest 55. A tally of 197 runs from six innings saw him head the batting figures.

The 1958-59 series against West Indies was not a very productive one for Manjrekar who was by now plagued with injuries. But no series can be played without at least one outstanding Manjrekar innings, and he provided this in the third Test at Calcutta. India, following on 490 runs behind were in a hopeless situation at 17 for four when Manjrekar walked in towards the evening of the third day. While Gilchrist and Hall, in venomous form, were striking down his companions one by one, Manjrekar not only stood firm but also carved out authentic strokes against the deadly duo. The first bouncer he received from Hall was hooked magnificently to the fence – a stroke so masterful and correct that it was straight out of some cricket manual. Gilchrist and Hall quickly decided in consultation with skipper Alexander not to bowl any more bouncers at Manjrekar. Unbeaten with 20 at stumps, Manjrekar continued on the fourth morning from where he left off. Dicky Rutnagar describes his innings thus: 'Manjrekar played cricket of rare beauty, the like of which has not been played by an Indian batsman in a Test since Mankad's heroic innings at Lord's, almost seven years ago. Drives, hooks and cuts came easily to Manjrekar. I believe that it was the finest exhibition of batsmanship seen in the entire series.' And this in a rubber in which Sobers hit three centuries and Kanhai had scores of 256 and 99. Indeed Manjrekar's 58 not out was the epitome of courage, class and skill.

For the next two years, Manjrekar's Test appearances were limited. A damaged knee saw him miss three Tests in England and the entire series against Australia at home in 1959-60. In the limited opportunities he had in England before the operation he did enough to show his class, and headed the tour figures with 755 runs at an average of 68.68 with a highest score of 204 against Oxford University. In the Tests, he had scores of 44 and 61. He came back to Test cricket for the contest against Pakistan at home in 1960-61 but now he was overweight, rather slow in the field and the long lay off seemed to have affected his batting. Still his experience saw him battle on and with scores of 73, 52 and 45 not out, he proved that he could not be written off as yet. But doubts persisted as to whether he would be the batsman of old again.

It did not take long for Manjrekar to show the skeptics that like wine he was getting better with age. He reached his peak in the 1961-62 series against England. Starting off with scores of 68 and 84 in the first Test at Bombay, he then made 96 in the next Test at Kanpur. And in the third Test at New Delhi, Manjrekar's batting blossomed like a flower in spring. Coming in at the fall of the first wicket at 121, Manjrekar batted right through the innings and when India were all out for 466 late on the second evening, he was unconquered with 189, surely the handsomest innings ever this great artist played in Test matches. In a stay of 440 minutes, he hit 29 fours, showing the Kotla crowd his full regalia of strokes. This eclipsed Mankad's 184 at Lord's in1952 as the highest innings by an Indian against England and remained Manjrekar's best Test score. Modest scores followed at Calcutta and in the first innings of the final Test at Madras, and it seemed that Manjrekar had played his typical knock of the series at New Delhi. But in his final outing of the series, Manjrekar played an innings that was the last word in batsmanship. The surface was fast crumbling, Indians were struggling and Tony Lock and David Allen were working havoc. Manjrekar, who with his technical proficiency, was the one batsman who could have made runs in these difficult circumstances, now took over the entire burden of the team's batting. He shrewdly shielded his teammates from the menace of the two spinners and took on most of the strike himself. Every time the ball did something awkward – and this was the rule rather than the exception – he had the angle of deviation covered. There really seemed no way the bowlers could get rid of him and indeed he was dismissed in the only manner that seemed possible – run out. When he came in the score was 15 for one. When he was out four hours later the score was 158 for nine. The highest score after his 85 was 17. Can there be a higher tribute to Manjrekar's batting? He tallied 586 runs, setting a record for a series aggregate for an Indian.

By the early Sixties, following the retirement of Umrigar, Manjrekar had become the elder statesman of Indian cricket. The youngsters looked up to him for guidance and inspiration. In scoring 108 against England in the first Test at Madras in 1963-64 Manjrekar proved that there was still a lot of cricket in him, even if the rest of the series wasn't very productive. But he had the backing of the then captain M.A.K. Pataudi who had a great regard for his classy batting and vast experience. And, indeed, it was in Pataudi's company that he enjoyed one of his great moments and played a vital role in a notable victory over Australia at Bombay in 1964. In a moderate scoring series he had already proved his worth by successive scores of 33, 40 and 59. But the crucial innings came in the second innings of the Bombay Test. Needing 254 runs for victory, India were on the ropes at 122 for six. Manjrekar joined Pataudi at this stage and the captain must have been the happiest man to have his company at this critical juncture. After all, who was better than Manjrekar in a crisis? One mistake by him would have knocked the fight out of India. But displaying immaculate defence, even by his own high standards, Manjrekar stayed till the total reached 215. His first mistake after more than two and a half hours of standing firm cost him his wicket when he was 39. But by then he had done enough to put India on the road to victory.

So in early 1965, Manjrekar even though he was in his thirty-fourth year and a bit bulky around the waist and a trifle slow in the outfield, still looked good enough for another year or so. In the first innings of the first Test against New Zealand at Madras, he was out for 19. At stumps on the penultimate day, India had not yet batted in their second knock. The team for the second Test was selected. Manjrekar was excluded but the team was not officially announced till the following evening. On the final day Manjrekar, batting with all the class and authority at his command, scored 102 not out. An hour later the team was announced – and the furore that followed was justifiably incredible. Manjrekar, deeply hurt, pondered over the situation for some time – and then announced his retirement from Test cricket. What else could any self-respecting individual do? 'Unwanted Manjrekar Retires' screamed the headlines in the newspapers. It did seem a pity that that his career came to an end so suddenly – and certainly prematurely. But on the other hand, at least it had a storybook finish. Merchant was the only other batsman to end his Test career with a century. And it seemed somehow right and proper that two of India's most technically perfect batsmen should jointly enjoy this enviable distinction.

Manjrekar continued to play in the Ranji Trophy with distinction. Being a professional, registered with the Indian Cricket Board, he played for Bombay, Bengal, Uttar Pradesh, Andhra, Maharashtra and Rajasthan over a period of almost twenty-five years. But in the last few years, he stayed with Rajasthan and along with other stalwarts like Hanumant Singh and Salim Durrani, helped make the state a force to reckon with. Rajasthan entered the Ranji Trophy final for four straight years from 1960-61 and again in 1965-66, 1966-67 and 1969-70. Each time, however, they came a cropper against Bombay, who were then in the midst of their world record fifteen-year run as champions. Manjrekar continued to be among the runs and suddenly there was talk of him coming out of retirement and touring England in 1967 and Australia in 1967-68 with Indian teams. He himself was keen to go and was ready to announce his comeback provided the selectors showed the intention to pick him. This never came about though, and Manjrekar's last few years were spent quietly around the domestic circuit.

Manjrekar's last few years were not particularly happy ones. He went as manager of the Indian schools team to England in 1973 and acquired the image of a martinet. His health too was rather indifferent. He lost weight and as he grew older, was hardly recognisable as the bulky player during his final days. He passed away suddenly, following a heart attack, in Madras in 1983. Gavaskar, in his tribute said that Manjrekar was a father figure to him. He surely meant this in more ways than one.

# 8

# Chandrakant Gulabrao **Borde**

## The Gentleman Cricketer

His playing career makes for interesting reading. He started out in the mid-Fifties as one of India's most promising batsmen. In the late Fifties and early Sixties, he was India's number one utility man. In the last few years of his fairly long career he was the sheet anchor of India's batting. In the meantime, he was the only Indian selected to play for the Rest of the World XI against Barbados in 1967, led his country in one Test and when he finally retired, Chandrakant Gulabrao Borde's record of 3061 runs, 52 wickets and 38 catches in 55 Tests marked him out as among the country's finest cricketers of all time.

There was no more beloved cricketer in his time than Borde. The public loved him for the manner in which he pulled India out of a crisis. He always received a good press for he was always accessible and there was nothing controversial about him. He did his job in his efficient, stylish way and was always pleasing, charming and modest in his talk and behaviour. His team members respected him for they knew they could always depend on him for valuable advice. There was, in his time, no greater team man than Borde. He was the most unselfish cricketer one could hope to come across. He could not do a mean thing even if he tried.

For example, I never saw Borde appeal unnecessarily. Time and again the batsman was rapped on his pads by a Borde delivery. While this might draw a response from some others on the field, Borde would just walk back quietly to his mark – until he was sure the batsman was out. He never tired to pressurise the batsman or the umpire and got his wickets through sheer skill, merit and hard work. In these days of catlike, almost rude, appeals for virtually every delivery, when players do everything to create pressure on the batsman or the umpire, when sledging is commonplace and behaviour is at an all-time low, it is nice to know that cricket was a gentleman's game – something epitomised by players like Borde. It was the same while batting. I don't think I ever saw Borde hesitate after being given out, let alone look at his bat or the stumps, or stare at the umpire, fielder or bowler or look back while walking to the pavilion. Even if he had some doubt about the decision, once the umpire gave him out, he never questioned the verdict. The young cricketer today could learn a lot about sportsmanship from Borde.

He could learn other things too. Borde could teach him how to play the square cut. Not since the days of Hazare had we seen a more perfect version of this lovely stroke. In a way, this somehow seemed correct for Hazare was Borde's mentor. Like the great master, he too possessed a flowing cover drive. His late cutting was as good as Mankad's. As his career progressed, he came to know how to make the most of leg side deliveries, and these he leg glanced in pretty fashion or drove past a gaping mid on or pulled and hooked past mid wicket and square leg with perfect timing and placement and a hidden power. He had a most hefty-looking pull drive, and used this stroke to enormous profit in the last few years of his Test career which stretched from 1958 to 1969. Before a shoulder injury in 1964 prevented him from bowling, Borde's leg spinners caused no little discomfort to India's opponents. Indeed, along with Durrani, he was the country's leading spin bowler in the early Sixties. While the additional bowling responsibilities did not affect his batting much, there is no doubt that his batting peaked after he gave up bowling.

Though Borde played his first Test only in 1958, he was a nationally known figure in cricket circles for about six years before that. Born in Poona in 1934, Borde made his Ranji Trophy debut as an eighteen-year-old schoolboy in 1952 when he made 55 and 61 not out for Maharashtra against Bombay. Based on potential rather than performance, he was selected for the tour of Pakistan in 1954-55. Borde, at twenty was the surprise choice. He did not play in any of the Tests, had quite an undistinguished tour and was promptly forgotten for the next four years. It wasn't till the West Indians came over in 1958-59 that the Indian selectors, on the hunt for promising young batsmen to make the team to play the touring side and subsequently go on the tour of England in 1959, realised that there was a bloke named Borde around. He played in the first two Tests but scores of seven, nought and 13 could not have helped his cause much. His electric fielding, however, saw to it that he was not summarily banished from the Test side. He was among the reserves for the third Test at Calcutta and was named twelfth man for the next Test at Madras.

Fate sometimes can be most unkind to someone. But then almost to balance the picture, it can be very kind to someone else. On the eve of the match, Gopinath and Manjrekar, who were both in the team for the Madras Test, reported unfit. Borde was among the players called upon to fill the breach. There seemed little hope of Borde making the team for the final Test – or the team to tour England – when, sent in at number nine, he was out for a duck in the first innings. In the second innings, injuries to Mankad and Kripal Singh meant that Borde was sent in at number five. His entire cricketing future seemed to hang in the balance when he went out to bat. India, chasing an unlikely victory target of 447 were 45 for three. The pressure on him must have been terrific. But Borde kept his composure. The first ball from Gilchrist was well pitched up and he effortlessly drove it towards the cover boundary. It was a splendid stroke in murky light and brought him three runs. That set the stage for one of the best innings of the series. Borde held on grimly and it was only when there was no hope of India drawing the game that he adopted aggressive gestures. He took ten runs in one over off Sobers and in the process reached his 50. When he was ultimately out for 56 made in three and a half hours and inclusive of nine boundaries, the cheering for his gallant knock in a losing cause in the face of a formidable bowling line-up was loud and long.

So Borde kept his place in the team for the final Test – and I don't think even the most casual Indian cricket follower needs to be told of his feat during that match at the Kotla. It was such a dream feat that every Indian schoolboy at the time knew about it as surely as he could recite his multiplication table. Within the space of a few short days,

Borde was transformed from just a promising young cricketer to a hero of national fame. His name was on everyone's lips – even of those who were not normally interested in the game. It is sufficient to say that against an attack which had ground India into absolute humiliation in three successive Tests, Borde hit 109 and 96 to come within a 'short head' of a feat performed only once before by an Indian – Hazare against Australia at Adelaide in 1948. How thrilling it would have been, especially for Borde, had he been able to equal his mentor's feat! He treated Hall and Gilchrist as if they were club bowlers, and played the stellar role as India, most unexpectedly, held on for a draw. His batting was hailed as 'classic' and he was immediately worshipped as a Messiah who had come to the rescue of the fragile and slipshod Indian batting.

With three superb knocks in a row behind him, Borde embarked on the tour of England with confidence and with the eyes of every cricket follower back home thrust hopefully on him. Against the background of the 'classic' knocks and the high expectations, he could be termed a disappointment on that disastrous tour. He only just about crossed the 1000-run mark even if he did head the bowling averages with a bag of 72 wickets. In the Tests, he was unfortunate to suffer a painful injury during his first innings of the series. When 15, his left hand little finger was fractured by a ball from Trueman and that kept him out of action for many matches including the second Test. In the third and fourth Tests he showed something of his true form with scores of 41 and 75, but overall it was a tour Borde could not have looked back on with much fondness.

Though he did not have a very profitable series against Australia in 1959-60, Borde showed that he could be depended on in a crisis. By scoring 44 at a crucial juncture, he played an important role in the famous victory at Kanpur. And by getting 50 at an equally vital juncture in the final Test at Calcutta, he had a major role to play in India holding out for a draw. And at the dawn of the Sixties, it had become obvious that Borde was now India's number one utility man and quite irreplaceable. Indeed, from Leeds, 1959 to Auckland, 1968, Borde had a record run of 49 consecutive Tests. During the period as utility man, his batting really peaked in the series against Pakistan in 1960-61. There were scores of 41, 44 and 45, and one more knock, which is recalled fondly even today by old timers fortunate to have seen it.

In the fourth Test at Madras, facing a Pakistan total of 448 for eight declared, India were 164 for four late on the third evening. Borde joined Umrigar and the two first defended dourly in the crisis situation and then as the partnership progressed, Umrigar really turned on the heat. As long as Umrigar was at the crease, Borde was content to play the supporting role. The fifth wicket stand, which realised 177 runs, the Indian record for that wicket against any country, was not broken till late on the fourth evening. After Umrigar was out for 117, Borde really went for the bowling. But there was more brilliance than raw power in his batting, and as one critic put it: 'He sought runs without ever appearing brutal.' How in keeping with the Borde image! After taking six and three quarter hours over his hundred, Borde hammered 77 runs in a little over two hours. His unbeaten 177 was a score he was never able to better during his Test playing days. He headed the averages for the first time with 330 runs at an average of 82.50.

Borde's utility qualities peaked during the series against England in 1961-62, as figures of 314 runs at an average of 44.85 together with 16 wickets at 28.75 apiece clearly illustrate. Scores of 69, 45, 68 and 61 underlined his consistency. While scoring 69, he shared a record 142-run stand for the fifth wicket with Durrani and during his 45 he shared a 132-run partnership with Manjrekar. His all round skills were instrumental in India sealing the rubber against England for the first time. But against the backdrop of his growing stature and his reputation of playing fast bowling with a degree of assurance, his aggregate of 246 runs from ten innings in the 1962 series against West Indies was a mite disappointing. He had just one innings of note – 93 in the second Test at Kingston.

By 1963-64 with the retirement of Umrigar, Borde was now one of the two principal batsmen of the side, the other being Manjrekar. And he was now widely tipped to take over the captaincy, following the near fatal injury to Contractor. But the selectors opted for Pataudi and Borde remained vice captain for the rest of his Test career, except on one occasion when he led the Indian team. In the series against

England that season, he was not at his best with the bat, his only innings of note being 84 at Bombay, when he rescued India from the quagmire of 99 for six with a seventh wicket stand of 153 runs with Durrani. It was around this time that a shoulder injury meant that he was ruled out as one of India's main bowlers. Borde, now free to concentrate on his batting, tightened up his defence and technique considerably. This, added to the fluency of his stroke play, made him a complete batsman. He was ready to take over the mantle of India's sheet anchor as, within a year, Manjrekar too had retired.

When the Australians landed in India for a three Test series in October 1964, Borde was in charge of the batting. And for the next few years, it was Borde to whom the Indian public, press and players looked to for a big score or a champagne knock. The greater solidity in his batting was immediately visible. In 33 Tests till then, he had scored 1700 runs. In the next ten Tests, he scored nearly 900 runs. In 57 innings he had made two centuries. In the next 16 innings, he accounted for three more. Moreover, there was no more shuttling between the batting order for Borde. He was by now more or less established at number four and from that pivotal position, guided the fortunes of India's batting.

In the matches against Australia, Borde came off in every Test. At Madras, he came in after five wickets had gone down for 76, scored 49 and helped Pataudi add 142 runs for the sixth wicket. At Bombay he was involved in a storybook feat, the kind that every schoolboy sees in his dreams of making the winning hit for your country. Requiring 254 runs for victory, India were 215 for seven when Borde walked in. Nine runs later, Pataudi left, leaving Borde with only the new wicketkeeper K.S. Indrajitsinhji and a very definite number eleven in B.S. Chandrasekhar for company. Making use of the psychological advantage, Australian captain Bobby Simpson applied the pressure but Borde rose to the occasion, thanks to his vast experience, his ideal, ice cool temperament and tactical skills. The final on drive off Tom Veivers heralded a famous two-wicket victory and brought the house down at the Brabourne stadium. The 40,000 holiday crowd (it was Dassera) went wild with joy, and Borde's final match winning stroke is still talked about by old timers lucky to have seen it. For the record, Borde remained unbeaten with 30 – perhaps the most famous 30 in Indian cricket! Carrying on in the same confident vein Borde top-scored in the only Indian innings in the rain affected final Test at Calcutta. Coming in when India at 133 for six were struggling against the spin of Veivers and Simpson, Borde in a thrilling counter attack took the total to 235, his own share being 68 not out.

Against New Zealand, later that season, he was at his attacking best. A scintillating century and three half centuries saw him finish the series with a tally of 371 runs from the four Tests. In every game, he had at least one partnership of note. At Madras, he scored 68 and shared a 88-run partnership with Durrani after five wickets had gone down for 114. At Calcutta, after four wickets had fallen for 101, Borde and Pataudi added 110 runs for the fifth wicket, Borde's contribution being 62. At Bombay, India following on 209 runs behind, were 107 for three when Borde entered. He dominated a fourth wicket partnership of 154 runs with Sardesai, hitting 109. At New Delhi, he scored 87 and added 138 runs with Pataudi for the fourth wicket.

With such consistency it was obvious now that Borde was at the zenith of his batting powers, and a lot was expected of him on the eve of the three match series against the all conquering West Indies team that visited India in 1966-67. But even the most optimistic Borde fan could not have bargained for his superb record in the contest. Against one of the strongest bowling attacks to have bowled against India – Hall, Griffith, Gibbs and Sobers all at their peak – Borde hit two centuries in three Tests. The rescue work started early. The series was hardly a few overs old when he walked in with India ten for two. Soon it was 14 for three. Borde nursed the innings through the critical phase. First with Pataudi he put on 93 runs for the fourth wicket. Then with Durrani he added 102 runs for the sixth wicket. Borde was out only on the second morning with India 242 for seven, his share being exactly half – 121. After three modest scores Borde was back in form in the final Test at Madras. This time he came in shortly after lunch on the first day with the score 131 for two and did not depart till shortly after lunch on the second day. The score was 377 for seven and Borde's contribution was 125. In the second innings too he was going great guns and it took an outstanding catch by Clive Lloyd to restrict him to 49. Borde finished the series with 346 runs – an Indian record for a three Test series – and the next best was Pataudi's 143.

It was shortly after this series that Borde received the invitation to represent the World XI to play Barbados at Bridgetown. So, when he took off with the Indian team a couple of months later for his second tour of England, he was confidence personified and great things were expected from him. On the contrary, the tour was a disaster both from the team's viewpoint and as far as Borde was concerned. Who could have foreseen that a batsman good enough to play for a World XI would end up with an average of 10.00? His aggregate was an incredible 60 from six innings and he finished below Chandrasekhar in the averages. He fell three times to pace and three times to spin, and his struggling form had a demoralising effect on the side. When the team's principal and most experienced batsman gets out for a series of low scores, it does have an adverse effect on the younger members.

The Indian cricket fan now began asking a question that would have seemed unthinkable just a few months back – is this the beginning of the end for Borde? After all, he wasn't getting any younger. In Australia that winter, Borde's lack of form gave rise to even more speculation. Two successes and six failures did little to redeem his reputation. In the first Test at Adelaide – the only game in which he led India in the absence of the injured Pataudi – he scored 69 and shared a 121-run fourth wicket stand with Rusi Surti. Then in the third Test at Brisbane, when India were chasing a tough victory target of 395, a sixth wicket partnership of 119 runs between Borde and Jaisimha gave the visiting team hopes of pulling off a remarkable win. However, Borde was out for 63, the rest of the batting crumbled and India lost by 39 runs. By the end of the series, there was a serious confidence crisis, illustrated by the fact that Borde was back at number seven and number eight. He did better against a weaker New Zealand attack and scores of 57, 33, 41 and 65 not out must have restored his confidence a bit, particularly since he headed the averages. But by now it was clear that this was not the Borde of the early and mid-Sixties. Then he was the commanding batsman, now he was struggling to maintain form. The Borde of old flicked the fastest of bowlers off his toes to the mid wicket boundary, but the Borde of 1968 was one with failing eyesight and slow reflexes.

In late 1969 on the eve of the return rubbers against New Zealand and Australia at home, Vijay Merchant was the chairman of the selection committee. He had definite views about 'the future belongs to the youth'. When the team to play New Zealand in the first Test was announced, a couple of newcomers were included – and Borde was dropped. This brought to an end the run of 49 Tests that started with the Leeds Test in 1959, an easy Indian record and a tribute to Borde's fitness and skill. However, this did not mark the end of Borde's Test career. He did have one last fling, a feeble one though. When some of the youngsters disappointed in the series against New Zealand, a hue and cry was raised in some quarters favouring the return of experienced players. Borde was recalled for the first Test at Bombay against Australia. His performance against McKenzie, Connolly, Gleeson and Mallett was pathetic. He was out for two and 18, and it was obvious even to the most inveterate Borde fan that it was the end of the road for him. Mercifully that proved to be Borde's last Test. He was one of the contenders for captaincy – along with Pataudi and Wadekar – for the tour of the West Indies in 1971. But going by his declining batting form, there was never any realistic chance that he would get the job.

Borde continued to play in the Ranji Trophy for a few more years. He still had one ambition – to lead Maharashtra to victory in the national competition. He came close to it in 1970-71 when he led a full strength state side against a depleted Bombay team in the final. Maharashtra were the clear favourites, but Bombay, in the midst of their dream fifteen-year run, pulled off an upset victory. Shortly afterwards, Borde retired from first-class cricket. But there was no way that Borde could give up his ties with the game he loved so much. He became a respected and well-liked manager of Indian teams, and in 1982-83 was a member of the selection committee that picked the victorious World Cup team. After serving on the committee the following year, Borde was elevated to the chairmanship in 1984, a post he held the following year too. He returned as chairman in 1999, a position he held till 2002.

# 9

# Mansur Ali Khan **Pataudi**

### Charisma Personified

Charismatic personalities are what cricket is all about – players who are responsible for spectators thronging to the stadium with their combination of handsome looks and dashing approach. And even with the presence of such cricketers like Salim Durrani, Farokh Engineer, Abbas Ali Baig and M.L. Jaisimha in the Sixties – style and elegance came naturally to all of them and they made cricket seem chic – can there be any doubt that the central figure and the leader in more ways than one was the Nawab of Pataudi, later known as Mansur Ali Khan Pataudi after the princes lost their privy purses and titles in 1971?

For many years Pataudi was not only the best batsman in the country, he was one of the leading players in the world. He attracted notice because of many factors – his aristocratic lineage, his background as the son of the elder Nawab of Pataudi, who had played for both England and India and captained the country on their tour of England in 1946, his English cricketing background, having had his education at Winchester and Oxford, his courage at coming back into the game and playing it with remarkable success at the highest level despite a serious eye accident, his ability to shine like a beacon even as the Indian batting collapsed time and again, and the manner of his batting which was bold and adventurous.

Indeed, to see 'Tiger' Pataudi bat was a revelation. He was such a gifted player that he could get away with the most remarkable of shots. That is why the purists in England, on seeing the early Pataudi bat in his university days, labelled him as 'unorthodox'. Nothing could be further from the truth. Pataudi's batting was based on scientific principles like all good batting is. But, in addition, he was such an artist that he could get away time and again with shots that were not strictly in the book. He never imitated anyone. He was an original and his style was all his own. Before he came on the scene, for example, the pull drive was a shot that was almost never played by any Indian batsman. And even if executed, it was not with a little hesitancy and uncertainty. Pataudi alone could get away with the stroke. There was no element of risk whatsoever in the manner he played it. His left leg was quickly forward and then those steely wrists and strong shoulders combined to give the ball an all-powerful heave which saw the ball land in the stands at deep mid wicket.

Like the pull drive, Pataudi also perfected the lofted shot over long on. The occasions were not infrequent when I saw him lift the best of spin bowlers for sixes via these two productive shots. He was also perfectly at ease against fast bowling – despite the eye injury – and was a fairly good hooker. If all this gives the impression that Pataudi was a stronger player on the leg side, it is correct. But that is not to say he was not a good player on the off side. His off drive and extra cover drive were strokes made with a touch of effrontery. He cut, square and late, with a blend of timing and power. Indeed, timing was the essence of all his strokes. But it is chiefly because of his leg side strokes that we shall remember Pataudi. It was said that the cares of captaincy burdened his batting but that was probably only late in his career. On the contrary, he thrived on the responsibility.

Pataudi was born in Bhopal in 1941 but we, in India, first heard of him when there came over from England a photograph in 1952 showing Alf Gover correcting an eleven-year-old boy's stroke at his famous indoor cricket school. That was also the year the elder Pataudi passed away. Then in 1957, John Arlott, always quick to spot talent, wrote: 'The 16-year-old Pataudi has followed in the footsteps of his late father in developing into a considerable batsman while still at school – in his case Winchester. Here he has come under the eye of H.S. Altham and G.H.G. Doggart. Turning out for the Sussex Colts in the 1957 season, the young Indian prince has already made a strong impression by the correctness of his play, his assured footwork and a cool temperament.'

The next we heard about Pataudi was in 1960 when he emulated his father by scoring 131 in the University match. The following year, he was again in rip-roaring form. Appointed Oxford captain, he had made 1216 runs at an average of 55.27 and seemed certain to pass his father's record of 1307 runs in a season. The English critics were in raptures about his batting, which they hailed as 'unorthodox but dazzling'. Then came the car accident on July 1 that threatened to ruin a career that seemed marked for great achievements. The car in which he was travelling collided with another vehicle and a splinter from the shattered windscreen entered Pataudi's right eye. The lens of the eye was destroyed and the whole eye shifted slightly out of alignment. Doctors said that he could not play for a long time and that he would never be the same player again. Some said he would never play again. They obviously did not know the supreme guts and the steely nerves of the young man. Displaying tremendous courage and a fierce determination, the young Nawab made some adjustments and within weeks was back practising at the nets.

In November 1961, Pataudi arrived in India, confident of playing for the country. Not many knew the extent of his injury or what effect it would have on his batting, but the selectors, on the tremendous promise he held out, made an adventurous move by including him in the Indian team to play against the MCC team led by Ted Dexter. It did not take long for Pataudi to display his talent and skill, class and enterprise, and in the final Test at Madras unfolded the kind of enthralling and innovative batting that is talked about even over forty years later. He entered when the score was 74 for two, and so breathtaking was his batting that even the normally stodgy Contractor was driven to make aggressive gestures. In an hour after lunch, the two slapped on 82 runs, a rate of scoring unheard of in Indian cricket in those days. The crowd at the Corporation stadium on that day – January 10, 1962 – sat spellbound for two and a half hours and were witness to batting, the like of which they had not seen before. In that time, Pataudi hit 103, which for its sheer audacity and freedom of stroke play was unsurpassed. He hit 16 fours and two sixes, lofted the ball with nonchalance and one particular shot – a six off Allen for which he took the ball from outside the off stump and pulled it right into the stands at mid wicket – brought the house down.

It was thus with more than a degree of confidence that Pataudi took off with the Indian team for the tour of West Indies in 1962, particularly as he had been promoted to the vice captaincy. But the near fatal injury to Contractor pitchforked him into the hot seat much sooner than expected. Among the first questions to be asked was whether the exceptional batting skills of the twenty-one-year-old Pataudi would be affected by the sudden burden of captaincy. Going by his scores in the three Tests that he played, it did not seem to be the case. He made 48 in one Test and 47 in the next. Both the times he came good in a crisis, showing that besides talent and technique, he had the ideal temperament.

Still, Pataudi had his critics who pointed out to his youth, the fact that he had spent much of his time in England and knew little of Indian conditions or players, and to the result of the three Test matches he led in the West Indies, all of which were lost. To make matters worse, he was on a lean trot just before the next series against England in 1963-64 was to commence. But the adverse situation brought out the best in Pataudi the cricketer. Playing for North Zone in the Duleep Trophy semifinal against South Zone, he scored 141 and that settled any doubts as to his claim as a batsman in the side. It also paved the way for him to be named captain – albeit on chairman Dutta Ray's casting vote.

The initial outings were so alarming that the selectors suggested that he take an eye test, convinced that something was wrong. Pataudi contemptuously rejected the idea though he wondered how long the bad patch would last. He need not have worried. In the second innings, he scored 203 not out, the first double century by an Indian against England. Even after granting that the second half of the ton was made when there was very little in the match as a contest, the fact that he had batted almost seven hours and made a major score boosted his confidence no end. Pataudi was out of the rut and it was obvious that Indian batting in the Sixties would revolve around him.

And so it proved. Throughout the decade Pataudi was the inspirational figure, and with the captain showing the way the Indian batting was not as brittle as it was in the Fifties. Pataudi was such a complete batsman that he could combine an array of strokes with sterling defence depending on the situation. Frequently he had to play the Horatio role and as far as courage in adversity is concerned, Pataudi probably ranked close to Hazare as time and again he pulled the Indian innings through a crisis with a superbly crafted characteristically brave knock. Against Australia in 1964, for example, he started off with an unbeaten 128 at Madras. It turned out to be the only century for both sides in the series, a rare feat. In the process, he emulated his father who had also scored a century in his first Test appearance against Australia in the infamous Bodyline series, thirty-two years before. In the second Test at Bombay came a notable double of 86 and 53 wherein he displayed his ability to play two very different innings. The first time around he unleashed his full array of strokes. In the second essay, coming in a crisis, he displayed his superb defensive technique in scoring 53 and sealing India's win in a fighting seventh wicket partnership of 93 with Vijay Manjrekar, after six wickets had gone down for 122 in quest of a seemingly distant victory target of 254.

By the mid-Sixties Pataudi was acknowledged to be among the leading batsmen in the world, and as a personality was second to none underscored by his selection as Sussex captain when Dexter was injured. Two sparkling centuries in the series against New Zealand in 1965 confirmed his growing stature, and even though he was restricted to scores of 44, 51 and 40 against the world champion West Indian team that Gary Sobers brought out to India in 1966-67, the aura surrounding Pataudi did not diminish one bit. In fact it only brightened on the 1967 tour of England when Pataudi considerably enhanced his reputation. Just mention 'Headingley 1967' and the eyes of any cricket lover will sparkle with delight, even thirty-eight years after the event. When the Indian team took the field for the first Test at Leeds, they were woefully short of practice as rain had dogged them ever since they landed in England. Then in the Test itself, injuries left two key players Surti and Bedi incapacitated. The Indians, facing an English total of 550 for four declared, collapsed to 86 for six by stumps on the second day.

There was a storm of protests in the morning's newspapers with critics hitting out at the Indians' lack of spine. Ian Woolridge wrote in the *Daily Mail* that 'If it were a heavyweight fight instead of a featherweight Test match, the referee would have shown humanity and stopped the contest to spare the Indians full punishment.' The *Daily Telegraph*, in its mocking headline, summed the situation aptly: 'INDIA 160 RUNS BEHIND BOYCOTT'. (Geoff Boycott had scored 246 not out in England's first innings.) Such was the pressure that Pataudi, on 14, faced as he resumed his innings on the third morning. Soon the Indians were 92 for seven. Pataudi stood like Horatio on the tottering bridge. He was middling the ball well but where was the support? Surti, inspired by his captain's pep talk that morning, hobbled his way to the wicket with Wadekar as the runner. He stayed 100 minutes, scored 22 and helped Pataudi to add 59 runs for the eighth wicket. Pataudi mixing caution and aggression judiciously, got to 64 before he was last out with the total 164. As events proved, this proved to be a most inspirational knock. With the captain having showed them the way, the Indian batsmen in the second innings were a transformed lot. Gone was the hesitancy in their stroke play, their insecurity in defence. Wadekar and Engineer put on a record 168 runs for the second wicket and Borde got 33, his highest score in what was a wretched series for him.

Still in the pre-lunch session of the fourth day, India were 228 for four when Pataudi joined Hanumant. A comprehensive defeat loomed large, for India had finished 386 runs in arrears on the first innings. But the two batsmen got entrenched without any difficulty and went on to add 134 runs for the fifth wicket. Hanumant got 73, Prasanna at number nine scored 19 and Bedi, the next man, made 14. And towering above everyone was the man who had inspired the fightback, which truly belonged to the golden age of cricket. When he was ninth out at 506 on the final morning, Pataudi had made 148. For its bravery, the quality of the batting under immense pressure, and the inspirational circumstances it was made in, the hundred takes its place among the most memorable Test centuries in Indian cricket. And England, which seemed set to win by an innings and plenty inside three days, finally won by six wickets late on the final afternoon. The man who almost single-handedly made this possible was the picture of modesty, but the English press wrote now in rhapsodic terms about the team in general – and of Pataudi in particular. The *Daily Mail* especially went rapturous over Pataudi and hailed him in a brilliant banner headline: 'HIS MAGNIFICENT HIGHNESS THE NAWAB OF HEADINGLEY AND OF PATAUDI'.

By now Pataudi had scored six hundreds in 22 Tests and seemed well on the road to breaking Umrigar's record of 12 centuries. Little could anyone have known then that the Leeds hundred was to be Pataudi's last in Tests. That epoch-making innings, however, guaranteed him a place as one of Wisden's five cricketers of the year – a rare honour then for Indian cricketers. But then the really great knocks need not have to be hundreds, as Pataudi proved in Australia in 1967-68. He was struck by misfortune early on the tour when while fielding at practice, he pulled a hamstring muscle and missed not only all the first-class games before the first Test, but the Test itself. It was not until the second Test at Melbourne that he played his maiden first-class match in Australia. It would be difficult for anyone to top a feat like the one at Headingley but in some ways, his double of 75 and 85 this time was to be as memorable – if not even greater. For one thing, it was his first experience of the fast and bouncy Australian pitches. Secondly, he had not yet fully recovered from the injury and this meant that his running was reduced to a gentle jog. His movements too were restricted while making strokes. In effect he had now one good eye and one good leg. Indeed the writers called him 'Long John Silver'. And yet there he was, defying everything that the bowlers could hurl at him.

Did I say defying? No, that should be flaying, lambasting, hammering away at them playing the innings of his life. 'If this is how he bats with one eye and one leg how would he bat with two good eyes and two good legs,' murmured many former cricketing greats while gaping in amazement. In a losing cause, his knock was a 'many splendoured thing'. It underscored his fighting qualities, a disinclination to buckle under the severest of pressures and a never-say-die attitude. He carried on gamely, making light of a handicap that would have prevented lesser mortals from even donning the gloves and pads. Pataudi tamed the attack, combining, according to Wisden, 'batting genius with courage in a manner which warmed the hearts of all. He was severely restricted in front foot play by his leg strain and refused many singles. Yet he executed aggressive strokes, including several pugnacious hooks.' The Australian spearhead Graham McKenzie, who took ten wickets in the match, was made to look ordinary by Pataudi, who once hit him off the back foot over his head for a near six - a truly remarkable stroke. Really it was all the kind of stuff that cricketing folklore is all about.

At the peak of his batting prowess and personal popularity, Pataudi was confidence personified on the eve of the return contests at home against New Zealand and Australia in 1969-70. But he struck a most unproductive patch with one success and five failures. He was even heckled by his hometown crowd at Hyderabad during the final Test, though of course, true to his aristocratic nature, he never betrayed his emotions in public. It was much the same story against Australia. In nine innings, he had two successes - scores of 95 and 59 - and seven failures. He again suffered abuse from the crowd, this time at Calcutta. Averages such as 21 (against New Zealand) and 24 (against Australia) were not something that one associated with Pataudi.

At the beginning of the 1970-71 season Pataudi was not at the top of popularity polls. India had lost matches in the past but Pataudi always remained supreme as a batsman. Now India continued to lose matches and Pataudi was no longer the master batsman. Perhaps it was a bad patch and a classy player like him would surely come out from it. Perhaps this would come about on the tour of the West Indies in 1971. Surprisingly, however, Wadekar was appointed as the captain. Pataudi had got the top job seven years before on the chairman's casting vote; he now lost it on the chairman's casting vote.

Would Pataudi retain his place as batsman, was the next question. It was answered quickly. Making himself unavailable for the West Indies tour, Pataudi stayed behind to contest the 1971 general elections unsuccessfully. Somehow, an Indian team without Pataudi looked very different. But the team under Wadekar won not only in West Indies but also in England. So, by the time the 1971-72 season got under way, there was a perceptible change in the Indian cricket scenario. Wadekar was firmly entrenched as the captain. All the batsmen had done well in West Indies and England. Pataudi now faced the unenviable - and unbelievable - task of fighting his way back into the Test team.

This Pataudi did with a run of sterling knocks around the domestic circuit, blending dash with discipline. And when the Indian batting failed in the first two Tests of the 1972-73 series against England, there was a clamour for Pataudi's inclusion. With the perfect timing that was the hallmark of his batting, Pataudi got a hundred for South Zone against the visiting team. When the team for the third Test at Madras was announced, Pataudi was back where he belonged. It was time for the 'Tiger' to roar again and he did not disappoint. I shall never forget the royal welcome he got from the capacity Chepauk crowd when he came in to bat. Batting as the Pataudi of old, he made 1969 appear as if it had been some bad dream. It was Pataudi who brought a touch of class to the Indian batting, which until then had looked anything but reassuring. He made 73 and looked good for a hundred when he was a trifle unlucky to be dismissed, out to a catch at deep mid wicket which substitute Tolchard took almost on the fence. He followed this up with 54 in the next Test at Kanpur and altogether there was little doubt that Pataudi still remained a world-class batsman.

Unfortunately he did not remain in this category for too long. The disaster in England in 1974 meant that Wadekar had to go and the selectors turned again to Pataudi to lead India against West Indies in 1974-75. And while he still possessed the cricketing acumen and led the side capably, unfortunately the same good things could not be said of his batting. He turned thirty-four during the series and it was now obvious that age had taken its toll on his physique. His reflexes were slow and even his remarkable one-eyed sight, which had seen him combat the fastest of bowling and cleverest of spin bowlers all these years, had considerably weakened. In seven innings, his highest score was 36 and he finished fourteenth in the averages. His stays at the crease were miserable for him – and equally miserable for the spectators who were shocked at seeing the shadow of a once great batsman. In the final knock of the series (incidentally his last Test innings) he was out for nine. For this, he batted 63 minutes – and was dropped thrice! It was a sight no one wished to see. And coming to terms quickly with the situation, Pataudi announced his retirement almost immediately afterwards.

Pataudi's final Test figures are a travesty of justice. Without the kind of pressure situations he had to face, it is inconceivable to think how much better the figures would be. He remains Indian cricket's most endearingly heroic figure. Today at sixty-four, he has aged gracefully – like his film star wife – and has remained a personality of utmost charm and dignity. He is perhaps Indian cricket's ultimate charismatic figure.

# 10

# Gundappa Ranganath **Viswanath**

The Supreme Artist

Gundappa Ranganath Viswanath appeared on the scene when Indian cricket was in desperate need of someone like him. The Indian batting order had little solidity, consisting of a couple of swashbucklers and a few aged artisans. What was needed was the presence of a true artist. The batting was becoming increasingly plebeian with hardly any sparkle. And then came this pocket-sized wonder from Mysore to brighten up the Indian cricket horizon. From then on, almost every day was like Diwali.

Viswanath's place in the pantheon of the great Indian batting stars is secure and unchallenged. He stood only five feet, four inches but that was the only thing small or little about him. He was a big-hearted cricketer who wore his patriotism on his sleeve. His gifts were varied and prodigious. He had marvellous eyesight and remarkably quick reflexes and this enabled him to play the ball that much early. He was held in awe by his opponents and was worshipped like a demigod by his countless fans. He had the prettiest of strokes. The bat in his hands was a wand through which he wove a magic spell that left bowlers and fieldsmen bewitched, bewildered and breathless. Power was not the essence of his batting, but timing was. He was an apostle of non-violence. If at all he had to execute the bowler, he preferred to do it gently. His tenures at the crease could be compared to that of a musician at a concert. Like Ravi Shankar and Bismillah Khan in their arts, he held you spellbound with his matchless craft. He was always a great favourite with the crowd, who cheered him loud and long every time he came to the wicket, for they knew that while he was at the crease, they would witness batting in its highest art form. I watched

Viswanath play several innings and not once can I remember the spectators booing him for slow scoring, though a Srikkanth or a Sehwag he was not. He was always watched with more than just keen interest. Even a defensive stroke – normally a dull thud of bat against ball – was a thing of beauty and grace when he played it. He sculpted his runs at the rate of roughly 25 an hour not with monotonous regularity but with strokes of ethereal beauty and grace. There were touches of Vijay Hazare when he drove and shades of Vijay Manjrekar when he cut. While these strokes were predominant in his repertoire, he was also a daring hooker and had the most attractive leg glance one could hope to see.

Viswanath appeared on the first-class scene about the same time as Sunil Gavaskar. He made his Test debut a season before Gavaskar. Viswanath was just a few months older and their careers ran parallel. Throughout the Seventies and till the early Eighties, the two were the batting kingpins. But while Viswanath was certainly the more gifted of the two, he was also more likely to give the bowler a chance by flashing unwisely outside the off stump. Otherwise, like Gavaskar, his judgement of line and length, his body balance and his footwork were superb. Viswanath had wrists of steel and hit the ball with a wondrous touch and a sense of timing and control that was unsurpassed.

Born in Bhadravati in 1949, Viswanath made his first-class debut in 1967 for Mysore against Andhra in the Ranji Trophy. The eighteen-year-old pint-sized lad could not have started off with a bigger bang, for his maiden score in first-class cricket was 230 not out. This marked him out as an uncommonly good batsman. In addition, the manner in which he continued to make runs in handsome fashion for the next two years did not go unnoticed. It was obvious the lad had class written all over him. A fighting unbeaten 51 in a losing cause for South Zone in the Duleep Trophy semifinal against North Zone at Madras at the start of the 1969-70 season – when he adroitly handled Bishen Bedi and Rajinder Goel on a turning track – confirmed this opinion. The Vijay Merchant led selection committee included him among the reserves in the series against New Zealand, and when Borde failed against Australia, Viswanath replaced him in the second Test at Kanpur.

Alan Connolly made Viswanath's Test debut a harrowing one. He hustled the young man with a couple of really fast deliveries. He then dealt him two bouncers and finally dropped a deceptive slower one. The result was a catch to short leg. When Viswanath, not having opened his account, made his way to the pavilion, Pataudi greeted him with an encouraging, 'Don't worry, you will get another chance in the second innings.' Well, in the second innings, when he came in at 94 for two, the bowler he had to face was Connolly. The tall and well-built Australian gave him a bouncer first ball. Viswanath made a thrilling hook to the mid wicket boundary and never looked back. The rest – as the cliché goes – is history. How he flayed the attack to hit 25 boundaries in his 137 before he was seventh out at 306. How he displayed deep concentration for 354 minutes to help India draw the match. How he dominated the batting to score his runs while five senior players scored only about 70 between them. Even in the nineties, Viswanath displayed the temperament of a veteran. While the spectators bit their nails, unable to bear the suspense, Viswanath was never affected. He serenely proceeded through this traditionally nervous period and finally square cut Connolly to the fence to go from 98 to 102. That shot also signalled the completion of a unique feat. No batsman in cricket history had scored a double century on first-class debut and followed it up with a hundred in his first Test. Scores of 29 and 44 not out in the next Test, followed by half centuries in each of the two remaining Tests, saw Viswanath leap to an aggregate of 334 runs and head the averages comfortably – in his first series! By the end of the season, Viswanath was a national hero.

At the start of the Seventies then Viswanath was not just a bright star on the Indian cricketing horizon, he was also going to be the fulcrum of the batting during the decade. The discovery of Gavaskar during the India Rubber year of 1971, however, meant that the two were going to be the joint pillars. And if it was Gavaskar who was now the new sporting hero, Viswanath was not far behind. Of particular significance was his batting in England where a combination of impeccable technique and a wide array of strokes saw him earn praise from the critics. He scored a gallant 68 in the first Test at Lord's while his 33 in three tension-packed hours at the Oval underscored his ideal temperament. During a vital period, he withstood all the pressure that the shrewd Ray Illingworth exerted on him, batted through the innings and was out while going for the winning stroke. Even the usually stern Keith Miller wrote that 'no praise can be too high for Viswanath's knock'.

It is amazing how fickle the Indian selectors can be sometimes. After Viswanath failed to come good in the first three Tests of the series against England in 1972-73, there was talk that he might be dropped. Admittedly, a tally of 104 runs from six innings made for a rather poor return, but as the cricketing adage goes: 'Form is temporary, class is permanent'. And if nothing else, Viswanath had class written all over him. He just about kept his place for the fourth Test at Kanpur. At the end of the penultimate day, it seemed almost sure that he would be dropped for the final Test for he had made only 25 in the first innings. Thankfully, however, he had another chance in the second innings on the final day and he grasped it with both gloves. With an unbeaten 75, he not only saved India from an awkward situation, but also batted with the fluency that brought him his maiden Test century at the same venue three years before.

Interestingly enough, when Viswanath scored that 137, the keener cricket fans brought up the subject of other Indian players who had scored a century in their first Test and remembered that none of the previous five who had performed the feat had made another Test hundred again. The hoodoo had followed Lala Amarnath, Deepak Shodhan, Kripal Singh, Abbas Ali Baig and Hanumant Singh. Would Viswanath be similarly jinxed? There was a tense suspense from November 1969 to February 1973. During that time, Viswanath played 13 Test matches without even approaching the three-figure knock. In fact, he had passed the half-century mark on only five occasions. Was Viswanath too going the same unkind way of the other five? The answer, a most emphatic 'no' was provided on February 7, 1973. That day, attacking the English bowling in the final Test as only he could and exhibiting the most dazzling array of strokes the Brabourne stadium crowd could ever hope to see, Viswanath went on to score 113 to break the hoodoo once and for all.

Having 'killed' the jinx, Viswanath now proceeded to greater things. And the timing could not have been better. By the end of 1974, there was a considerable change in the Indian batting scenario. Ajit Wadekar had called it a day at the end of the disastrous tour of England, Dilip Sardesai had retired, and Salim Durrani had played his last Test. At the start of the 1974-75 series against West Indies it was obvious that India would rely overmuch on Gavaskar and Viswanath. As luck would have it, Gavaskar was injured in the first Test and did not take part in the series till the final Test. The pressure on Viswanath was enormous, but he responded to the added responsibility in a befitting manner with a performance that is recalled fondly even today.

And yet Viswanath's greatest series had a modest start. Scores of 29, 22, 32 and 39 led one to believe that he lacked both confidence and concentration. But in the second phase of the series, there underwent a metamorphosis in his batting. A fighting 52 in the first innings of the third Test at Calcutta heralded the new turn of events. And he followed this up with a knock that was rated pretty high even in his long and illustrious career. His 139 was the backbone of the Indian innings. He top-scored both times, and his great double was the chief reason for India's unexpected victory after the first two Tests had been lost by margins that brooked no argument. At Madras in the next Test, the run continued. And how! His unbeaten 97 in the first innings, for its grace and defiance, is acknowledged as one of the greatest batting displays by an Indian in a Test. Even by Viswanath's own high standards, it was a truly superlative innings and critics ran out of adjectives in trying to describe it. Viswanath alone tamed Andy Roberts, then at his fastest, and no other batsman got even into the twenties. It remained Viswanath's greatest innings – for all the centuries and the one double century to come – and I consider myself fortunate for being at Chepauk on that day. In the second innings, he displayed his superb defensive technique to good effect in getting 46. The fabulous run culminated in a splendid 95 in the first innings of the final Test at Bombay. Viswanath finished the series with 568 runs. The next highest was Engineer's 222. He also stood at the top of the averages like a Colossus with 63.11 while the next best was Anshuman Gaekwad's 36.67.

Topping this record would take some doing, but it is to Viswanath's credit that for almost a decade after this he continued to play sparkling strokes in every country and in every clime and against the best bowlers. On the dual tour of New Zealand and West Indies in early 1976, Viswanath maintained his reputation. Scores of 83 and 79 in the second Test at Christchurch meant that he was in good form, something that was imperative for the Indian team on the tougher tour of the Caribbean, which followed immediately. In keeping with his reputation that 'the higher the level of competition, the better he is', Viswanath rose to the occasion against West Indies. A delightful 62 in a losing cause – the first Test at Bridgetown – was a prelude to an outstanding knock in the third Test at Port of Spain. No one gave India a chance of winning when they were set a target of 403. Gavaskar brought forth a glimmer of hope with a splendid 102 but when he was second out at 177, India's hopes receded considerably. Viswanath joined Mohinder Amarnath and batted with all the regality at his command. While Amarnath played the sheet anchor role, Viswanath made strokes, which somehow as if by magic, always eluded the fielders. He almost caressed the bowlers to the boundary and out of a third wicket partnership of 159, Viswanath made 112 before he was run out after a four-hour stay. By the time he left, he had put India firmly on the road towards an unbelievable victory.

One of Viswanath's finest innings was played against New Zealand at Kanpur in 1976-77. The bowling, with the exception of Richard Hadlee, was not very strong but the fact remains that a major part of the knock – he scored 103 not out – was made in indifferent light. This brought out the excellence of his sight and his remarkably quick reflexes. For sheer mastery and dominance over the bowling, as well the timing of his strokes, it was one of Viswanath's best efforts. He took only just over two and a half hours to reach his hundred.

As if to show that the artist in him was after all human, Viswanath had to endure an eclipse of sorts being restricted to 175 runs in the five match series against Tony Greig's MCC team in 1976-77. But, of course, it was nothing but a bad patch, something that has affected the game's greatest players, and it was taken for granted that Viswanath would shrug it off sooner rather than later. Sure enough, the wretched series against England proved to be only a passing phase. And Viswanath's brilliance was again seen in Australia in 1977-78. He did not score a century, but five successive scores over the half century mark in nine innings gave him a tally of 473 runs, putting him once again where he belonged – at the top of the batting figures for the Tests. Having displayed his charming batting style on various grounds in five countries, Viswanath now proceeded confidently to spread his elegance to a sixth nation – across the border in Pakistan the following season. Viswanath scored 145 in the first Test at Faisalabad, becoming the first Indian to score a hundred against all five of India's opponents. The knock also gave him a sixth successive score over the half-century mark in Tests and also surpassed his previous Test best of 139.

It was against the West Indies at home later in the season that Viswanath came up with one of his best hundreds. Indeed when discussion centres round his 14 Test hundreds, the one made at Madras in January 1979 ranks very high. The attack was a good one with Sylvester Clarke and Norbert Philip no mean fast bowlers. But its chief feature was that it was made on a pitch that West Indian captain Alvin Kallicharan classed as 'dangerous and one of the fastest wickets I have played on anywhere'. Every time the two fast bowlers – and Vanburn Holder was also around – made the ball rise disconcertingly from the good length spot, Viswanath was right behind it. And whereas the others made hurried and uncomfortable jabs, Viswanath played the full regalia of strokes with all the time at his command. The next highest score after his 124 was 33. Even Gavaskar, in the midst of a personal run feast, was reduced to scores of four and one. That India could win only by three wickets – the only decisive result of the six match series – puts Viswanath's innings in proper perspective. He rounded off the series with a monumental 179 – his highest Test score till then – in the final Test at Kanpur and embarked on the tour of England in 1979 with his confidence sky high.

In England Viswanath brought all his expertise, besides his well known technical perfection and ethereal stroke play into action. And the apotheosis of these qualities came about – fittingly enough – at Lord's in the second Test. India, after being shot out for 96, finished 323 runs behind. At 99 for two, they were staring at an innings defeat. Viswanath joined Vengsarkar, and the two shared a partnership that brought back strong memories of the legendary rearguard action by Willie Watson and Trevor Bailey at the same ground twenty-six years before. Certainly it has taken its place as one of the greatest partnerships in Indian cricket. For 326 minutes, the two held firm against Lever, Botham, Hendrick and Edmonds, and by the time the stand was broken they had added 210 and India had earned an honourable draw. Vengsarkar got 103, the first of the three successive hundreds he was to get at the game's headquarters, while Viswanath went on to score 113. The strong, silent man of Indian cricket, as Viswanath had come to be known, had again showed that as a saviour of lost causes through artistic batting, he had no equal.

During the busy 1979-80 season, when India played 13 Tests at home, Viswanath was at his best against Australia before running out of steam against Pakistan and in the Golden Jubilee Test against England. He scored two handsome centuries at Bangalore and New Delhi, in addition to 96 at Calcutta in the six Test series against Australia, finishing with an aggregate of 518 runs at 74.00, statistically his best since the series against West Indies, five years before. But a run of lean scores thereafter saw the experts predicting that it was the beginning of the end for the supreme artist. They hoisted the alarm bells and noted that his legendary concentration was not the same and the twinkling footwork and superfast reflexes had slowed down. Viswanath could do little for some time to quash this theory. He redeemed his reputation somewhat by a courageous 114 against Australia in the final Test at Melbourne on the 1980-81 tour, a vital innings in the context of the sensational Indian victory. But the critics were back with their doomsday predictions, when in the series that followed against New Zealand he had the scores of nought, nine, seven, two and 46, easily Viswanath's worst outing ever.

When in the first two Tests against England the following season, Viswanath got only 48 runs there was a serious threat to his place in the side. The talk was that one more failure in the third Test and the selectors would drop him. Viswanath rose to the challenge as only he could. In the face of an England total of 476 for nine declared, India were 49 for two when Viswanath walked in early in the post lunch session on the third day. As the middle order crumbled one by one,

Viswanath not only stood firm but also ticked off the runs in his inimitable style. The pressure on him was immense but he played his strokes with all the calm assurance that was his trademark. The England quartet of Botham, Willis, Underwood and Lever did not have any idea of what to bowl to him. When he was finally sixth out at 237, Viswanath had scored 107, a gem of an innings. England captain Keith Fletcher paid a handsome tribute by saying, '...in all the years I have watched him I don't think I have ever seen him play better. His hundred was a classic.' Well-known English writer Scyld Berry hailed it as 'the finest innings of the series'.

Talk about dropping him ceased immediately and in the fifth Test at Madras, Viswanath's batting bloomed like a flower in spring. He came in shortly after lunch on the first day with India 51 for two. With Vengsarkar he took the score to 150 before Vengsarkar was hit on the head by a ball from Willis and retired hurt. Yashpal Sharma joined Viswanath shortly after tea. The next wicket did not fall till shortly before lunch on the third day. The two batsmen put on 316 runs before Yashpal was out for 140. In the process, they became the seventh pair of batsmen in Test history to bat through an uninterrupted day's play. Viswanath scored 222 in 638 minutes with 31 boundaries, equalling the Indian record set by Budhi Kunderan during his 192 against England in 1963-64. It was Viswanath's highest Test score and the highest by an Indian against England, surpassing Gavaskar's 221 at the Oval in 1979. In an attempt to end his yearlong bad run, Viswanath had shaved off his beard and had invoked divine aid. Excusing himself from the second one-day international between the two teams, Viswanath went to a temple on a hill in southern India. His prayers were now answered in a most emphatic manner, and it was now obvious that the fears about his lapses in concentration or his footwork or reflexes having slowed down were premature.

At thirty-three, Viswanath was good enough to make another tour of England. He maintained his reputation by getting successive scores of 54, 56 and 75 not out. Certainly there was no indication of any technical fault in his play or that he was nearing the end of his international career. Astonishingly, however, in the next eleven innings, he could get only one half century. The run drought started with the one off Test against Sri Lanka at Madras where his scores were nine and two. Crossing over to Pakistan, the drought became even more severe. His scores in the six matches make for sorry and unbelievable reading: one, 24, nought, 53, nine, nought, 37 and ten. A total of 134 runs from eight outings at an average of 16.75 could only mean one thing – that the premature predictions made by the cynics a couple of years ago were finally coming true. With his never-say-die attitude, his ability to rise to any challenge, and his own artistic gifts, Viswanath had carried on gloriously from early 1980, when such talk first surfaced till early 1983. Now, age seemed to have finally caught up with this seemingly ageless artist. When the series ended, he was days away from his thirty-fourth birthday. He had played 91 Tests – more than any other Indian cricketer and had played the last 87 of them consecutively – a figure that surpassed the long-standing record of 85 held by Gary Sobers. Had he now come to the end of the road?

When Viswanath was finally dropped on grounds of form for the first time since he made his debut in November 1969, for the tour of West Indies, it was certainly not taken for granted that he had played his last Test. The general opinion was that he still had a lot to offer Indian cricket and would be back, perhaps even for the twin home rubbers against Pakistan and West Indies in 1983-84. Sadly, this did not happen. There were failures in the middle order but the selectors chose not to recall Viswanath. In another year, as Mohammed Azharuddin, a direct descendant from Viswanath was discovered, it was finally accepted that the Mysore magician would no longer grace India's Test teams.

At the time he played his last Test, Viswanath's run tally was next only to Gavaskar's. His 14 hundreds too were second only to Gavaskar. As is well known, when Viswanath got a hundred, India never lost a match. It helped in a victory four times and on ten occasions, his ton helped India to draw the match. Perhaps no other single statistic can adequately convey his value to the side during his long career.

Viswanath will find a place in anyone's list of top ten Indian batsmen. Gavaskar himself has openly admitted over and over again that he could not be compared to Viswanath. Hailing him as India's best batsman at a time when the two ruled Indian cricket together, Gavaskar only found fault with him now and then for lacking confidence in his own ability and for giving undeserving bowlers the chance to take his wicket. As only to be expected from someone like him who always liked to keep a low profile, Viswanath, after his Test career was over, was out of the scene for some time. But in the Nineties he served as national selector before taking over as chairman of the committee, a post he held for four terms. In more recent times Viswanath has earned a name for himself as an ICC match referee known for his fair and balanced rulings.

Well known cricket writer Raju Bharathan once wrote, in comparing Gavaskar and Viswanath: 'While Gavaskar was the bulwark of India's batting, Viswanath was its showpiece. Gavaskar waited for things to happen. Viswanath made things happen. Gavaskar was a miser hoarding runs, Viswanath was a millionaire spending them. Gavaskar was all prose, Viswanath all poetry. Gavaskar planned an innings, Viswanath sculpted it. With Gavaskar, batting was a science, with Viswanath, it was an art form.' It was Indian cricket's good fortune that for a full dozen years the artisan and the artist were both around. For, it was a combination that spelt disaster for the best bowlers all around the world.

# Mohinder Bharadwaj **Amarnath**

## The 'Comeback King'

The career of Mohinder Bharadwaj Amarnath has to be one of the most fascinating and enduring tales in the history of Indian cricket. It had everything that would be ideal for a hit film script – ups and downs, many heroic triumphs and a few outright disasters, numerous comebacks that made him the Muhammad Ali of the game in India, and at the centre of it all, a personality almost as colourful as his father. He generally preferred to suffer in silence, but when the need arose, he too was not afraid to court controversy. Like Lala, he was always news, on and off the field. He certainly was a worthy son to a great cricketer, in more ways than one.

Amarnath's international career stretched from 1969 to 1988. On sheer longevity itself, he is clearly one of the most durable of Indian cricketers. Here too, he was a match for his father, whose career lasted from 1933 to 1952. Like his father, he too was a more than handy medium pace bowler, capable of turning a World Cup final around. But his chief claim to fame is that of a courageous right-handed batsman, with a particularly good record against pace bowling. And considering the fact that this mode of attack had been a major headache for Indian batsmen over the years, his fearless and consistent hooking of pace bowlers and scoring centuries off them was no minor triumph. At his peak in 1982-83, he was considered the best batsman against pace bowling in the world, and for an Indian to be handed that accolade was as unlikely as an Indian opening bowler being the highest wicket-taker in Tests. Certainly, during the nadir years of the Fifties and Sixties, when the problem of pace bowling plagued Indian cricket, it did not seem likely that the country would one day produce a batsman about whom Vivian Richards would say in 1983, 'since 1976, no other batsman has faced the pacemen with such an abundance of confidence and determination as Mohinder Amarnath'. Certainly few Indian batsmen can boast of a difference of more than 21 runs between the home average (30.44) and the average overseas (51.86) – the ultimate proof that the bigger the stage, the better Amarnath performed. When the going was tough, the team knew, it could depend on this doughty warrior.

And yet a batsman of his calibre, skill, guts and an impressive record to boot, was kept out of the Indian team repeatedly, was in and out of the squad many times, and at one time was not considered for more than three years even as the Indian team were going around the international circuit without any conspicuous success. The crying need was for a batsman who could not only just face pace bowling squarely but also score runs handsomely off it. But while Amarnath played Ranji and Duleep matches, batsmen with considerably limited skills and far less courage were donning the India cap. This is the kind of irony that has retarded the progress of Indian cricket.

The second son of Lala, Amarnath was born in Patiala in 1950. Like elder brother Surinder he too made his mark at the schools level, with a doting father, who was determined that his sons should play for India, guiding them. He turned out for Northern Punjab in the Ranji Trophy in 1966 while still at school and was a member of the highly successful Indian schools team, which toured England in 1967. The next step to progress was taken at the varsity level where his solid, orthodox style, which was a hallmark of his batting, evolved. He developed a free and straight flow of the bat even as elder brother Surinder was emerging as an elegant and natural stroke player. That he was talented, had a sound technique and good strokes and a down to earth approach could not be denied. But when he made his Test debut at nineteen against Australia at Madras in 1969, the general opinion was that he was being rushed. Scores of 16 not out and nought seemed to confirm this view, even though he made sure that the debut was not a total disappointment by sending Keith Stackpole and Ian Chappell packing, bowled by deliveries the experienced batsmen knew nothing about.

Through the Seventies, Amarnath worked hard on his game. He had an excellent record in the Vizzy Trophy and his progress was more pronounced after he shifted to Delhi in the mid- Seventies. By now he was a more complete batsman and had developed an ideal temperament. His sterling performances in the Ranji Trophy and Duleep Trophy could not be ignored any longer and in 1975 Amarnath made the first of his many comebacks. After participating in the inaugural World Cup with modest success, he was back in the Test arena during the tour of New Zealand and West Indies in early 1976. In the interim he had missed 21 Tests.

Amarnath was straightaway into his stride. With scores of 64, 45, 30 and 26 in the three Tests against New Zealand, he proved to be invaluable in the middle order. By the time the team had moved over to the Caribbean islands, Amarnath had so impressed the tour management with his sound technique, the impeccable timing of his strokes and ice cool temperament, that he was promoted to number three. And it was in this position that he played his first notable knock for the country. This came about in the course of the memorable victory chase of 403 runs at Port of Spain. Entering at 69 for one, Amarnath dropped anchor while Gavaskar, Viswanath and Patel made the runs at the other end. The tactics worked to perfection and India duly completed a famous win with six wickets to spare. Amarnath's broad blade brought back memories of Trevor Bailey and 'Slasher' Mackay and frustrated the bowlers no end. For 442 minutes, Amarnath batted with great skill, rugged determination and deep concentration. A natural attacking batsman, he eschewed stroke play for the team's sake and took on the role of anchor man at a pivotal position still new to him. He was fourth out for 85 at 392. As he sadly went off the field dripping with sweat, the only regret was that he could not be there at the crease for the moment of victory which he had striven so hard towards and had worked so gallantly for. In the Kingston 'bloodbath' Amarnath stood his ground firmly against the blatantly unfair bowling to score 39 and 60. The assurance he displayed in playing Roberts and Holding showed that India had discovered a batsman who would not flinch in the face of fast bowling.

In the return rubber against New Zealand at home during 1976-77, Amarnath carried on his good form. Scores of 45, 30, 70 and 55 augured well for him, particularly with a tougher series to follow against England. But a jaded looking Amarnath was easy prey for the English bowlers and after scores of nought, 24, nought and 12 he was dropped – interestingly enough, to be replaced by Surinder. But he regained the number three spot from his brother, when Surinder was injured early on the tour of Australia in 1977-78. Not only that, he enjoyed a great series. Scores of 47, 90, 100, 72, 41 and 86 featured his impressive tally of 445 runs. The second Test was particularly memorable. He not only hit 90 and 100 but shared in two big stands for the second wicket – 149 runs with Chauhan in the first innings and 193 runs with Gavaskar in the second. In the third Test, he rescued the Indian innings after both Gavaskar and Chauhan had fallen without a run on the board. And in the final Test, he led the seemingly impossible victory chase. When India were set to get an improbable 493 for victory, Amarnath and Viswanath with a third wicket partnership of 131 runs set them firmly towards the target, which finally eluded the Indians by 47 runs.

Losing the number three slot again to his elder brother in the series in Pakistan the following season, Amarnath found runs hard to come by in the middle order. Sent in at number three in the final innings of the series, Amarnath finally found his touch, scoring 53 and sharing a second wicket stand of 117 runs with Gavaskar. Midway through the series against West Indies, which followed, Vengsarkar had taken over the number three spot following a record 344-run second wicket stand with Gavaskar. But Amarnath, going in at number six in the final Test at Kanpur, had the satisfaction of getting his second century in Tests – an unbeaten 101. He, however, had only modest success on the tour of England in 1979, played in two Tests without doing anything of note and in the last first-class match before the final Test, suffered a hairline fracture of the skull after being hit by a bouncer from Richard Hadlee. Recovering from the blow, he lost his place temporarily. But when brought back for the final Test against Australia at home in the winter, his confidence seemed to be shattered. He was most uncomfortable against Rodney Hogg before being out hit wicket to the same bowler while trying to negotiate a bouncer, after having scored only two. The awkward manner of his dismissal shocked onlookers and seemed to have convinced the selectors that Amarnath lacked the courage and determination to counter pace bowling and stand up to rising deliveries.

This was the start of the unhappy phase of Amarnath's career. Over the next three years, he was constantly overlooked. India played 23 Test matches without him. The team went on tours of Australia, New Zealand and England and played against Pakistan, England and Sri Lanka at home without him. In the meantime, Amarnath, the last person to lose heart, started practising and playing with a helmet. By the early Eighties, the old confidence was back. The ultimate proof of this came when he scored 185 for Delhi against Karnataka in the famous Ranji Trophy final in 1981-82. The bat was so dominant that the match was decided only on the first innings – and that, after the match had gone to a sixth day. Karnataka led off with 705 and most opponents would have given up. After all, no team in first-class cricket anywhere had overhauled a total of 700. Amarnath, whose middle name was courage, was never one to give up, however hopeless the cause. He led his team by personal example, taking six hours over a heroic 185. Taking the cue from the skipper, Delhi ended up with an unbelievable score of 707 for eight. When, even after this, he could not make the Indian team, which toured England in 1982, the selectors' decision was roundly condemned. A lesser cricketer would have probably announced his retirement, but then Amarnath, both as a batsman and a person, was made of steely determination. At the start of the next season, he presented scores of 207, 80, 67 not out (in the Duleep Trophy) and 127 and 52 (in the Irani Trophy) before the selectors. When the team to tour Pakistan was selected, Amarnath was finally back where he belonged.

The lion-hearted cricketer did not take long in displaying his courage, skill and polished strokes. In the first Test, he came in when India had slid from 105 for no loss to 123 for three. Amarnath nursed the innings thereafter like a doctor tending a patient. When the innings terminated at 379, Amarnath was unconquered with 109. There was an extremely rare double failure in the next Test at Karachi where he was dismissed for five and three. Scores of 22 and 78 in the third Test boosted both his morale and his average. Contributions of 61 and 64 followed in the next Test. And he rounded off a highly successful series with 120 in the fifth Test and 103 not out in the final game. While most of the other batsmen succumbed meekly before the pace and swing of Imran Khan, who had a haul of 40 wickets, Amarnath not only stood firm but also made fluent strokes. In ending the series with 584 runs at an average of 73.00, Amarnath exposed the folly of the selectors who had kept him out for so long. Midway through the series he took over the pivotal number three slot and retained the position for the series to follow in the West Indies.

From one triumph to another was the continuing success story of Mohinder Amarnath during his golden period. In the West Indies, all eyes were now on Amarnath. Could he repeat his deeds in Pakistan on Caribbean soil, against the fearsome pace quartet? The answer was provided in the affirmative in the most emphatic manner. Modest scores of 29 and 40 (top score) in the first Test were only a prelude to the great knocks that were to unfold from his bat. In the second Test, he came up with scores of 58 and 117 to enable India to draw the Test after they were in arrears by 219 runs. After a rare failure in the third Test the apotheosis of Amarnath's courage was witnessed in the fourth Test. The Indians were subjected to a barrage of short-pitched fast bowling. Amarnath, as he had been for the past few months, was again the one shining star. He top-scored with 91 in the first innings with no other batsman getting 30. In the second innings, he was forced to retire when he was 18. He tried to hook a short, ultra fast snorter from Marshall, missed and the result was a cut upper lip. He resumed his innings the next morning at the fall of the fifth wicket at 139 and was last out at 277 after scoring 80 of the bravest runs ever he made. A double of 54 and 116 rounded off this, undoubtedly his greatest series, even after taking into account his heroics in Pakistan. In finishing the series with 598 runs at an average of 66.44, Amarnath had registered undoubtedly the finest performance by any Indian batsman against pace bowling. No one else could have played the fearsome quartet of Roberts, Holding, Marshall and Garner with greater confidence, courage or skill. Such was his dominance through the 1982-83 season that he crossed the 1000-run mark in a calendar year on May 3, the final day of the series in the West Indies – the earliest any batsman has reached the mark. In all, he scored 2355 runs during the season, a record outside England.

The golden period extended to the World Cup in England in the summer when he starred in India's unexpected triumph both with bat and ball. Man of the match awards in the semifinal and final were testimony to this. At the height of his cricketing prowess and popularity, Amarnath came back to India, riding a crest of success. He was suddenly the most instantly recognisable cricketing personality, and even his trademark red handkerchief in his back pocket became a major point of discussion. But then cricket, like fate, is a great leveller. And the 1983-84 season for him became the antithesis of all what happened the previous year. A big cheer went up as he went out to bat in the first Test against Pakistan at Bangalore. But he scored only four runs. In the second Test at Jalandhar he was restricted to seven. Suddenly, his confidence was shattered and he was mysteriously omitted from the third Test at Nagpur at the last minute. Still one was sure that this sudden loss of form was only temporary and he would be back among the runs in the series against West Indies to follow. What actually happened was the unthinkable and the unbelievable. In the first Test at Kanpur, he got a pair. In the next Test at the Kotla, he got one and nought. Dropped for the next two matches, he came back for the fifth Test at Calcutta. The result? Another pair. One run from six innings was the kind of figures that would not even be associated with B.S. Chandrasekhar. And yet, this is what 'the best player of fast bowling in the world' was reduced to. He fell three times to Marshall and once each to Holding, Winston Davis and Wayne Daniel. Whatever the reasons, the West Indians had wasted little time in getting even with him.

Amarnath was suddenly confronted with a heavy barrage of criticism and many uncharitable remarks – some of them unreasonably personal. The cynics, of course, were ready with the usual question – was Amarnath finished? It takes nerves of steel to come out unscathed from this kind of adversity and Amarnath did not take long to show that he possessed this quality in abundance. After missing out on the final Test of the series, Amarnath was picked for the tour of Pakistan in 1984-85 and back to his best battling form. Despite the severe reverses of the previous season, Amarnath was taken largely on his record-breaking performances on the last tour of Pakistan. The selectors knew that he was just the man required to combat the adverse conditions in Pakistan and Amarnath did not disappoint. In the first Test he came in at 94 for two and while wickets fell in a heap, he as his wont, stood firm before he was last out for 41 in a total of 156. But it was in the second innings that he played a match saving knock that was superlative even by Amarnath's standards. By now the umpiring had become a major controversy. Gavaskar charged that the umpires were rather over-enthusiastic about lifting their fingers when the Indians batted and pointed out to three successive leg before decisions in the first innings. As if this was not enough, India were now forced to follow on 272 runs behind with two full days left. This time the score was 114 for two when Amarnath came in to bat on the fourth afternoon. By the evening it had become 164 for four. Amarnath, like he did on the famous occasion at Port of Spain in 1976, dropped anchor. Ball after ball, over after over, hour after hour, he played each delivery with the deadest of bats. He was careful not to use his pads for it would give the umpire the opportunity to lift his finger. He played only with the bat and frustrated the bowlers no end. Try as they might, they could not get past it, could not find its edge. There was no way Amarnath was going to get out that day. And so it proved. India saved the match thanks chiefly to his six and a half hour vigil that saw him remain unbeaten with 101.

His confidence fully restored by that heroic knock, Amarnath shrugged off 1983-84 as a bad dream and surged on to a splendidly consistent performance against England at home. Scores of 49, 42, 64, 42, 78 and 95 saw him end with a tally of 407 runs. By this time, of course, he had proved to be indispensable in the limited overs game and was one of the stars of the triumph in the World Championship of Cricket in Australia in early 1985. Then in Sri Lanka in 1985-86, he came up with scores of 60 and 116 not out. In Australia, later the same season, scores of 37 and 45 were the prelude to his tenth century in Tests in the final game of the series – a stroke filled 138 during which he added 224 runs for the second wicket with Gavaskar. On then to

England and in the two Tests he played, Amarnath had scores of 69 and 79. Like wine, Amarnath seemed to be getting better with age. A timely innings of 51, coupled with a century stand for the second with Gavaskar on the final day of Tied Test II against Australia at Madras in 1986-87 paved the way for the sensational finish to the game. Against Sri Lanka later that season, Amarnath notched up his 11th and last Test hundred. Scoring 131 in the second Test at Nagpur, he put on 173 runs for the third wicket with Vengsarkar. A little over a month later, came another big third wicket partnership with Vengsarkar, this time against Pakistan at Madras. The two added 185 runs with Amarnath getting 89.

That was Amarnath's 63rd Test match. And the knock was the last score over the half-century mark that Amarnath would get in a Test. He did get 49 in the third Test of the series at Jaipur. After that, his career was strictly downhill. His last eight innings in Test cricket read: seven, 13, nought (against Pakistan) and one, eight, 43, three, one (against West Indies the following season). He had come back so many times, had proved the cynics wrong time and again. But now at thirty-seven, age was against him. Perhaps he was still good enough for the one-day game and even though he had not been picked for the Reliance World Cup squad in 1987, which just preceded the series against West Indies, he was in good form with the bat during the Asia Cup in Bangladesh in October 1988. However, his days as a Test batsman were numbered and he possibly hastened the end by calling the selectors a bunch of jokers when he was omitted from the team to play New Zealand in 1988-89.

The end was a pity in more ways than one. But then, of course, in a long, glittering career, marked generally by ups, there are bound to be a few downs. Too much should not be made of the tail end of Amarnath's career. His overall figures in Tests, Ranji Trophy and first-class cricket are remarkably consistent. But then consistency was always among his manifold qualities. In retirement he has proved to be multi-talented – taking up a coaching assignment in Bangladesh, promoting the game in Morocco, becoming well known as a shrewd cricketing analyst on TV and being involved in various business interests. There never is a dull moment when 'Jimmy' is around!

# 12

# Sunil Manohar **Gavaskar**

## The Master

March 6, 1971. On the face of it, this is not a date of any great significance. Perhaps only the really die-hard Indian cricket fan will understand the importance of that date, after some prodding. But as far as Indian cricket is concerned, this is a landmark day. If the history of mankind is divided into two eras – BC and AD – the history of Indian cricket is divided into two eras – BG and AG. The thirty-nine years before the date in question were generally marked by defeats, disasters and debacles and very few triumphant moments. The thirty-four years after the date in question has generally been marked by glorious victories, rare individual feats and greater respect for Indian cricket and cricketers in the international arena. Sure, there have been the low points but these have been comparatively few.

March 6, 1971. It was the day a certain Sunil Manohar Gavaskar made his Test debut. He first fielded most of the day as West Indies were all out for 214 on the opening day of the second Test at Port of Spain in Trinidad, a ground which over the years became his favourite for obvious reasons. And then he opened with Ashok Mankad to bat for a few overs before the end of the day's play. He himself recalls in *Sunny Days* his first moments with the bat in a Test: 'As I took strike after Ashok had got three runs, I was a little afraid that I might not be up to the mark. Holder thundered down and bowled on the leg stump. The ball struck my leg guards and went down to fine leg for two leg byes. But I was surprised to see that the umpire did not make any signal so I was off the mark with two runs when actually I should not have had any. This helped me to get rid of the fear of failure and

I was soon middling the ball and clipped Holder to the square leg fence for my first boundary in Tests.'

Today, with his awesome record in the international game familiar to cricket fans the world over, it would seem incongruous that Gavaskar had a fear of failure and that he was afraid he might not be up to the mark. But much more significant than all his accomplishments is the fact that he is the father figure of Indian cricket. He was the pioneer, the man who proved that fast bowlers could be hit and not menaces against whom one flinched. He was a batsman who proved that it was possible to get 13 Test hundreds against the West Indies – including three double centuries. He showed that it was possible to break the 10,000 run barrier in Test cricket and to overtake Don Bradman's record tally of 29 hundreds. Most important, he inspired his teammates not to wince against fast bowling or falter against the turning ball. Thanks to him, many others learnt about the essential qualities of dedication and determination, technique and temperament, patience and perseverance, concentration and commitment. And soon the upward swing in India's fortunes was there for the cricketing world to watch and admire.

Before Gavaskar came on the scene, the chief image of Indian cricketers was that of 'dull dogs' who took an inordinately long time to get their runs. They lacked the will to fight and were technically and temperamentally ill equipped. The history of Indian cricket was punctuated – all too frequently – by shameful reverses. On one infamous occasion at Leeds in 1952, India lost their first four wickets without a run on the board. In the same series, at Old Trafford, India became the first team in Test cricket to be bowled out twice in one day – and for totals of 58 and 82. In the next Test at the Oval, India lost the first five wickets for six runs. A few years later, India lost a Test to West Indies at Calcutta by an innings and 336 runs – the second biggest margin of defeat in Test cricket. In 1959 and 1962, India lost all five Tests of the rubber to England and West Indies. In the period 1967-68, India lost seven Tests on the trot.

It might not be exactly right in saying that one man changed this depressing scenario. But that would be close to the truth. Gavaskar's entry itself coincided with India's first ever victory over West Indies, followed by a triumph in the series. Gavaskar was mainly responsible for this, scoring 774 runs with four hundreds, including a century and a double century in the final Test. His deeds inspired the greater triumph that followed in England the same year. And so the saga continued till 1987. And along the way, there were individual and team feats that none would have thought the Indian team and Indian cricketers were capable of. Scoring 400 plus to win a Test, running up totals of 600 plus more than once, making the bowlers sweat it out for more than a day to earn a wicket. And inspired by the greater solidity in the batting, the bowlers have risen to the occasion and shaped many notable triumphs.

Indeed, before Gavaskar came on the scene, India had won only 15 of 117 Tests. In the next 129 Tests, till Gavaskar played his last game at Bangalore in 1987, India won 25. As regards losses, India in the period 1932-1970 suffered 49 defeats, while in the period 1971-1987 India lost 35 Test matches. Before 1971, India won five rubbers – three against New Zealand and one each against Pakistan and England. From 1971 to 1987, India won ten rubbers, four times against England, twice against West Indies and one each against Pakistan, Australia, Sri Lanka and New Zealand. Before 1971 India had won only one series abroad – against a none too strong New Zealand side in 1967-68. After Gavaskar came on the scene India won rubbers in West Indies and England (twice). Notwithstanding some reverses in the post-1987 period – in itself a tribute to the great man – there is little doubt that Gavaskar's legacy endures. And today's champion Sachin Tendulkar would be the first to admit the inspirational role that Gavaskar has played and the exalted status SMG enjoys in the history of Indian cricket.

Gavaskar was born in Bombay in 1949 and as only to be expected from a lad with prodigious gifts, made his mark early. In the mid-Sixties, while still at school he was reeling off centuries and double centuries in inter-school matches. This immediately marked him out as an exceptional prospect. What's more, he loved to play a long innings and hated getting out. There was nothing slap-dash in his approach. Winning mattered very much to him even at this stage. Discipline, determination and concentration were his mantras at a very early age. These qualities, along with his superb defensive technique and natural stroke play, sustained him throughout his varsity days and the early days of his first-class career, and saw him put on 472 runs for the first wicket with Ramesh Nagdev in an inter-collegiate match at Bombay in 1966.

By 1969-70 he had progressed to make his maiden century in the Ranji Trophy, against Rajasthan in the final, when he and Ashok Mankad put on 279 runs for the first wicket – a competition record. The next year, he made the highest individual score in the Rohintan Baria Trophy – his 327 surpassing Ajit Wadekar's 324 notched up twelve years before. By now, there was little doubt that this twenty-one-year-old opening batsman was an automatic selection for the tour of West Indies in early 1971. And while it was expected that he would be among the runs, no one could have bargained for what actually happened. We all expected, at best, a steady 'stream' of runs from his bat. What we got was a non-stop 'cascade'. After missing the first Test due to a finger injury, Gavaskar started off his career with 65 and 67 not out to play a leading role in India's great triumph at Port of Spain, graduated to his maiden Test century in only his second match, added a second hundred in the next Test and in the final Test came his well known double of 124 and 220. An unbelievable tally of 774 runs – at an average of 154.80 – left him with a host of records that had statisticians in a tizzy. From just a promising cricketer, Gavaskar was transformed, overnight as it were, into a national hero well known even to those not normally interested in the game and an international celebrity.

But, of course, even now there had to be the skeptics who dismissed all this as a fluke and wondered whether he would go the way of so many young cricketers who had started off in sensational fashion only to fall like a faulty meteor, who asked whether he could repeat such feats again. And when he 'failed' in the Tests in England later that year – only two half centuries in six innings – the cynics had a field day. And the number of skeptics grew when, in the 1972-73 series against England at home, Gavaskar's aggregate after the first six innings, was just 60 runs at an average of 12.00. For a player hailed as a new star on the cricket horizon, figures like these were alien. There seemed to be a strange hesitancy in his shots as though he had lost confidence in himself. Scores of 69 and 67 in the last two Tests saved his face somewhat but he still finished as low as sixth in the Test figures.

What is wrong with Gavaskar, was the question now being asked, not only in India, but all over the world for by now he had attracted international attention. His career average had slid to just over 57 and after the West Indian exploits, in 16 innings, he had just four fifties with a highest score of 69. Would the scoffing opinion held by the cynics hold good? Gavaskar answered that question in the one way he knew best – with his bat. At Old Trafford in 1974, he came up with a knock that even in a long and illustrious career like his is ranked very high. Many knowledgeable critics in fact put it at the top of his 34-century list. Former England captain Tony Lewis described it thus: 'Quite unforgettable was his 101 out of 246 against England in 1974. Cold north-west winds drove in squalls, bringing only the seventh day of rain in Manchester since mid-February. The pitch was firm and bouncy. Willis, Old and Hendrick were hostile, whacking in the short balls. Underwood and Greig were the slower bowlers and they gave nothing away. Gavaskar first demonstrated how brave he was. He kept his eye on the ball and swayed either side of the high bounce, but when the ball was pitched up, he was immediately forward to drive it straight. This is where Gavaskar was a better player than Boycott overall. Boycott lost his strokes or maybe through parsimony he cut them out. Gavaskar reduced risk too but never lost the spring off the back foot which sent him firmly into the drive.'

His first Test century in England in alien, seaming conditions convinced even the cynics that, in racing parlance, Gavaskar was a stayer, not a sprinter. No more would there be any doubts about any aspect of Gavaskar's batting. He was India's most totally organised batsman since Merchant. Indeed, he was a product of the Merchant school of batting and he was a student who had passed out with distinction plus. The two would be the unanimous choice to open the innings in the greatest Indian XI of all time.

His confidence no doubt restored by that unforgettable hundred, Gavaskar was now the batsman the cricketing world admired and the bowlers dreaded. From the final Test at Bombay against West Indies in

January 1975 to the first Test against Pakistan at Madras in February 1987 Gavaskar had an unbroken run of 106 Tests, which he voluntarily put to an end by withdrawing from the Test against Pakistan at Calcutta in 1987 due to personal reasons. For a full dozen years, a supremely fit Gavaskar displayed the rare combination of total technique, impeccable body balance and scintillating strokes to spectators in Madras and Melbourne, Lahore and Leeds, Colombo and Christchurch. Over the years, he left a trail of frustrated bowlers who, with a gesture of helplessness, turned to their captain as if to implore, 'Please take me off. There is no use bowling to this bloke. He's never going to get out.' Indeed, so impeccable was his technique, so insatiable was his appetite for runs, so uncanny was his knack at building an innings brick by brick, that he gave the impression of batting all day and every day.

As if this was not enough, Gavaskar had so many strokes that he was ruthlessly unsparing on the bad ball. There was no bowler who could say with any certainty that Gavaskar was weak against such and such a delivery. No bowler could have a pet theory and say, 'If we pitch the ball this way and move it that way, he will be in trouble.' There are some, for example, who would be better players of pace than spin or vice versa. If there is one batsman who played both with equal felicity, it was Gavaskar. He was at ease in attack and defence, off the front foot and back foot, against all bowling known to the cricket book – fast, medium, swingers, cutters, leg spin, off spin, googlies, top spinners, full tosses, long hops. He was so well organised that he was able to encounter any delivery with ease and comfort, giving the impression of having all the time in the world to play the stroke – the hallmark of the greatest of batsmen. His excellent eyesight saw any minute change in the bowler's action and his nimble footwork enabled him to get to the pitch of the ball, faster and more effortlessly than almost any other batsman. If the bowler forced him on to the back foot, Gavaskar's feet would quickly get into the perfect position to essay a square cut, a glance, a pull, a hook or a drive to all parts of the ground. Off the front foot, he was a peerless driver. No shot was his pet stroke; he played them all, handsomely, felicitously and lucratively. There was an element of power in his batting. But it was not total, naked power but controlled power. Timing was the essence of all his shots.

By the mid-Seventies then, it was accepted even by the skeptics that Gavaskar was no fluke and that he was here to stay the course and guide the Indian batting fortunes for an extended period. By the time he exited the stage, a dozen years later, he had become the bowlers' bugbear and the statisticians' delight. He had earned a name for himself as one of three or four outstanding opening batsmen of all time and had earned a new respect for Indian cricket. The team was no longer the whipping boys of international cricket and the players were no more the dull dogs of the game. The opponents realised that an Indian team with Gavaskar around could be taken lightly only at their own peril. Like Clive Lloyd realised at Port of Spain in 1976. He declared the West Indian second innings closed leaving India to get 403 runs for victory. Such a target had been achieved only once previously and that side had Bradman playing for them. Gavaskar got 102 to spearhead India's spirited challenge that saw them reach the target with seven mandatory overs to spare. His unique chemistry with the most Indian of grounds in the Caribbean is well known and led to a new mathematical equation: Gavaskar + Queen's Park Oval = century.

No Indian had crossed the 1000-run figure in Tests in a calendar year till Gavaskar came long. He achieved the feat in 1976 and then repeated it in 1978, 1979 and 1983 – the only batsman till then to have done so four times. Inspired by Gavaskar, many Indian batsmen have recorded the achievement since then. By January 1978 Gavaskar had already notched up 13 hundreds in 35 Tests, surpassing Umrigar's record of 12 in 59 matches. And around this time he struck the kind of sunny patch that only the greatest of batsmen can bask under. It extended for a year – from October 1978 to September 1979 – during which he played 13 Tests, amassed 1721 runs at an average of 86.05 with seven hundreds and seven fifties. Included in this out of this world run were two double centuries, a century in each innings on two occasions, and a knock that was arguably the greatest he ever played. Even by Gavaskar's monumental standards, the 221 he scored against England at the Oval in 1979 was a tremendous achievement. It is not every time that a batsman gets a double hundred in the fourth innings of a Test match. George Headley did it against England in 1930 and

Bill Edrich against South Africa in 1939. Both, however, were timeless Tests. The Oval Test was limited to five days and Gavaskar's 221 inspired one of the most famous run chases in cricket history.

Requiring a prohibitive 438 runs for victory, India were off to a great start with openers Gavaskar and Chauhan putting on 213 runs. Vengsarkar helped Gavaskar maintain the tempo with a second wicket partnership of 153 runs. At 366 for one, India were the favourites to win even though the mandatory overs had started with the Indian score on 328 for one. But the dismissal of Vengsarkar and the promoted Kapil Dev in successive overs put a spanner in the works. Gavaskar battled on until he drilled Botham to Gower at mid on, fourth out at 389 – but not before he had notched up the highest score by an Indian against England. It was also his 20th hundred in only 50 Tests. At his going, India needed 49 runs off 7.4 overs. But with the fulcrum gone, the lever snapped, the momentum could not be maintained and India, at final draw of stumps were 429 for eight. Gavaskar had batted gallantly for 490 minutes, faced 443 balls and hit 21 fours. But besides the gallantry, what particularly attracted notice was the manner in which he played his strokes. Wisden noted: 'Gavaskar masterminded the show, doing all the thinking and playing most of the shots.' Runs and minutes were all in relation to each other, for on the final morning India required 362 to win in six hours. So the runs had to be obtained at a nifty rate and it was Gavaskar, dominating the scoring throughout with his technically flawless batting, who initiated the momentum by playing an array of strokes, which had even the most learned English critics scouring the dictionary. Little wonder then, all things considered, it is widely regarded as the jewel in King Gavaskar's crown.

The yearlong outstanding run saw Gavaskar's overall average leap from 48 to 57. And even as he turned thirty, there were no indications that Gavaskar's appetite for runs was satiated. In January 1980 against Pakistan at Madras he batted 593 minutes for 166 – the longest innings for India in Test cricket. Two years later, he himself was to surpass this record by batting 708 minutes for 172 against England at Bangalore. In 1982 the number of centuries went past the 25 mark and Bradman's long standing record of 29 hundreds came sharply into focus. Every time he endured a bad patch – which fortunately never lasted for very long – the critics were out gunning for him. Had age finally caught up with him? Was his eyesight failing or had his reflexes slowed down? Was there something faulty with his technique? Did he have it in him to cope with the fastest of bowlers? And it did not take long for Gavaskar to come up with a timely hundred to convert the skeptics into cheerleaders.

No Indian batsman before Gavaskar had achieved the feat of carrying his bat. Fittingly enough he did so against Imran Khan and Sarfraz Nawaz at Faisalabad in January 1983. That was hundred number twenty-six and before the year was out the most coveted record in Test history was his. After more than a dozen years of international cricket, Gavaskar still had lost neither the skill nor the temperament required to perform at the highest level. Yes he did make one concession as a gesture to advancing years. At thirty-four Gavaskar finally took to wearing the fibreglass skullcap, which from now on became one of his trademarks. It was lighter than a helmet and he could wear his favourite sun hat and have protection as well. It was an admission that he wasn't getting any younger and as he himself put it: 'My reflexes were not getting any sharper and there was too much cricket being played, with the result that the mind had become jaded.'

But there was nothing jaded about his batting that, in fact, was on the verge of a new phase. But before this metamorphosis came about he had to endure ridicule following the manner of his dismissal in the first Test against West Indies at Kanpur in October 1983. That he was out for nought 4and seven – falling both times to Malcolm Marshall – was bad enough. But when his bat was knocked out of his hand in the second innings alarm bells rang all over the country. Even the most fervent of Gavaskar's supporters were convinced that his career could well and truly be over. To the majority among the millions who saw him getting out in this manner on television, it was unbelievable. How could he be dismissed in this way? It was abject surrender, they argued. To most, age had caught up with him. The Gavaskar of old would never have got out this way, they said.

Gavaskar had to bear the brunt of criticism and many uncharitable comments and as such on the eve of the next Test at New Delhi, which was to start in three days time, his confidence must have been at its lowest. Secretly, however, he had decided on a plan and put very simply, it was to counter-attack. And on October 29, 1983 it was a new Gavaskar that the cricketing world witnessed. Gone was the diffidence, the hesitancy, the pushing and prodding. It was cut and thrust cricket. Gavaskar drove, cut and hooked – and hooked and hooked! Whenever Marshall, Davis, Holding and Daniel bowled short, he was in position to play the lucrative shot, which of course, is not without its dangerous element too. Driving the ball fluently to the off side, working the ball to the mid wicket boundary, Gavaskar did pretty much what he liked. Sure, he had his moments of good fortune. But batting in the manner he was on that memorable day, Gavaskar surely deserved some luck. Finally he flicked a ball from Marshall wide off mid on and it raced to the boundary, signalling his 29th century. The hundred had come off just 94 balls. His first fifty had come off 37 balls. At 104, he became the third batsman after Sobers and Boycott to pass the 8000-run mark in Tests.

Along with the joy, Gavaskar also felt a lot of relief. For, he had been under tremendous pressure for some time to get to the magic figure. As he himself admitted: 'Ever since my return from West Indies, people were eager for me to score the 29th century and so whether it was a plane, taxi, office, hotel lobby or restaurant, strangers would walk up and offer their good wishes for me to score that hundred. Much as I appreciated their sentiments, the cry "we want your 29th" was becoming a little strident to the ears. It was therefore a great relief to get that century and see the delight on the face of my countrymen.'

One prestigious landmark was reached. But now others beckoned. And during the series, calmly, coolly and methodically, Gavaskar achieved these too. In the next Test at Ahmedabad, Gavaskar glanced Holding for his 83rd run of the innings to overtake Boycott's world record aggregate of 8114 runs. Boycott had played 108 Tests and 193 innings. Gavaskar was playing his 96th Test match and 168th innings. Batting in much the same vein as he had done at the Kotla, a couple of weeks before, Gavaskar reached 50 out of 67 from 58 balls. Now the focus shifted to his 30th hundred. When would he get that? Would it be at his hometown of Bombay, or at the Eden Gardens in Calcutta or at the M.A. Chidambaram stadium in Madras? Or would cricket fans have to wait till the following season?

Bombay and Calcutta were quickly put out of reckoning as the lucky venues. Gavaskar was out for 12 and three at Bombay and nought and 20 at Calcutta. After all the hoopla over his record-breaking feats at New Delhi and Ahmedabad, it was back to mundane times again. Would Madras provide the turn in Gavaskar's fortunes again? In the meantime, India had already lost the series with a humiliating thrashing at the Eden Gardens. So while the team was playing only for pride, Gavaskar still had something to play for. He had requested to bat lower down the order to get some rest, physically and mentally. He was put down at number four but hardly got any time to relax for India lost two wickets without a run on the board. In fact, Gavaskar came in on a hat trick after getting ready in a hurry and then making his way slowly to the crease in an effort to calm down after the rush. He joined young Navjot Sidhu, playing only his second Test and the two started the repair work. But Sidhu, Ashok Malhotra and night watchman Shivlal Yadav did not last long and early on the morning of the fourth day (rain had washed out the first day's play), India were 92 for five. Gavaskar had just crossed his half-century and was looking good but he needed someone to stay with him. Ravi Shastri was just the man. Displaying the patience and doggedness that became his trademark, Shastri's broad blade frustrated the bowlers while Gavaskar proceeded along smoothly. As he neared his century, the 40,000-strong crowd greeted every run. Finally, Gavaskar placed Davis to mid-wicket for a single to bring up the new record that would now be the benchmark for future generations. His 30th century was warmly applauded by the Chepauk crowd, which gave him a standing ovation. So the final frontier had been reached. 'Move over Don, it's Sunny now' was the headline that summed it all up.

The following day Gavaskar reached his fourth double hundred. Now the figure 231 came into focus. With all the excitement surrounding the 30th century, there was really no thought given to Gavaskar breaking Vinoo Mankad's record of the highest score by an Indian in Test matches. It was also made at Madras, but at the Corporation stadium, against New Zealand in January 1956. Gavaskar, now with Mankad's figure firmly in sight, accelerated and at tea, he had all but overhauled it for his score was 229. Minutes after the interval, Gavaskar crossed Mankad's mark and when the innings was declared, he remained unbeaten with 236. He had become the first batsman to score 13 hundreds or three double centuries against West Indies.

Gavaskar had now scaled all the peaks any batsman can hope to achieve. Most runs, most centuries, the highest score by an Indian in Tests – all the major records now stood in his name. What more could he achieve now? How many more centuries could he score? What would be his final aggregate? And most important, could he be the first to cross the hitherto unthinkable 10,000 run barrier in Tests? And as methodically as ever Gavaskar with his objectives in sharp focus never faltered. In Australia in 1985-86, Gavaskar first notched up century number thirty-one. In the course of his 166 not out at Adelaide, he became the first batsman to cross 9,000 runs in Test cricket. In the third and final Test at Sydney, came century number thirty-two when he made an entertaining 172. At thirty-seven, he was still fit and full of zest on the eve of the 1986-87 season. He notched up century number thirty-three against Australia in his home town even as the Bombay Cricket Association, during the Test, arranged a function to felicitate him for getting 32 hundreds! Two months later, came century number thirty-four against Sri Lanka at Kanpur. This was another marathon innings of 176.

Then came the eventful series against Pakistan in February-March 1987. At the start of the series, Gavaskar needed 173 runs to reach the 10,000-run mark. He started off with 91 in the first Test at Madras, putting on 200 runs with Srikkanth for the first wicket. He opted out of the next Test at Calcutta, a personal decision, which sparked off much debate. Back for the third Test at Jaipur, he was out to the first ball of the match for the third time. But in the second innings he got 24. The countdown had started in real earnest. He now needed 58 more to reach the all-important figure. There were two more Tests to be played. Gavaskar did not waste any further time. At Ahmedabad, playing in his 124th Test and his 212th innings, he reached his 50 and then with the crowd going wild with every run, he finally late cut Ijaz Faqih for two runs to reach 58 – and the five figure mark in Tests! He could not restrain himself, and his bat and fist went up in the air in an ecstatic and triumphant gesture. As he himself aptly put it, 'Others might cross that figure, but the person who gets there first is remembered.' The pressure over, Gavaskar was out for 63. And in the final Test, of course, came the matchless innings of 96 on a treacherous pitch, in a losing cause and against Tauseef Ahmed and Iqbal Qasim. He gave a supreme exhibition of temperament and technique lasting 323 minutes. The quality of that knock is best illustrated by the fact that the next highest contribution was extras with 27.

No one knew at this stage that the Bangalore match was to be Gavaskar's last Test. But timing had never been his problem anyway, on and off the field. Invited to take part in the MCC Bicentenary match at Lord's in August 1987, Gavaskar achieved his last cricketing ambition – to score a century at the game's headquarters. With a handsome 188, Gavaskar showed that even at thirty-eight, he was still in form. So what better time to announce one's retirement? Stating that this was his last five-day game, Gavaskar said he would retire from all cricket after the Reliance World Cup, to be staged in India and Pakistan later that year. It was then that one realised that Gavaskar could not also have said goodbye to Test cricket in a more befitting manner. That 96 was his signature tune and the perfect way to bow out of the game he had adorned for so long.

High profile as a player, Gavaskar could not remain out of the game in retirement. Even during his playing days, he was a well known syndicated columnist and his writings bore the same stamp of authority that one associated with his batting. His succinct analysis and shrewd comments always make for interesting reading. Author of four books and editor of cricket and sports magazines, Gavaskar also dabbled in acting in films. Of course, he was the first cricketing superstar as far as TV and print commercials were concerned. Currently he is best known as an expert commentator on TV and his tongue-in-cheek humour is a delight. He has various business interests and has also held important posts in the ICC, BCCI and CBFS. A man of varied interests surely, but Gavaskar's chief image will be that of Indian cricket's most commanding personality, the country's greatest opening batsman and one of the world's best of all time. And I know that there are many, who despite the greatness of Tendulkar, still swear by Gavaskar as India's number one batsman of all time. After all, the pioneer, the man who shows the way, always has a special aura.

# 13

## Dilip Balwant **Vengsarkar**

Grace and Power Personified

Few batsmen in Indian cricket have combined the twin qualities of power and grace so effectively as Dilip Balwant Vengsarkar. Basically he was the emblem of charm and elegance, driving gracefully, playing the cut shot according to the book and glancing the ball in pretty-pretty fashion. But when the mood got to him, he could murder the best of bowlers, whatever the conditions or the situation. The bowling never looked more helpless when Vengsarkar was in this chilling form.

Vengsarkar was born in Rajapur (Maharashtra) in 1956 and first made his mark at the varsity level. A tall, slim orthodox right-handed batsman who loved to go for his shots and was not afraid to play the lofted drive, Vengsarkar's gifts blossomed very early, thanks to imaginative selectors who pushed him in the line of fire, so to say, when he was just nineteen. He made his Ranji Trophy debut for Bombay against Gujarat in 1975-76 and then was included in the state team to play Rest of India in the Irani Trophy game at Nagpur. The teenaged Vengsarkar played an innings that has achieved the status of folklore in domestic cricket. Bedi and Prasanna, then at their peak, were in the Rest team and they were astonished at the way they were treated by this newcomer to first-class cricket. Vengsarkar sailed into the attack, hitting Bedi for four sixes and Prasanna for three on his way to a hurricane 110 in 113 minutes, which also included eleven fours. Since the knock was played at C.K. Nayudu's birthplace, Vengsarkar was nicknamed 'Colonel' and it was a name that stuck right through his career. Bedi and Prasanna immediately spoke about 'that Bombay lad' as 'an India prospect'. The press too went gaga over the innings and the result was that Vengsarkar was rushed into international cricket – first against Sri Lanka and then for the dual tour of New Zealand and West Indies. Moreover, he was seen as a prospect good enough to be Gavaskar's opening partner.

For all his precocious gifts, Vengsarkar was not ready for Test cricket – yet. In the three Tests against New Zealand, he aggregated 83 runs, with a top score of 30 in the course of which he and Gavaskar put on 60 runs. Scores of nought, 39 and 21 that followed in two Tests against West Indies seemed to confirm that Vengsarkar had been rushed into international cricket, even though the manner in which he stood up to Holding and company in the midst of the 'bloodbath' at Kingston did not go unnoticed. During the 1976-77 season he played in only one of the eight Tests without success.

It was on the tour of Australia the following season that Vengsarkar really came of age. Well meaning critics had pointed out in 1975, when Vengsarkar was rushed into the international arena, that perhaps he needed to wait for a couple of years. And this was not far off the mark for in 1977, Vengsarkar was ready to prove his worth. Of course, there were a couple of additional points in his favour. For one thing, with Surinder Amarnath having returned home following an injury early on the tour, he was assured of a place in the side. Secondly, he was relieved of the pressures of opening the innings with the return of Chetan Chauhan. In the more familiar number five slot, he was more at home. He did open in the first Test, scoring 48 and one. But from the second Test on, he batted in the middle order and was a picture of consistency. Scores of 49, 37, 48, 44 and 78 underlined his arrival as a mature stroke player. In making 589 runs at an average of 32.72 on the tour, including 320 in the Tests at 35.55, Vengsarkar established himself in the Indian side.

On the tour of Pakistan the next season, Vengsarkar took another firm step towards making himself invaluable to the side. In the first Test he got 83, adding 166 runs for the fourth wicket with Viswanath. In the first innings of the second Test, he was the only batsman to stand firm against Imran and Sarfraz in top scoring with 76 out of a dismal total of 199. Failures in the three remaining outings of the series did not diminish his growing stature much. And in the series that followed against West Indies, he ended a search that the selectors had started in

1974 following the sudden retirement of Wadekar. Mohinder Amarnath had no doubt filled the breach at number three admirably but it was obvious that he was a stopgap. What was needed was a permanent one-drop batsman and in the absence of Amarnath, Vengsarkar went in at this pivotal slot in the second Test after the first ball dismissal of Gavaskar. He and Gaekwad added 170 runs for the second wicket. It was in the next Test at Calcutta that he really established himself as the country's permanent number three batsman. Vengsarkar and Gavaskar put on an Indian record of 344 runs (unbroken) for the second wicket with the former getting 157 and the latter 182. Finally, the search for a suitable batsman at the number three slot had ended. Not only that, he was hailed as the most exciting young batsman the country had produced since Gavaskar. Incidentally, it was Vengsarkar's maiden century in his 17th Test.

Vengsarkar experienced the full face of the ups and downs of cricket over the next two Tests. At Madras, he got a pair, falling to Sylvester Clarke both times. At New Delhi, he scored 109 and put on 151 runs for the second wicket with Gavaskar. Having scored 417 runs at an average of 59.57 in the series, Vengsarkar embarked on his first tour of England in 1979 with a lot of confidence. This was somewhat dented after the first three innings of the series saw him reduced to scores of 22, seven and nought. But in the second innings of the Lord's Test, Vengsarkar played an innings that was the last word in skill and courage. India, 323 runs in arrears, were facing an innings defeat when they were 99 for two. Viswanath joined Vengsarkar and in one of the finest rearguard actions in Indian Test cricket, the two added 210 runs for the third wicket to help India save the match. Vengsarkar got 103 and Viswanath scored 113. In the next Test, temporarily dropping down to number six, he played an aggressive innings of 65 not out, playing Willis, Hendrick, Botham and Edmonds with more than a degree of assurance. In the final Test at the Oval, came his timely second wicket partnership of 153 with Gavaskar that built on the 213-run opening stand between Gavaskar and Chauhan. Vengsarkar made a compact 52 which helped him finish the series with 249 runs at an average of 41.50.

That the tour of England had done him a world of good became obvious when he batted at home during the winter against Australia and

Pakistan. Starting off with a breezy 65 in the first Test, he moved to scores of 112, 52 and 89 against Australia. But the masterly performance of the season – and one of his greatest knocks – came against Pakistan at New Delhi. India required 390 for victory and their best hope was to play out for a draw. But thanks to Vengsarkar's great knock, India were pressing hard for a win and when the match ended, the home team were 364 for six. Vengsarkar who came in when the first wicket fell at 37, batted throughout. His century took 437 minutes and while compiling it, he completed 1000 runs for the calendar year to become the second Indian after Gavaskar to accomplish the feat. Vengsarkar went on to make 146 not out in 527 minutes, the longest innings by an Indian in a Test match.

On the tour of Australia and New Zealand in 1980-81, Vengsarkar enjoyed only moderate success. Two half centuries – both against New Zealand – in 11 innings was scant reward for a batsman of his class. But he shrugged off the indifferent form in the next series against England. With scores of 43, 70, 71 (retired hurt) and 46, he recovered some lost ground and was confidence personified when he went with the Indian team to England in 1982. In the three Tests, he registered scores of two, 12, six, 16 – and 157. He became one of the few non-English batsmen to get a second Test hundred at Lord's, and it was one of those knocks that mingled power and elegance in the best Vengsarkar tradition. India were following on 305 runs behind and Vengsarkar came in at six for one. What followed was one of the most commanding hundreds made by an Indian in England. Wickets kept falling at the other end but Vengsarkar just kept going with shots all around the ground. The five-man attack of Willis, Botham, Pringle, Edmonds and Allott just did not have any idea of what to bowl as Vengsarkar simply sailed into them. After four wickets had gone for 110, Yashpal Sharma helped Vengsarkar add 142 runs for the fifth wicket. Vengsarkar dominated the partnership to such an extent that he got 100 while Yashpal scored 37. Vengsarkar was seventh out at 254, having made 157 out of 248 scored while he was at the crease.

Back home, a breezy 90 in the one off Test against Sri Lanka during which he added 173 runs with Gavaskar for the second wicket, put him in the right frame of mind for the sterner tests ahead in the protracted season. In Pakistan he was neither a success nor a failure. For a batsman of his skill and class and experience, it was almost shocking how he fell time and again to Imran. Six times in a row did the Pakistan captain take his wicket in the midst of his greatest series, which saw him end with a 40-wicket haul. Like most other Indian batsmen, he too failed repeatedly but there were contributions of 79, 58 not out and 89, which symbolised his courage and technique. His final series figures of 241 runs at an average of 34.42, however, were not the kind he would have been happy with, nor also the fact that the Imran bogey saw him drop down the order for the latter half of the series to number five. He fared little better on the tour of West Indies that followed. A total of 279 runs at an average of 31.00 was not the kind of figures he was generally associated by now. But the run did contain one knock, which Vengsarkar has included in his top five innings – 94 in the final Test in Antigua. As Vengsarkar has been quoted: 'It came on a St John's wicket as lively as could be. On the opening morning I was up against the combined pace might of Roberts, Holding and Marshall. Each one of them bowled the fastest yet I middled the ball sweetly from the moment I took guard. I rate that innings highly as it was a score to which I just blazed away against quality quick bowling.'

Astonishingly, after such an innings, Vengsarkar was dropped for the next Test, which was played following India's victorious World Cup campaign in England of which he was a member. When the team to play Pakistan in the first Test in 1983-84 was announced, Vengsarkar was missing, bringing to an end a run of 28 successive Tests. It was an inexplicable decision but Vengsarkar took it in his stride and showed his true form in the series against West Indies that followed. In five Tests, Vengsarkar scored two hundreds, and one of them, his 159 at New Delhi was so satisfying that he placed it among his five top innings. He made the most fluent strokes against the fiery quartet of Marshall, Holding, Davis and Daniel, and the knock was only overshadowed by the fact that Gavaskar had notched up his famous 29th Test hundred earlier in the day. Incidentally, Vengsarkar was his partner during the big moment, and the two shared a stand of 178 runs for the second wicket. In that

Test, he top scored in the second innings too with 63. He followed this up with a century at Bombay. Earlier, in the first Test at Kanpur, he showed his fighting qualities by top scoring with 65 in the dismal Indian innings of 164. In aggregating 425 runs at an average of 53.12, Vengsarkar proved that his standing in Indian batting as second only to Gavaskar was undiminished. It was much the same Vengsarkar the next season against England, knocking up his customary hundred and averaging 40.57 for an aggregate of 284 runs. His 137 at Kanpur was a fine innings, full of pleasing strokes.

With his natural attacking approach, Vengsarkar was one of the few players who could boast of an outstanding record in both Test cricket and the limited overs game. He played a notable part in India's triumph in the World Championship of Cricket in Australia at the end of the season. And as if to prove his versatility, at the start of the following season, he came up with one of his best rearguard innings. India were facing an embarrassing defeat against Sri Lanka at Colombo. In arrears by 129 runs, they lost wickets at regular intervals but Vengsarkar stood firm. On this occasion he curbed his natural stroke play and batted for 406 minutes for an unbeaten 98. Thanks to his heroics, India just about managed to save the match. A stroke filled 62 in the final Test at Kandy rounded off another lucrative series and prepared Vengsarkar for the greatest phase of his long career.

Indeed, the period between December 1985 and December 1987 was the time when Vengsarkar touched Bradmanesque heights. No exaggeration this, as the figures will indicate. In 19 Tests and 28 innings (ten not out) Vengsarkar scored 1751 runs at an average of 97.27 with eight hundreds and six fifties. This surpassed even Gavaskar's golden run during 1978-79 when he scored 1721 runs in 13 Tests (20 innings) at an average of 86.05 with seven hundreds and seven fifties. The dream run commenced in Australia when he scored 120 runs in four innings (two not out) to average 60.00. In England in 1986 he was at the peak of his powers. In the first Test at Lord's, he got an unbeaten 126 to become the first non-Englishman to score three hundreds at the game's headquarters. In the next Test at Leeds, he top-scored in both innings with 61 and 102 not out. His first hundred helped India gain a psychological advantage; his second enabled India to build on it and win the series. Moreover, the hundreds were made in bowler friendly conditions, especially the hundred at Leeds. The fact that no one else got more than 31 puts Vengsarkar's knock in the proper perspective. He batted in a manner born to command, and handled the pace of Dilley and Lever and the spin of Edmonds and Emburey in regal fashion. Wisden noted that 'Vengsarkar's hundreds were the platform from which India pushed for victory. In both the Tests, he was rarely forced to play a false stroke and made every movement elegant.' Little wonder then that by the end of the tour he was christened Lord of Lord's. In England, where Indian batsmen have found it most difficult to bat on with the alien wicket and weather conditions, Vengsarkar in ten Tests spread over three tours, averaged over 57, a phenomenal achievement which eluded even players like Merchant, Hazare, Manjrekar, Gavaskar and Viswanath.

Back home, Vengsarkar continued from where he left off in England. An injury kept him out of the first Test against Australia, but scores of 22 and 164 not out in the remaining two games of the series meant that he was still in the midst of the Bradmanesque run. In the course of his unbeaten century, he and Shastri shared a record unbroken stand of 298 runs for the sixth wicket. Later in the same season he took it out on the Sri Lankan attack. A modest 57 in the first Test was only an appetiser. For the main course, he served up successive knocks of 153 and 166 in the next two Tests. In the course of the first century, he figured in a 173-run third wicket stand with Mohinder Amarnath. But it was the second hundred that really caught one's imagination for it was made on an under-prepared pitch. Sri Lanka themselves were all out for 191 and 142 with Maninder, Shastri and Shivlal making the ball do things. There was only one other half-century in the entire match. But even on this surface, Vengsarkar batted for seven hours with all his usual poise. In his own words, 'The Barabati stadium strip was the most difficult Test pitch I ever encountered in India. It's bounce was confidence shattering and the ball turned almost at right angles.' Little wonder then, that Vengsarkar placed this knock as next only to his 102 not out at Headingley in his list of outstanding innings.

Nothing, it seemed, would stop Vengsarkar from getting a third hundred in successive innings when he reached 96 in the first Test in the series that followed against Pakistan. Unusually, he was stumped at this stage but he was not to be denied his customary hundred, which came up in the fourth Test. It is uncanny how many times he hit a century at a time when there was a more notable feat. At New Delhi in 1983, Gavaskar's 29th hundred put his effort in the shade. At Kanpur in 1985, Mohammed Azharuddin got his world record third consecutive century in Tests and Vengsarkar's elegant 137 was relegated to the background. And now when he got a handsome 109 at Ahmedabad, Gavaskar picked this occasion to get his 10,000th run in Test matches. In the next Test, he displayed the superiority of his batting technique by getting 50 on a minefield of a strip in Bangalore. Gavaskar, with that memorable 96, was the only other batsman in the match to pass the half century mark. The runs continued to flow like a cascade the next season, by which time Vengsarkar had taken over the captaincy. A brave 102 against Patterson, Walsh and Davis in the first Test at New Delhi saw the tempo being maintained. His aggregate improved by leaps and bounds and his average rose even higher. In the next Test at Bombay came more courageous batting. On a fast wicket with Patterson, Walsh and Davis in their elements, Vengsarkar produced batting that constituted bravery of the first order in scoring 51 and 40 not out, helping India to draw a match that seemed lost. In the third Test at Calcutta, Vengsarkar completed his 17th – and as it proved, last Test century. On 102, his left hand was fractured by a rising delivery from Davis. He retired hurt and was ruled out of the match – and also the rest of the series.

Thus ended his Bradmanesque run, which saw Vengsarkar's Test average leap from 38 to 46. Anything after this would have to be anti-climactic, and indeed Vengsarkar did little of note thereafter though he played 18 Tests in India, West Indies, New Zealand, England and Australia. He had just five fifties with a highest score of 75. He failed against pace in the West Indies in 1989, scoring only 110 runs at an average of 18.33. It was amidst great expectations that he went again to England in 1990 and the focus was on him when he went out to bat in the first Test at Lord's. But this time, he was restricted to scores of 52 and 35. His last tour to Australia compounded the disaster cycle. In his thirty-sixth year, Vengsarkar found runs difficult to come by against the pace of McDermott, Hughes, Whitney and Reid. In the midst of the run famine there were two successive fifties, but a scoreline of five, nought, 23, 54, 54, 13, four, one and four for a total of 158 runs at an average of 17.55 could mean only one thing – it was the end of the road for Vengsarkar. And when he was dropped from the squad to take part in the World Cup immediately after the series, Vengsarkar took the hint. Shortly after coming back home, he announced his retirement, even though he needed only 132 runs to reach the 7000-run mark. His tally of 6868 was at the time second only to Gavaskar.

Interestingly enough, Vengsarkar called it a day just after he had hit his highest score in first-class cricket – 284 for Bombay against Maharashtra in the Ranji Trophy. Indeed, in the national competition he was a tower of strength to Bombay and stood out even in that strong batting side. He also had an excellent record in the Duleep Trophy, and was not one of those established Test batsmen who took domestic cricket lightly. Ruthlessly efficient, Vengsarkar made the most of every opportunity to score runs and make them handsomely. His aggregate in the first-class game is second to Gavaskar among Indians, and in the list of century makers he is fourth behind Gavaskar, Hazare and Tendulkar. As regards the career average, among Indians who have scored over 10,000 runs in first-class cricket, Vengsarkar stands eighth. Is there any doubt as to Vengsarkar being one of the batting giants in Indian cricket history? He now coaches young players, whom he hopes will be future giants, at the Elf Cricket Academy in Bombay besides being closely involved with the Talent Development Policy of the Indian Cricket Board.

# 14

# Navjot Singh **Sidhu**

## Colourful and Courageous

He has helped coin a new phrase in cricket commentary – Sidhuisms. Certainly there are two very divisive views on Navjot Singh Sidhu, the commentator. He is either very good or very bad. There is no grey area here. He has either come up with fresh and innovative ideas and given a whole new dimension to the art of cricket commentary, or he has debased and cheapened the rich and noble tradition associated with immortal names like John Arlott, Brian Johnston, Alan McGilvray and Jim Swanton.

There are, however, no two views about Navjot Singh Sidhu, the batsman. There is total unanimity that the tough, yet amiable even colourful sardar from Punjab was one of the most courageous opening batsmen ever to don the India cap. Besides possessing guts of a very high order, Sidhu was aggressive and enterprising and a peerless player of spin bowling. The manner in which he softened up Shane Warne for Sachin Tendulkar to complete the humiliation in the 1997-98 series against Australia, was an exemplary lesson in handling top class spin and his part in the rout of the Australian leg spinner was emphasised by both Tendulkar and the Australians. Besides, Sidhu was one of the few players to enjoy equal success in both Test cricket and the limited overs game, and for long he was among a handful of cricketers to average 40 in both forms.

Born in Patiala in 1963, Sidhu was equally good in studies and cricket at an early age and was a gold medal winning college student. Very keen on cricket, Sidhu worked hard on his game. Initially, he concentrated on having a tight technique and a good defence. It was as a cautious batsman that he played in junior cricket, touring Sri Lanka with the Under-19 team and Zimbabwe with the Under-25 side. He made his first-class debut for Punjab in the Ranji Trophy in 1981 and impressed everybody with his tidy approach. Two years later came an important innings. In scoring 122 for North Zone against the West Indians in 1983-84, Sidhu took a major step towards earning an India cap. Displaying deep concentration and fierce determination for 370 minutes, Sidhu hit 11 fours and a six. Three weeks later, he made 58 in a stay of about four hours against the tourists, playing for the Board President's XI. The selectors, duly impressed, included him in the Indian team for the Ahmedabad Test match. Going in at number three, he made 15 and four. In the final Test at Madras, with Gavaskar opting to go lower down the order, Sidhu opened the innings, scored a sedate 20, was dropped and promptly forgotten.

Suddenly, four years later, when the focus was on the Indian team to be announced for the World Cup, one name that started making the rounds was Sidhu. Hadn't we heard that name before, cricket followers wondered? Wasn't he that strokeless wonder who batted for hours to gather his runs painstakingly? Well, not exactly. For in the intervening four years, Sidhu had worked hard to transform himself into a sixer-hitter. He had realised the wisdom behind the dictum, 'Attack is the best form of defence'. People who had seen him in 1983 could not believe at the metamorphosis. There was no dull thud of bat against ball, no forward defence or backward defence – no blocking, period. Instead he jumped yards out to lift the bowler not just into the untenanted parts of the field but also into the stands. And while he was assured and composed against pace, he showed scant respect for the best of spin bowlers. With four successive half centuries, all struck in his inimitably new style, Sidhu announced that he had arrived on the international scene in a big way. Only Gavaskar with 300 in seven innings, scored more than Sidhu who hit 276 in two innings less.

By a strange irony, Sidhu was now considered too attacking a batsman for the longer version of the game and was not played in any of the Tests against West Indies that followed the World Cup. However, he was back in the Test arena, after a five-year interlude, and celebrated in style against New Zealand in 1988-89. Going in at number three,

Sidhu made 116 off 195 balls with 12 fours and four sixes, negotiating the pace and swing of Richard Hadlee admirably. In keeping with his new reputation, he took three sixes in an over off spin bowler Evan Gray. But it was on the tour of West Indies early in 1989 that Sidhu displayed his trademark courage in facing up to the likes of Marshall, Walsh, Ambrose and Bishop. Starting off with 42 not out in the rain affected first Test, Sidhu's perseverance paid off after four failures. By now he was opening the innings, and in the final Test on a fast and fiery Sabina Park pitch, Sidhu batted six hours and faced 237 balls in getting 116. Just prior to this Test, Sidhu had hit a mighty 286 against Jamaica – the highest score by an Indian outside India. He faced 464 balls and hit 27 fours and two sixes. Sidhu's marathon lasted nine hours and 22 minutes before he was ninth out at 568. He easily headed the tour figures with 596 runs at an average of 66.22.

It was clear that Sidhu had now established himself as an opening batsman, and he consolidated his position further in the series in Pakistan the following season. Fighting knocks of 85, 51 and 97 against Imran, Waqar, Akram and Qadir propelled him to an aggregate of 269. He had wretched luck on the tour of New Zealand that followed, though. Displaying a tight technique and his trademark guts, Sidhu was shaping well against Hadlee and Morrison in the first Test before he was struck on the wrist by a ball from the latter. Sidhu stayed on to get 51. However, it was later discovered that the wrist was fractured and he was ruled out of the tour. Back for the tour of England in the summer, Sidhu enjoyed little success in the Test, scoring just 56 runs in five innings at an average of 11.20. But he fared better on the tour, finishing with an aggregate of 639 runs at an average of 45.64 with two hundreds. The wretched run in the Tests continued in Australia in 1991-92 with Sidhu restricted to 102 runs at an average of 20.40. By now, his overall average had dipped to 28.83 and he was still to top the 900-run mark after 20 Tests.

Dropped for the tour of Zimbabwe and South Africa the following season, Sidhu stayed at home to work his way back to form, and paved the way for Punjab's maiden title triumph in the Ranji Trophy. By the time England came over for the second half of the season, Sidhu was ready. And the first few months of 1993 saw Sidhu back at his sparkling best. Recalled to the side, Sidhu started off with 13 and 37 in the first Test, hit a splendid 106 in the second, and rounded off a productive series with 79 in the final Test. A tally of 235 runs at 58.75 did much to boost both his morale and his average. As the icing on the cake, he also struck fine form in the one-day games and played a leading part in India pulling back a 1-3 deficit to draw level at three matches all with a superb unbeaten 134 in the crucial fifth match of the series. An attacking 61 in the one off Test against Zimbabwe and more good work in the one-day games against the same opponents saw Sidhu set the seal on a most successful season in which he aggregated 736 runs in all first-class matches at an average of 46.00.

Sidhu carried this form forward to the next season. In the Test series in Sri Lanka, he was one of the stars of the victorious campaign with scores of 82, 104 and 39. He and Manoj Prabhakar had now established themselves as a successful pair with successive stands of 171 and 86. In the return series at home, Sidhu was even more prolific, with successive scores of 124, 99 and 43. During his century, Sidhu was particularly severe on Muthiah Muralitharan, hitting him for six of his eight sixes – easily a record for an Indian and only two short of Walter Hammond's Test record of ten sixes against New Zealand in 1932-33. In the next Test, Sidhu was given out leg before, not the best way to be dismissed at 99. In fact, Sidhu had already taken off for the vital single when he was adjudged out. By now, Sidhu was at the peak of his batting powers and popularity, and further proof of this came about when the West Indies toured India in 1994-95. In the Tests, Sidhu had scores of 18 and 12 (first Test) and nought and 11 (third Test). But in between he had a grand double of 107 and 76 in the second Test and this kept boosting his morale and his average. He also played his part in India's victory in the one-day series, notably with an unbeaten 114 in the third match at Vizag. Incidentally that was his fifth century, which was an Indian record, surpassing Srikkanth's mark of four.

Sidhu did reasonably well in the Wills World Cup in 1996 scoring 178 runs at an average of 35.60 with two half centuries. He went to England in the summer as the elder statesman but early on the tour, there was the sensational news that Sidhu was coming back following serious differences with captain Azharuddin. According to Sidhu, he had been 'insulted and humiliated' and he could not take it any more. Opinion was clearly divided as to which of the two stars was in the wrong but given Sidhu's soft and studious nature, it was believed that he would not have taken this extreme step, unless he had a very valid reason. The other school of thought was that, whatever the provocation, Sidhu should have stayed behind for, after all, he was representing the country and he should not have allowed personal misunderstandings to cloud his decision.

At the start of the 1996-97 season then Sidhu was no longer in the team – for the first time since 1992-93 – while Tendulkar replaced Azharuddin as captain. Sidhu missed the one off Test against Australia and the home and the return series against South Africa. But following a compromise initiated by the Indian Cricket Board president I.S. Bindra he was back for the tour of the West Indies in 1997 and showed that he had shrugged off the controversy of the previous year by hitting 201 in the second Test at Port of Spain. It was an uncharacteristic Sidhu innings in that he batted over 12 hours, showing monumental patience, before he was sixth out at 387. A few months later, another three figure knock, his eighth in Tests, was added to Sidhu's growing list when he took 111 off the Sri Lankan attack at Colombo – the match in which the home team recorded the highest ever total in Test matches, 952 for six. And before the year was out, Sidhu got his third century in 1997 by hitting 131 against Sri Lanka in the first Test of the return contest at Mohali. Scores of 79, 35 and 43 gave him an aggregate of 288 runs at an average of 72.00 for the three match series. By now he was averaging well over forty in Test cricket.

A couple of months later, Sidhu showed why he was ranked among the best players of spin bowling. On the eve of the three-match Test series against Australia, the contest was billed as Tendulkar vs Warne. But Sidhu made it that much easier for Tendulkar to win the duel hands down. It was to Sidhu who took it out on Warne first during his two innings of 62 and 64 in the first Test at Madras. Warne, already demoralised by the sight of Sidhu stepping out and hitting him to the straight field, was already down and virtually out by the time Tendulkar came in. And as Tendulkar himself admitted, Sidhu did make it easier for him. The Australians too, after the series was over, were of the view that proper credit had not been given Sidhu for his pioneering efforts in quelling the menace of Warne early. Scores of 97, 74 and 44 followed in the next two Tests and Sidhu had by now more than comfortably perched himself in the opening slot, whoever his partner was, Prabhakar having been discarded after the 1996 World Cup. For the Australia series, for example, it was Nayan Mongia in the first Test and V.V.S. Laxman in the second. But a change in the opening partner did not deter Sidhu, who put on 122 with Mongia and 191 with Laxman.

At the start of the 1998-99 season then, there was no indication that it would be Sidhu's last hurrah in international cricket. He was thirty-five but still fit and confident and with all the recent scores to boost his morale. However, as events unfolded, it was clear that all was not well. In Zimbabwe, in the one off Test, he got only six and nought. Against New Zealand on the tour that followed, in the two Tests, Sidhu was again restricted to nought, 34, one and 13. Finishing eighth in the averages among the bowlers was a new experience for him and his career average fell from 44.97 to 42.13. Soon after he came back in January 1999, the selectors picked a left-handed opening batsman from Tamil Nadu, Sadagopan Ramesh to play in the first Test against Pakistan later that month. The erudite Sidhu was quick to see the writing on the wall and a few months later, announced his retirement from first-class cricket and soon afterwards commenced his new career as a TV commentator.

The statistics associated with Sidhu – whether at the Test level, in ODI's or the first-class game – are very interesting in that they exhibit a certain consistency. But more than the impressive figures, Sidhu will be remembered more for the manner in which he made those runs. Whether the going was smooth or rough, he made them with panache. These days, of course, he regales fellow members of Parliament with his Sidhuisms having been elected from Amritsar on a BJP ticket last year.

# 15

# Mohammed **Azharuddin**

## A Flawed Genius

'Heights of glory, depths of humiliation'. That headline was used in an obituary reference to Richard Nixon in 1994 while summing up his career. Probably no other Indian cricketer would qualify for a similar epitaph than Mohammed Azharuddin. He was hailed at the start of his international career in 1984 as 'an absolute diamond' and 'cricket prophet', enjoyed the status over a long period of being the leading batsman in the country along with Sunil Gavaskar, Dilip Vengsarkar and Sachin Tendulkar, and savoured success for a long stretch in the Nineties as no Indian captain did. But in 2000, all this came to nought when it emerged, following Hansie Cronje's revelations and various enquiries, that he was alleged to be one of the key figures in the match fixing scandal which by then had stunned the cricketing world. Banned for life by the Board of Control for Cricket in India, Azharuddin has taken the matter to court but whatever happens, the stigma attached to his name for his alleged role in the scam, is bound to affect his overall record in international cricket in the eyes of the cricket follower anywhere in the world. Which is a pity because till the scandal broke out in the open, Azharuddin had taken his place in anyone's top ten list of greatest Indian batsmen as well as one of the most gifted and dazzling batsmen of his time.

Born in Hyderabad in 1963, Azharuddin displayed his talent early and made his first-class debut in 1981. The selectors, quick to spot the lad's prodigious gifts, wristy stroke play and brilliant fielding, pushed him into the South Zone side after he made just one century in the Ranji Trophy. Azharuddin's response was to hit 226 in his first knock in the Duleep Trophy tournament in 1983-84. A tour with the India

Under-25 team to Zimbabwe in 1984 sharpened his skills. At the beginning of the following season, he got a century in each innings against Andhra in the Ranji Trophy and a sparkling unbeaten 51 for the Rest of India against Bombay in his team's successful run chase in the Irani Trophy game. This brought him that much closer to the India cap and he clinched his place by getting 151 for India Under-25 against the visiting England team. By now he was being christened as the Hyderabad sensation and his Test debut was keenly awaited. In style and his wristy stroke play, especially while cutting or working the ball away square or fine off the wicket, he seemed a direct descendant of Viswanath, who had played what turned out to be his last Test the year before.

Azharuddin made his Test debut at Calcutta. India were not in a very good position at 126 for three when he entered on the first afternoon. Soon it became 127 for four. Shastri joined Azharuddin and the two proceeded to set up an Indian fifth wicket record stand of 214. Azharuddin reposed the selectors' confidence by hitting 110 off 288 balls, the seventh Indian batsman to score a hundred in his first Test. Two weeks later, in the next Test at Madras, he got 48 and 105 becoming only the fourth batsman after Bill Ponsford, Doug Walters and Alvin Kallicharran to score hundreds in each of his first two Tests. And then a fortnight later, he was on the peak all by himself, becoming the first batsman to score hundreds in each of his first three Test matches. In scoring 122 and 54 not out in the final Test at Kanpur, he raised his aggregate for the series to 439 runs at an average of 109.75.

The remarkably unique feat made Azhar, as he was by now popularly known, a household name. Even people not interested in cricket, were able to identify a face that became the most recognisable in Indian cricket, for the moment eclipsing those of the two superstars Gavaskar and Kapil Dev. After the Kanpur Test, police in ceremonial attire, escorted him home from the airport at the head of a throng, which held up posters simply reading: Azhar. The name came very close to Hazaar, which in Hindi, means, appropriately, thousand. Moreover, his interesting background attracted considerable attention. Mild mannered and soft-spoken, Azhar came from a lower middle class family, unlike most Indian cricketers. Brought up in strict tradition by his maternal grandfather, who died shortly before Azhar made his Test debut, he was very much a humble, shy and well behaved youth with his feet planted firmly on Mother Earth despite his tremendous achievement. Praying five times a day and maintaining all the fasts required by the Muslim faith were a traditional part of his upbringing. A college graduate with a commerce degree, the simple-minded Azhar started out playing street cricket like so many other lads in the country, but even then he was convinced that he was going to make cricket his career. 'I played the game seriously, never for the heck of it,' he was to say in later interviews.

Off to Australia for the World Championship of Cricket after his first Test series, Azhar went with a tremendous reputation. He was an instant success in limited overs cricket too and by now was a national hero. Of course he was aware of the fact that he would not enjoy a run like he did against England all the time, and he came face to face with reality when he enjoyed only moderate success over the next couple of years. In 12 Tests following the series against England, Azhar got only three half centuries and his average plummeted to 48. Despite his dream start, Azhar could complete 1000 runs in Test cricket only in his 16th game. And he picked this occasion to get his fourth hundred and his first since the Kanpur Test in early 1985. It came about almost two years later, in December 1986 against Sri Lanka, interestingly enough, also at Kanpur. Scoring 199, he became only the second batsman to be dismissed at that score in Test cricket. In the process, he and Kapil Dev shared an Indian sixth wicket record stand of 272 runs off just 49.3 overs.

Having tasted success after a long time, Azhar now went from strength to strength. By now, he had become a more complete batsman. While still retaining his artistic touch, he had tightened up his technique considerably and his defence was much more secure. So, while scoring runs at a brisk pace with his trademark skill and grace, he was also proving to be a hard batsman to dismiss. Seeing the ball early and playing it late – the hallmark of a truly great player – Azhar charmed audiences and frustrated bowlers the world over. At least, a new generation, which never saw Viswanath bat, was now fortunate to see his direct descendant. Against Pakistan towards the end of the 1986-87 season, he reeled off centuries in successive innings – a classy 141 at Calcutta and a more sedate 110 at Jaipur. But a mundane run against West Indies in 1987-88 and New Zealand the following season, followed by failures in the West Indies in 1989, not only brought his average down further to 46 but also raised doubts whether Azhar was susceptible to bowling that was really quick. In 12 Tests in the period 1987-1989, Azhar got only two half centuries. Moreover, fast and short-pitched bowling in the West Indies seemed to have created some sort of a chink in his batting armour.

It was uncanny how every time doubts were raised about Azhar, he did not take long in quelling them in his own inimitable style. Fortune favours the brave and certainly a class player like Azhar deserved his share of good luck. Following his failures in West Indies – he averaged 28.25 in the Test series and 20.75 on the tour – he was now reduced to the level of having to fight for his place in the middle order. On the eve of the first Test against Pakistan in November 1989, he was dropped and only made it on the morning of the game when Raman Lamba sustained a toe injury and had to pull out. Azhar grabbed the opportunity and made the most of it – not so much with the bat as in the field. He held five catches, scored 35 and 35 and just about retained his place. In the first innings of the second Test, he was out for a duck but that turned out to be his only real failure for some time. In the next three innings, he reeled off scores of 109, 77 and 52. He treated Imran Khan, Wasim Akram and Abdul Qadir with disdain, driving, cutting and flicking them off his toes in imperious fashion. The century in particular was a gem as he faced only 175 balls, hitting ten fours. With figures of 312 runs at an average of 44.57 Azhar emphasised his newfound confidence. He looked ahead eagerly to the New Year and the new decade, particularly now that he had been appointed captain, quite unexpectedly, for the tour of New Zealand.

Would the burden of captaincy put curbs on his natural batting style was the initial doubt raised by cynics. During the year, Azhar proved that if anything his batting improved with the responsibilities of leadership. One breathtaking innings in the third and final Test of the series was enough to underline this. In the face of a New Zealand total of 391, India had lost three wickets for 71 runs when Azhar entered. Despite the grim situation, he counter-attacked in a thrilling manner.

Wickets fell at regular intervals at the other end, but Azhar continued to bat in 'Nawabi' fashion treating the New Zealand seam trio of Hadlee, Morrison and Snedden with absolute disdain. He stroked the ball with silken ease and his 192 came up off only 259 balls with as many as 26 fours. Lack of support at the other end made Azhar adopt desperate measures towards the closing stages of the innings, and he miscued a big hit to be caught in the deep, being the last batsman to be dismissed by which time the total had reached 482. Thanks chiefly to Azhar, the run rate was staggering. In two hours before lunch on the third day, 148 runs were scored and the first five overs of the new ball cost New Zealand 50 runs. For the first time since his debut series five years before, Azhar again topped the Test figures with 303 runs at an average of 75.75.

This was now a new Azhar the world of cricket was seeing. In addition to his wristy elegance, his pretty-pretty late cuts and leg glances, Azhar was now fluently playing the drives, hitting powerfully to the leg side and was unafraid to loft the ball to the untenanted places in the field. Mixing power and elegance in the ideal measure, Azhar was now in impeccable form, and proof of this was seen in England. Wisden noted that 'a new definition was given to oriental artistry as Azharuddin, time and again, placed the ball through square leg and mid wicket with a wristy turn of the bat at the instant of impact. It was the return of the touch which had launched his international career five years ago so spectacularly.' Indeed Azhar reached the very heights of artistic batting on the tour. On his century in the first Test at Lord's, Wisden observed: 'The Indian captain's breathtakingly audacious hundred signified the difference between the English straight bat, wielded with control rather than subtlety, and oriental wristiness which lends itself to innovation.' When he came in to bat, Azhar was already under severe pressure for his decision to put England in to bat, which had led to the home team rattling up 653 for four declared. But he batted in charming fashion from the first ball. As time went by, he enraptured the Saturday crowd with strokes of ethereal beauty. With a razzle-dazzle approach that bordered on audacity, Azhar cruised to three figures off only 88 balls. He had come in at 191 for three and by the time he left after getting 121 on the fourth morning, the score had leapt to 393 for seven.

The entertainment spread over to the next Test at Old Trafford. In the face of an England total of 519, India lost three wickets for 57 late on the second day. Helped by Sanjay Manjrekar and Sachin Tendulkar in putting up century stands for the fourth and fifth wickets, the captain proceeded to carry on from where he left off at Lord's two weeks before. By the time he was fifth out at 358, Azhar had batted in his by now trademark dashing-cum-elegant style for 281 minutes and scored 179 with 21 fours and a six. Between lunch and tea on the third day, he became the first Indian batsman to score 100 runs in a session in a Test match. Nothing it seemed would stop Azhar from posting his fourth century in as many Tests but at the Oval he was restricted to 78. However, it did not prevent him from heading the Test figures for the second time in a row with 426 runs at an average of 85.20. He also headed the tour figures with 770 runs at an average of 77.00. As the icing on the cake, India won both the Texaco Trophy ODI's, and Azhar was adjudged the Indian man of the series for his scores of 55 not out off 50 balls and 63 not out off 44 balls. Verily, for Azhar, this was a tour that dreams are made of.

His career average having jumped from 46 to 51 as a result of his outstanding run over the previous year, Azhar looked forward with a lot of confidence. But then his career, till now, had had its share of ups and downs. Just when things were looking down for Azhar, there would be an upward swing in the fortunes. And just when things were looking bright, there would be a downward swing. So it proved again, for the period 1990-1992 was a really testing one for him. The one off Test against Sri Lanka in 1990-91 was duly won but he scored only 23. And though he enjoyed a successful season for Derbyshire when he turned up for the English county in 1991, scoring 2016 runs at an average of 59.29, the charge that he was susceptible to fast, short pitched bowling on bouncy tracks returned to haunt him on the tour of Australia during the winter. He was plainly in distress against McDermott, Reid, Hughes and Whitney and could only struggle to come up with an aggregate of 192 runs at a miserable average of 21.33 in the five Tests. There was only one gallant innings in nine, 106 in the fourth Test in a losing cause at Adelaide, when he indulged in a daring counter-attack. For the rest of the time, he was hopping around, falling five times to McDermott. He redeemed himself with a splendid record in the World Cup, which followed the series, heading the figures with 332 runs at an average of 47.42 with four half centuries.

Overall, however, it was a most disappointing experience, exposing once again a certain vulnerability in Azhar's ability to play genuine pace bowling. This view gained further credence when he failed against Donald, McMillan and company in South Africa the following season, reduced to just 120 runs at an average of 20.00. For first-class matches, the figures were even worse – 132 runs at an average of 14.66. At the end of the tour, his overall Test average had come hurtling down to an all-time low 43. Would he be able to resurrect his career, now that a cloud hung over his captaincy as well, was the question uppermost in everyone's minds as the Indian team returned in January 1993 to battle it out with England.

There comes a turning point in everyone's career – for good or for worse. Azhar's turning point – for the good – was now around the corner. Astonishingly, despite the successive reverses, he kept his job as captain and perhaps that was the morale booster he needed. Or maybe even the fact that the first Test was to be played at his favourite venue – the Eden Gardens at Calcutta. He had never failed on the ground since his historic debut eight years before and his scores in the three Tests he had played so far were 110, 141 and 60. Under pressure, in more ways than one, Azhar entered on the opening day of the series with India at some difficulty at 93 for three. By close of play, he was unbeaten with 114 and raised this to 182 on the second afternoon. By the time he was out, India were 362 for seven. It marked a decisive turn, not only in the match but also the series. India won all three Tests, even if Azhar did nothing of note in the remaining games. He also played a leading role in India levelling the one-day series at three matches all after being down 1-3, reeling off successive scores of 74 and 95 not out (off just 63 balls).

For the next couple of years, Azhar could not put a foot wrong. As a captain he was the monarch of Indian cricket. And as a batsman, with Vengsarkar too having followed Gavaskar into retirement, he and Tendulkar were now the twin bulwarks. In the home series against Sri Lanka in 1993-94 Azhar was at the height of his artistic powers. With successive scores of 47, 108 and 152 in the three Tests, all of which were won by an innings, he showed that he could bat admirably even under adverse conditions. On turning tracks, which caused a lot of heartburn among the visitors and on which the spinners revelled, Azhar displayed exemplary batting in scoring 307 runs at an average of 102.33. Particularly outstanding was his 152, for which he batted a minute over six hours. His batting was described as 'near miraculous', for the next longest stay at the wicket was three hours by Sidhu. Wisden noted that 'he looked as if he was on a plumb pitch, dispatching the bad balls for four while keeping out the good ones with polished defence'. With virtually no support – the next best score was Kambli's 57 – Azhar, virtually on his own, battled it out against Muralitharan and Anurasiri. Coming in at 123 for three, he was ninth out at 355. To emphasise the greatness of Azhar's batting it is worth pointing out that the Sri Lankans could make only 119 and 222 in their two innings. Back in England in 1994 for a second season with Derbyshire, Azhar started off with a scintillating 205 from 192 balls with 21 fours and six sixes against Durham, but was called back by the Indian Board in mid-season to prepare for a one-day competition in Sri Lanka. He had the satisfaction of heading the averages with 712 runs from nine games at 44.50. Against West Indies the next season, Azhar had to be content with a tally of 178 runs from six innings, but there had to be a trademark knock and this came about at Nagpur when he got 97 and added 202 runs with Tendulkar for the fifth wicket.

Throughout his first decade in international cricket, Azharuddin also maintained very good form in limited overs cricket. By the time he played his last ODI he had played in more matches (334) and scored more runs (9378) than anyone else. He was one of the few players to have a splendid record in both forms of the game but somehow could not rise to the occasion in both the 1996 and 1999 World Cup competitions. Indeed, the lack lustre, rain affected Test series against New Zealand in 1995-96 and the Wills World Cup started another downward slide in Azharuddin's career graph. He did not do anything of note in the Test series, failed in the World Cup and his form touched rock bottom in England in 1996. On the tour, he finished eighth in the first-class figures with 439 runs at an average of 39.60. But he really plumbed the depths in the Tests, scratching around for 42 runs at an average of 8.40. As if all this was not enough, came the Sidhu controversy with Azhar copping most of the blame for the return of the experienced opening batsman to India. His personal life too was going through turmoil for this was the time he divorced his first wife and married actress-cum-model Sangeeta Bijlani. He was, of course, still indispensable as a batsman for he was capable of striking form at any time, given his class and experience, but he was very much dispensable as a captain. In 1996-97 then, his long reign finally over, Tendulkar became captain and Azharuddin could concentrate on his batting. Given his recent record, it seemed a very healthy development.

Azhar really bloomed in the second Test at Calcutta – where else? – against South Africa. In the face of a total of 428, India had lost seven wickets for 161 when Kumble joined Azharuddin. For the next three hours, the formidable attack of Donald, McMillan, Cronje, Symcox, Adams and Klusener did not know what hit them. The two just sailed into them and did pretty much what they liked. The partnership yielded an Indian record eighth wicket partnership of 161 before Azhar was out at 322 for 109 while Kumble went on to score 88. In the disaster of the second innings, which saw the Indians shot out for 137, Azhar again top-scored with 52. Continuing from where he left off, Azhar hammered a spectacular unbeaten 163 in the final Test, again putting the famed attack to rout, as India surged towards victory in the match and the series.

Displaying a taste for South African bowling, Azhar proceeded to flay them on their own turf during the return contest. In the second Test, he and Tendulkar authored one of the most astonishing fightbacks in Indian cricket. Replying to South Africa's total of 529 for seven declared, the visitors lost half the side for 58 before the captain and the former captain turned the innings around with a thrilling counter-attack that yielded 222 runs for the sixth wicket. Tendulkar got 169 and Azhar

115. This unforgettable knock, however, was sandwiched by five failures and his shocking run in the West Indies continued. In the tour that followed early in 1997, nothing went right for Azhar. He got only a measly return of 63 runs at an average of 12.60 in the Tests and again was plainly in distress even against new pace bowlers in Rose and Dillon. A few months later, however, back on familiar subcontinental terrain, Azhar was a transformed batsman scoring 126 and 108 not out in successive Tests in Sri Lanka.

Regaining the captaincy early in 1998 against Australia, Azhar's way of celebrating was to get his customary hundred at Calcutta. In scoring 163 not out with 18 fours and three sixes, Azhar got his fifth century in six Tests at the Eden Gardens. At the start of the following season it was clear that age had not dimmed his artistic skills for against New Zealand, one of his favourite opponents, Azhar notched up scores of 103 not out and 48 at Wellington. This boosted his confidence as the Indians prepared to take on Pakistan in early 1999 in the first Test series between the two countries in almost ten years. His form was patchy in the two Tests as well as the two matches of the Asian Test Championship, the only notable knock being 87 against Sri Lanka. His lack of form in the World Cup also added to his worries. But soon he had more important things to worry about.

A shoulder injury, for which Azhar stayed back in England for treatment took some time to heal. He was lost to Indian cricket for about six months during which time the Indian team, besides playing a host of one day matches, hosted New Zealand in a three Test series and then toured Australia again for three Tests. Having recovered from his injury, Azhar was recalled for the first Test against South Africa at Mumbai in February 2000. But a finger injury he sustained in the three-day match prior to the Test ruled him out of the big game. Thus it was that Azhar's 99th Test was the second and final match of the series at Bangalore. Making light of his thirty-seven years, he scored a stroke filled 102, which brought back memories of the vintage Azhar and showed that he was still fit and skilful. He was also the epitome of consistency in the Ranji Trophy and ran up a tally of 815 runs at an average of 81.50 with two hundreds and six fifties. His splendid form had much to do with Hyderabad making the final for the first time since their title triumph in 1986-87.

By the time the final was being played, the match fixing scandal had already broke open, thanks to the Delhi police having come across the taped conversation Hansie Cronje was alleged to have had with bookie Sanjay Chawla. A few months later, Cronje named Azhar in his testimony before the King Commission. In the meantime, the Indian government had asked the CBI to conduct an inquiry and the BCCI also had their inquiry conducted by former CBI official K. Madhavan. Azhar himself appeared before the inquiry and the evidence seemed to be building up against him and a few others. Finally, the CBI came up with their report and Azhar was one of the names mentioned. The BCCI for their part met in Chennai in December and took the decision to slap a life ban on Azhar, who promptly went to court challenging the ban.

Given the manner in which his career came to an end, can there be any doubt that Azhar was a flawed genius? There will be the tendency to look down upon his achievements, particularly in the last few years, in the wake of the match fixing controversy. It does seem that even Fate was against him towards the end. But for the injury, he would have played 100 Tests. Now, he will be the only player to be stuck on 99 Tests, a truly unique figure. Which may be fitting if one remembers that he also burst upon the scene twenty years ago with a unique feat.

# 16

## Sachin Ramesh **Tendulkar**

Numero Uno

I t was a signal honour that remained elusive for an Indian batsman for sixty years. To be adjudged as the best batsman in the world was for years the prerogative of an Englishman or an Australian, a West Indian or a South African. The leading Indian batsmen of their day, however good they were technically and statistically, could never aspire for the title. For example, greats like C.K. Nayudu, Vijay Merchant and Vijay Hazare were the leading lights in the Thirties and Forties and earned accolades galore even internationally. But then their peak period coincided with that of Don Bradman, Wally Hammond and George Headley. And however good Polly Umrigar and Vijay Manjrekar were in the Fifties, there was never any chance that they would be considered the best in the world – not with the likes of Len Hutton, Peter May, Neil Harvey and the three W's around. The Nawab of Pataudi was the best Indian batsman of the Sixties and was acknowledged to be one of the leading players in the world. But then his heyday coincided with the peak period of Gary Sobers, Rohan Kanhai, Graeme Pollock, Bobby Simpson, Colin Cowdrey, Ken Barrington, Ted Dexter and Hanif Mohammed. Even when Sunil Gavaskar made his big splash on the international stage there was not much chance of him being adjudged undoubtedly as the best batsman in the world. Sobers was still around and about the same time that Gavaskar played his first Test, Greg Chappell, a twenty-two-year-old Australian made his debut a memorable one by hitting a hundred and went on to become one of the finest batsmen of all time. And even as Gavaskar and Chappell were vying for honours there appeared on the scene a certain West Indian batsman who answered to the name of Isaac Vivian Alexander Richards.

As long as he remained on the international scene he would hold centre stage despite competition from such greats as Javed Miandad, Zaheer Abbas, Gordon Greenidge, David Gower and Allan Border.

Richards played his last Test in 1991 and the title became vacant. But not for long. And glory be! It was an Indian who acceded to the throne. And it was not that he did not have competition. From the early Nineties to the early years of the new millennium represented the decade of Brian Lara, Richie Richardson, Martin Crowe, Steve and Mark Waugh, Matthew Hayden, Inzamam ul Haq, Gary Kirsten and fellow Indian Rahul Dravid. But can there be any doubt that the number one batsman in the world for a decade now has been Sachin Ramesh Tendulkar – something acknowledged by fans, media representatives and fellow players the world over a d augmented if need be by statistics. But figures, however important they may be, are something that Tendulkar's achievements should not be measured by. He should be judged by the manner of his batting that is an impeccable blend of full-blooded strokes and immaculate defence, utmost determination and intense concentration and a single-mindedness of purpose in achieving his mission. The ultimate tribute to the Indian maestro, of course, has to be the one paid by none other than Don Bradman, who remarked that Tendulkar's method of batting, his style and approach to the game, was the closest to the greatest of them all.

And yet such an exalted title sits lightly on the shoulders of Tendulkar, as well as all the fame, the adulation, the heady praise and other accolades that he has received over the past decade and a half. But then Tendulkar is not just another great cricketer. He is arguably the greatest Indian cricketer ever, pipping Gavaskar and Kapil Dev to the post. After watching Gavaskar and Kapil Dev, besides a few others before them, I was convinced that in my lifetime I would never see a greater Indian cricketer than the terrific twosome. I am happy to say that Tendulkar proved me wrong. Going beyond Indian cricket, Tendulkar, simply put, is one of the greatest players in the history of the game, symbolised by Bradman naming him in his dream team of all time.

Tendulkar really has everything that is there in any cricket manual and he has added a few chapters of his own. After fifteen years in international cricket, he has carved a niche all his own, and run up a record of runs, centuries and double centuries that will take some beating. The truly amazing point is that the entertainment for the cricketing world could still be only around the three quarter mark. As it is, his figures are mind-boggling and one really can let his imagination ran amok as to where it will all end around five years from now. He has all the strokes – and then some! He has humbled purveyors of pace and swing, cut and spin and has scored a mountain of runs in the limited overs game and in Test cricket. He has got runs on slow pitches in India and fast tracks in the West Indies, on bouncy wickets in South Africa and Australia and in whirling conditions in New Zealand and England.

The thought of having Tendulkar as an opponent gives bowlers bad dreams, and according to some reports, Shane Warne does not even want to hear his name mentioned! After all, Tendulkar has been giving him nightmares. The story doing the rounds a couple of years ago was that the Aussie leg spinner, voted among Wisden's five cricketers of the century, was willing to come again to India, provided Tendulkar was not in the home team! On the tour of India last year he quite enjoyed himself in the absence of Tendulkar from the first two Tests. After taking ten wickets in three Tests on each of his first two visits in 1998 and 2001 at over 50 apiece – thanks principally to the mauling he received from Tendulkar – he took ten wickets in the first two Tests at a little over 30 apiece – including his first five wicket haul against India.

Certainly no Indian batsman has inflicted such psychological damage to bowlers at any time, and no batsman in the world has had this kind of negative, almost frightening, impact on bowlers since Vivian Richards. Ultimately, the manner in which Tendulkar takes them apart, it drives them to a nervous depression. He has them in such a tizzy with a trail of devastating shots that at last, in desperation and disgusted with life as it were, the bowler has to either look at the Heavens for Divine help or closer to earth, implore with the captain to take him off. 'There is no use bowling to his bloke,' has been the general refrain of bowlers the world over. When you bowl to him, there aren't enough tricks. Similarly, when you write about him, there aren't enough words.

Tendulkar is such a complete batsman that he can bat all day and every day if the need arises. After all, he is not a stranger to long stays at the crease in Test matches. However, in one-day cricket, aware that only a maximum of 50 overs are available, Tendulkar makes the most of these with shots that enthral, excite and entertain – and boost the run rate. He has so many strokes at his command that he does pretty much what he likes with the bowling. There is no real weakness in his armour. No bowler can say with any justification that Tendulkar is weak against such and such a delivery. Nor can there be any theory which is based on an opponent saying 'pitch the ball here, move it that way and Tendulkar will be in trouble'. All this is sheer nonsense.

Watching Tendulkar bat, I am reminded of Neville Cardus' appreciation of the 1930 Don Bradman. Just substitute Tendulkar for Bradman as you read the following passage: 'When Bradman passed 200 at Leeds I felt that my interest in his play might break out anew at the sight of one miscalculated stroke. But none was to be seen. His cricket went along its manifold ways with the security, which denied its own brilliance. Every fine point of batsmanship was to be admired; strokes powerful and swift and accurate and handsome; variety of craft, controlled by singleness of mind and purpose. Bradman was as determined to take no risks as he was to hit boundaries from every ball the least loose. And his technique is so extensive and practiced that he can get runs at the rate of fifty an hour without once needing to venture romantically into the realms of the speculative or the empirical. The bowler who had to tackle Victor Trumper, was able to keep his spirit more or less hopeful by some philosophy such as this: "Victor is moving at top speed. Well, I am bound sooner or later to send along a really good ball. Victor will flash at it in his ecstasy – and I will have him!" The bowler toiling at Bradman cannot support himself by a like optimism. For hours, he will see his ordinary balls hit for fours along the grass; then his good one will wheel from his arm, by the law of averages, which causes every bowler to achieve one moment of excellence in every hour. But is Bradman ever likely to be so blinded by the radiance of his own visions that he will throw back his head at the good ball, confuse it with the others, and lose his wicket through a royal expense of spirit? Not he;

he sees the dangerous ball with eyes as suspicious as those of a Makepeace. Down over his bat goes his head; the blade becomes a broad, protective shield – and probably two pads will lend a strong second line of defence. It is not a paradox to imagine some bowler saying to Bradman, with strict justice, after Bradman has punished five fours in one over and cannily stopped the sixth ball: "For the Lord's sake, Don, do give a fellow a chance and have a hit at her!"' What Cardus wrote about Bradman, nearly seventy-five years ago, applies very much to Tendulkar today.

Tendulkar is a peerless player of any bowling. There are some batsmen who are better players of pace bowling than spin or vice versa. If there is one batsman about whom I cannot say the same thing, it is Tendulkar. I have seen him bring out the most fantastic of shots against all bowlers – fast, medium, swingers, cutters, leg spin, off spin, googlies, top spinners, honest straight balls. You name it, he's hit it. His technique is so well organised that he is able to encounter any delivery with ease and comfort, giving the impression of having all the time in the world to play the stroke – the hallmark of the greatest of batsmen. His excellent eyesight sees any minute change in the bowler's action and his nimble footwork enables him to get to the pitch of the ball faster and with much less effort than most batsmen. Should the bowler force him on the back foot, Tendulkar's feet are in perfect position to essay a square cut, hook, pull or the lofted drive. No shot is his pet stroke; he plays them all, handsomely, felicitously and lucratively. There is an element of power in his batting. However, it is not total, naked power, but controlled power. Timing is the essence of all his shots. His concentration is legendary, his determination is fierce and the hunger to succeed is insatiable. Even today, he takes even club matches seriously, something driven home by the fact that he averages over 90 in the Ranji Trophy. When he assured coach Ashok Mankad that Mumbai would win the Ranji Trophy in 1999-2000, the former Indian batsman could just relax. He was confident that having set his goal on something, Tendulkar would definitely achieve it. On the way, he played an innings of 233 not out against Tamil Nadu in the semifinal, which will rank very high even in the little big man's long list of great knocks. A batsman who scores all 41 runs added for the last two wickets and gives his side the lead with the last man at the crease, has to be one who possesses exceptional qualities.

But then again something has to be mentioned about his stupendous feats before he became an international cricketer to underscore that Tendulkar possessed his special, even unique qualities at a precocious age. Indeed, if there is one prodigy in Indian cricket, it is Tendulkar. Like Gavaskar, he was nationally known in cricket circles even before he played first-class cricket. In the mid-Sixties, a boy named Gavaskar made headlines by scoring double centuries regularly while still at school. Twenty years later, Tendulkar became known as the schoolboy with the Midas touch. Even at twelve he was totally focused on the game and never missed a chance to further his batting skills. And displaying his amazing mental toughness – which he later was also to show in the international arena – Tendulkar made his Ranji Trophy debut at fifteen a memorable one by hitting a century against Gujarat. He was the youngest to hit a century on debut in the championship. Already there was talk of including him in the Indian team to tour West Indies in 1989. But the selectors resisted the temptation and Tendulkar did not make the trip.

During the summer, Tendulkar paid a visit to the MRF Pace Foundation Academy in Chennai and got a few tips from Dennis Lillee after facing up to the Australian fast bowling great and other young hopefuls with more than a degree of assurance. Lillee, duly pleased by what he saw, predicted a great future for the young lad. By now, it was taken for granted that Tendulkar would don the India cap sooner rather than later. And a century for Rest of India against Delhi in the Irani Trophy game just prior to the selection of the Indian team to tour Pakistan in 1989-90 was just the passport Tendulkar needed to make his entry into the international arena. At sixteen, he was the youngest to play in his first Test and it was one debut that was eagerly awaited.

It wasn't a sensational debut. There was no century in his first Test like a few Indians had done. There was not even a half-century. He made only 15 before being bowled by another debutant Waqar Younis. In the second Test, he improved to 59, adding 143 runs for the fifth wicket with Manjrekar. It did not matter to him that the bowling was in the hands of Imran Khan, Wasim Akram and Abdul Qadir. Not one to honour reputations, Tendulkar impressed by facing up to the bowling squarely and by displaying an ideal temperament. A neat 41 in the third Test gave him further confidence. And he rounded off his first Test series with scores of 35 and 57, during the latter innings, sharing a fifth wicket stand of 101 runs with Sidhu after four wickets had fallen for 38 runs. The manner in which he stood firm for three and a half hours in the face of repeated bouncers by the paceman – enough for the umpire to warn Akram for intimidatory bowling – spoke volumes for the teenager's courage, skill and technique. Indeed, early in the knock, a snorter from Younis hit Tendulkar on the nose and blood started dripping profusely. It was suggested that he go off for treatment but Tendulkar, already made of sterner stuff, stayed put and after a hasty patch up job, settled into his stance again to face the remainder of the over. Noted journalist Ayaz Memon gives an eyewitness account: 'Younis' next delivery, swinging but full pitched, was gloriously square driven for four. The delivery after that was a trifle short outside the off stump, to which Tendulkar, on his toes and striking the ball on the up, hit past a rooted cover for yet another boundary. This, a spectacular riposte from a player who had just been felled, established not merely Tendulkar's pedigree but also his gumption. Within five minutes, as it were, he had made the transition from boy to man.' In scoring 215 runs at an average of 35.83 in the four Test series, Tendulkar did not exactly set the Jhelum on fire, but as in the case of so many great cricketers of the past, anyone who saw Tendulkar make even 30 was aware that he was watching a player of uncommon gifts.

That was the modest start to his career. And over the next fifteen years, Tendulkar has exhibited his ethereal batting qualities all over the world, on all surfaces and climes, against every type of bowling known in the game. But however prodigiously talented he was as a teenager and however much the experts were convinced very early that here was a cricketer bound to rewrite the record books, none could have bargained for Tendulkar to scale the heights he has reached over a decade and a half.

It somehow seems fitting that it was in the home of cricket that Tendulkar first showed signs of greatness, where he really unfolded the full range of his strokes, along with the skill, technique and temperament. Let's hear what Wisden has to say about his first Test century crafted at Old Trafford in 1990: 'Of the six centuries scored in this fascinating contest, none was more outstanding than Tendulkar's which rescued India on the final afternoon. At 17 years and 112 days, he was only 30 days older than Mushtaq Mohammed was when against India at New Delhi in 1960-61 he became the youngest player to score a Test hundred. More significantly, after several of his colleagues had fallen to reckless strokes, Tendulkar held the attack at bay with a disciplined display of immense maturity. He remained undefeated on 119 having batted for 224 minutes and hit 17 fours. He looked the embodiment of India's famous opener Gavaskar and indeed was wearing a pair of his pads. While he displayed a full repertoire of strokes in compiling his maiden Test hundred, most remarkable were his off side shots from the back foot. Though only 5 feet, 5 inches tall, he was still able to control without difficulty short deliveries from the pacemen.' Tendulkar really drew heady praise even from hard-boiled critics and old timers who had seen them all – from Hobbs to Richards.

Incidentally, one of those to be impressed by Tendulkar during that Old Trafford century was Mushtaq Mohammed. And as he said in praise of Tendulkar, 'I would easily trade that record of mine to play an innings like this'. And reviewing the tour, Wisden noted that, 'there should be many more Test hundreds for Tendulkar'. Actually it did not require Wisden to make such a prediction for everyone knew that Tendulkar would get many more three figure knocks. What probably no one was prepared for was the commanding manner in which he batted through the next decade, the giant strides he made in world cricket and the exalted status that he reached. And to think that no one really knows to what extent he will reach when he finally quits the game! Whichever way one looks, however, there is little doubt that the England tour marked a watershed in Tendulkar's career.

By 1991, when Tendulkar reached adulthood, there was little doubt that he was the most exciting young talent in international cricket, his precocity matched by his single-mindedness to succeed in his career. Like Gavaskar, he came from a middle class Maharashtrian family – his father was a professor in Sanskrit and his mother a clerk in the Life Insurance Corporation. Gavaskar himself observed at this stage that 'Tendulkar is more talented than I was at the same age'. And while at this time, comparisons were made between the two, it could be seen that except in physique, there were certain basic differences in their approach. Gavaskar's concentration was legendary and he could bat on and on. And though he played long innings in Test matches even up to 708 minutes for 172 runs, there were times he would go into a sort of stupor. One could not ever imagine Tendulkar batting for ten hours or so or taking that long over his innings. An ardent admirer of Vivian Richards, Tendulkar even at a young age, had fashioned his batting on the West Indian great, believing that primarily the ball was meant to be hit. Defence, for him was something to turn to only as a very last resort. But his technique was such that it was not just a dull thud of bat against ball; even his defensive strokes and pushes got him runs thanks to faultless timing and impeccable placements.

In South Africa in 1992 Tendulkar at 19 years and 217 days became the youngest batsman to reach 1000 Test runs, displacing Kapil Dev (21 years, 27 days in 1979-80). Soon of course these landmarks – and greater achievements – were to become commonplace. Indeed from 1993 Tendulkar's career really took off like a Concorde. From now on, there were no more moderate figures associated with him. From now on, the century ratio increased, the runs came more easily – and handsomely as ever – and it was inevitable that Tendulkar was going to be a bigger bugbear for bowlers. By early 1994 he had added another landmark to the burgeoning list – the only batsman in Test history to make seven centuries before turning twenty-one.

Of course, alongside his awesome Test record, his figures in one-day internationals were also improving by leaps and bounds. He had shown very early in his career that he could adapt himself to the intricacies of limited overs cricket very successfully. On his first tour of Pakistan, Tendulkar had hit Qadir for 26 runs in an over in a one-day game on his way to a blitzkrieg innings of 53 not out, placing his captain and non-striker Srikkanth, himself no slouch when it came to fast scoring, in the role of a spectator. Since then, he had played a notable part in India's victories in various such competitions around the world. But on the short tour of New Zealand in early 1994, something happened that was to have a tremendous influence on India's fortunes in the one-day game in the future. He usually batted at number four or five but in a moment of inspiration, he opted to open following a neck strain to Sidhu. What followed was an astounding innings of 82 not out off just 49 balls with 15 fours and two sixes and India, chasing a moderate target of 143 rushed to victory using up less than half of their allocated 50 overs. Tendulkar smashed three fours and a six off Larsen's first over before being third out at 126. Subsequently, with Tendulkar's awesome record in one-day cricket, together with his famous opening partnerships with Sourav Ganguly and Virender Sehwag, this otherwise inconsequential game at Auckland in March 1994 has achieved a special status. Indeed, this match was a sort of re-birth for Tendulkar in limited overs cricket, for six months later, he scored his first century in his 78th one-day match in the Singer Cup against Australia at Colombo. And as the whole world knows, the century list has burgeoned into an unbelievable number by now.

When the West Indies came over in 1994-95, the series was billed as 'Tendulkar vs Lara'. The West Indian superstar had earlier in the year set up records for both Tests (375) and first-class cricket (501 not out). By the end of the series Tendulkar had left Lara far behind – 402 runs at an average of 67.00 compared to Lara's 198 at 33.00. That was Tendulkar rising to the challenge as only he could – as he proved again when he got the better of Shane Warne in the much touted about 'Tendulkar vs Warne' duel three years later. Tendulkar's stature kept growing and by 1995 he was signing a lucrative deal with a sports management firm that made him the world's richest cricketer and the biggest name in international cricket – a title he holds till this day.

It's hard to get to the top; it's harder to stay there. And it is a tribute to Tendulkar's fitness, class, skill and enterprise that he continues to be perched at the top for so long. And besides the above-mentioned qualities the one quality that has remained uppermost is his equanimity. He is least affected by nefarious aspects of the game like sledging or gamesmanship. While bowlers have been able to get under the skin of many other batsmen by needling them, they are plainly wasting their time whenever they have tried to unsettle Tendulkar. How he manages this calmness of mind with sage like single-mindedness of purpose! He just shuts himself off from the world so to say, ignores the baiters whether it is the bowler or the fieldsman, withdraws towards square leg and then concentrates on the next ball. In a game corrupted by ill-mannered and loutish behaviour and allegations of match fixing, Tendulkar has remained the squeaky clean mascot.

For all his inborn talent and classy batsmanship, Tendulkar also remains a deep thinker of the finer points of the game. He has always been aware of the importance of mental preparedness – a quality he proved to the hilt on the eve of the 'Tendulkar vs Warne' duel in 1998. If Tendulkar was at the height of his powers as a batsman, so also was Warne as a bowler. To have the leading batsman in the world play the leading spin bowler in the world was obviously going to be a battle for the gods. Moreover, their personal duel was going to govern which way the series went. The preparation then was all-important and Tendulkar showed why he was well versed in the intricate strategies and tactical manoeuvres of the game. Fully aware of how important it was to the team that he wins the duel with Warne, Tendulkar arrived in Madras, the scene of the first Test a few days before the commencement of the game, and asked for former Test leg spinner L. Sivaramakrishnan to bowl to him at a spot outside the leg stump which Tendulkar had marked. When the series started, Tendulkar was ready – and easily won the contest underscored by the figures – 446 runs at an average of 111.25 and a strike rate of 80.65 runs per hundred balls as against Warne's ten wickets at a cost of 54 runs apiece (his career average prior to the series was 23.81). Little wonder then that Warne following an Indian one-day triumph in Sharjah shortly afterwards – largely shaped by Tendulkar's back to back hundreds – sought his autograph on his shirt, a gesture that signalled his respect for the Indian superstar.

By the late Nineties Tendulkar had reached the stage when even hundreds hardly merited attention. The tally of runs and centuries both in Test cricket and the shorter version of the game just kept bulging. And in the new millennium the achievements just went soaring and his batting records stretched vast and almost unsurpassable like a distant view of the Himalayas. In 2001, for example, he became the first batsman to cross the 10,000-run mark in ODI's. At twenty-eight and after a dozen years on the international stage, Tendulkar had lost none of his hunger for runs and his ability to rise to the occasion when the chips were down was still far from diminished. Staleness had not crept into his play and he still commanded a worldwide audience every time he came out to bat. Moreover, he was already a sort of father figure to whom everyone looked up to for inspiration. So much so that when he was forced to miss the tour of Sri Lanka early in the 2001-2002 season because of a heel injury, the Indians missed his calm and all pervading influence – as admitted by Indian captain Ganguly – and lost the three Test series by two matches to one. And it must not be forgotten that it took Tendulkar's return for India to win a Test against Australia in the recent series at home last year.

In the last few years Tendulkar has had to battle fitness problems – as only to be expected with non-stop cricket for more than fifteen years. But service to the team's cause has always been uppermost in his mind, the ultimate proof of this being witnessed during the 1999 World Cup in England. Soon after the commencement of the big event, he had to return to India as his father suddenly passed away. Speculation was rife as to when he would be back but Tendulkar missed only one game. The true professional representing his country that he was, after the funeral was over he flew back and was in time to play against Kenya. With an awe inspiring 140 not out, his highest World Cup score which he dedicated to his father's memory, Tendulkar brought a lot of cheer to the Bristol crowd. One also recalls how he batted on despite a back strain in the course of one of his greatest innings – the 136 against Pakistan in Chennai in January 1999. But when any injury has become serious he has preferred to stay away and take proper treatment and come back refreshed. He has never played with a hidden injury – testimony to Tendulkar's commitment and fair-mindedness.

Tendulkar's Test average crossed the fifty mark for the first time in the mid Nineties. By 2001 it was up to 57. Captains, coaches and strategists had to come up with some tactic or the other to curb Tendulkar's run scoring capabilities. Nothing really worked – not even Nasser Hussain's negative tactics on the English team's tour here in 2001-

2002. In a way it was a tribute to Tendulkar that Hussain concentrated on a negative strategy almost from the moment he came out to bat. It was the England captain's way of admitting that he could not get Tendulkar out with conventional methods. Though well within the laws of the game, Ashley Giles' tactics of bowling well down the leg stump was certainly not within the spirit of the game and did much to kill the game as a spectator sport. All this, however, did not stop Tendulkar from making his usual packet of runs complete with his customary hundred. And then there was this theory that the Pakistan team management worked on before the crucial game against India in the 2003 World Cup. They reckoned that if they bowled fast deliveries at Tendulkar's midriff he would make a false stroke. Tendulkar's reply was a blistering 98 off 75 balls against Akram, Akthar and Younis that virtually assured an Indian victory in the first few overs itself. Wisden rated it as 'an astounding innings – perhaps the best of the tournament and undoubtedly one of his best in ODI's. Against a testosterone propelled pace attack he hit a vivid and memorable stream of shots none so perfect as the cut six and two fours – one swirled into the leg side, one pushed down the ground – which concluded Shoaib Akthar's first over.'

As he turned thirty, cricket fans noticed a perceptible change in Tendulkar's approach to batting. The swashbuckling, aggressive style was slowly being eased out and in its place was seen a new, more mature Tendulkar the batsman. He was not obdurate or defence oriented but he was a bit more selective in his stroke play. In short, he was more solid and cut out some shots from his repertoire and this meant he would take more time over his innings. The transformation from 'spontaneous marauder to a purposeful innings builder' as Wisden had noted when commenting on his 176 against West Indies at Kolkata in 2002 was more marked during the 2003-2004 season. There was no stonewalling but it could be observed that he had cut out some of the shots that in the past had led to his dismissal. It was this knock that displayed Tendulkar at his best, for attack and defence were both equally important. Occupation of the crease alone was of no use; runs too had to be scored. And in his inimitable masterly manner Tendulkar with the ideal mixture of strokes and defence held the West Indian attack at bay. As Wisden noted: 'A common criticism of Tendulkar has been that at the crunch he crumbles. As if to counter that he has transformed himself from spontaneous marauder to a purposeful innings builder. His average has not suffered but his aura has diminished. In the daunting situation would he dig in or hit out? He did both imperiously progressing to 176, his maiden Test hundred at Kolkata and occupied the crease for seven hours to save the match. He did this with minimum risk and to maximum effect. Unlike lesser batsmen, he looked least likely to get out when most dominant. This was Tendulkar of old re-emerging when India most needed him.'

But if he was going to take a longer time to get his runs, it did not mean that the big scores would not come or that the entertainment value would be any less. If any proof was needed it was seen during the 2003-2004 season in both Australia and Pakistan. After a relatively modest start he was in full bloom in the final Test at Sydney. Batting like the Tendulkar the cricketing world has known, loved and admired, Tendulkar made mincemeat of the formidable Aussie attack spearheaded by Brett Lee. In finishing with 241 not out, Tendulkar made the highest score by an Indian abroad – a mark broken a couple of months later by Virender Sehwag's 309 at Multan. For good measure he added an unbeaten 60 in the second innings to silence the critics who advocated the rather laughable view that Tendulkar's best days were behind him. And if at all more proof was needed came his unbeaten 194 against Pakistan at Multan. During both these knocks he shared 300-plus partnerships with V.V.S. Laxman and Sehwag to underline the fact that he had lost none of his insatiable appetite for runs, that even with Dravid, Ganguly and Laxman around he was still the master and even with the entry of the swashbuckling Sehwag in the line up things had not really changed. India still needed the maestro and when he was not around the Indians would struggle. Even on the rare occasion when he has not been among the runs, Tendulkar's presence in the side is a great source of confidence and inspiration to his teammates and there can be no higher tribute to a selfless, dedicated sportsman, an ornament to the game who enjoys iconic status in the cricketing world. In this country, of course, Tendulkar is not merely a great cricketer, he is a great Indian, idolised and worshipped with a frenzied fan following that few sportsmen have had.

So what peaks does Tendulkar still have to climb? He has crossed the 10,000-run mark in Tests following his record tally in ODI's in which the figure just keeps going up every season. It is now 13,000 plus and in the tally of runs and centuries he is well above everyone else already. Then of course Gavaskar's record 34 hundreds beckons – and Tendulkar is just one short of the mark. It is only a matter of time as surely it is only a matter of time that he overtakes Allan Border's all time run tally of 11,174. After all this of course he will set his own marks and one really cannot imagine what other records he will run up and where it will all end and whether they will be surpassed at all. Verily the sky is the limit for Tendulkar as he marches on to fresher pastures. And the encouraging aspect for Indian cricket is that like wine he seems to be getting better with age. Long may the king of cricket regale his willing and joyful subjects!

# 17

# Sourav Chandidas **Ganguly**

## Blending Power and Elegance

I s there really any doubt that Sourav Chandidas Ganguly is the finest left handed batsman ever in Indian cricket? With batting that is the perfect blend of power and elegance, Ganguly has earned a name for himself as one of the leading batsmen in the world. His chief image is still that of a graceful player, who caresses the ball to the boundary in ethereal fashion. But when the mood strikes him – and this is not just the case in limited overs cricket – he can really 'murder' the bowling. Rarely have I seen any bowling look so helpless as when Ganguly is in command. Like the veritable Bengal tiger, he leaps upon his prey – the bowler – and dispatches him in no time. No amount of strategy by the opposing captain, no change in the bowling or the field placing, no shift in the bowler's tactics is going to make any difference. When Ganguly has decided to really go for the bowling, there is nothing that can be done to halt the cascade of runs, the free flow of fours and sixes. And while there are many instances of Ganguly in this mood, the prime example must still be Taunton, May 26, 1999. On that day, the Sri Lankans took the kind of hammering they would not like to remember even for an instant. It was a bruising the World Cup champions never really recovered from and the defence ended then and there. Ganguly just toyed with the attack, doing pretty much what he liked, bisecting the field at will, lofting the ball wherever he wanted. Long before a tired Ganguly virtually gifted his wicket away in the last over, Ranatunga and his men had hoisted the white flag of surrender.

Like in the case of a few other cricketers, Ganguly's career would make a good script for a successful film. It really has everything – rich boy, angry young man, very talented, gets his break too early, is ignored for four years, comes back with a story book feat, stays on to become a leading batsman, is then elevated to the captaincy, emerges as an aggressive, no nonsense leader, earns notoriety for his ill-tempered behaviour, marries a classical dancer, settles down to marital bliss and becomes a proud and happy father. Indeed, on and off the field, Ganguly's career is just begging to be adopted as a TV soap opera.

Ganguly was born in Calcutta in 1972 and made his first-class debut in the Ranji Trophy final of 1989-90. Bengal won the premier national competition after fifty-one years and the seventeen-year-old lad, even if he did not do anything extraordinary, was considered as a good luck charm. Coming up through the India junior ranks, he hit a century of high quality in the Asia Youth Cup in 1989 and another against Pakistan in the Under-19 series. The signs of a healthy temperament were in evidence early. The next season, he followed this up with hundreds in both the Duleep and Deodhar Trophy tournaments. It was now obvious that Ganguly was not just another promising cricketer and deserved a closer look. All the same, when he was suddenly thrown into the hard, tough world of international cricket in 1991-92, as a member of the Indian team, which toured Australia, it was a stunning decision by the selectors, criticised as being part of the quota system. The cricketer himself was lambasted for being an undeserving candidate. Ganguly, then nineteen, was certainly unnerved by the experience. Mentally, he was just not ready, he did nothing of note and it turned out to be a traumatic trip for him.

Not unexpectedly, Ganguly was discarded and for some time was a forgotten man. Over the next four years, he worked hard on his game, and the result was greater consistency and some big scores including a couple of double hundreds. Still he seemed far away from regaining his India cap, and it came as a major surprise when he was included in the Indian team to tour England in 1996. Again the quota system charge was repeated but this time the criticism was more strident, even personal. Ganguly, by now almost five years older since he had suffered the same treatment on his initial selection to the Indian team, this time took the adverse comments in his stride. At twenty-four, he was physically and mentally more mature and decided to hit back at his detractors in the best possible manner – by being silent and letting the bat do the talking.

At this stage, Ganguly perhaps had only a few believers who were convinced that he was deserving of a place in the side. But even the most optimistic of these followers could not have bargained for the fiction like feat that followed. Almost a decade later, Ganguly's feat has been well-chronicled as part of Indian cricketing folklore and still makes for fascinating and inspiring reading for the generations to come. The Bengal tiger roared at the game's headquarters, becoming the first Indian to get a century on Test debut at Lord's. For good measure, to make it look even more story bookish, he followed his 131 with 136 in the next Test at Nottingham. He headed the Test averages easily with 315 runs at 105.00 and topped the tour figures with 762 runs at an average of 95.25 with three hundreds. Suddenly the cricketer, whose selection had been criticised in vehement terms, was the main topic of discussion among the cricketing public. Suddenly he was a national hero. For a time, even Sachin Tendulkar was pushed aside – as indeed, Ganguly had pushed the master batsman to second place in the Test and tour figures.

Predictably enough, Ganguly came back from the tour, riding a wave of popularity. But the doubts remained among a few die-hard cynics who wondered whether his feats in England were a fluke. Could he keep it up, they wondered. Over the next year, such fears seemed to be justified for in 11 Tests, Ganguly passed the half-century mark only three times. Moreover, he had the dubious distinction of being the only batsman to be out for a duck in the run feast at Colombo in 1997 when Sri Lanka ran up their record total of 952 for six and as many as 1489 runs were scored for the loss of only 14 wickets at an average of 106.35 runs per wicket. But Ganguly dispelled all doubts in his next innings. Batting with all the elegance at his command and with stroke play and timing that brought back memories of his first two centuries in Test cricket, he knocked up 147 for which he batted 426 minutes, hitting 19 fours and two sixes. He was last out after taking India to a first innings lead of 43, which looked hardly possible when he had entered at 126 for four in reply to Sri Lanka's 332. By now, the Ganguly-Tendulkar pairing had become a fait accompli in one-day internationals, and the two commenced on what was to be a world record breaking partnership in more ways than one over the next few years. They gave a clear indication of this by putting together their world record partnership of 252 against Sri Lanka at Colombo which they themselves put in the shade later in the Standard Bank Series against Kenya with a stand of 258.

It was in the return series at home a few months later that Ganguly really cemented his growing status as among the world's leading batsmen. No more were there any doubts; Ganguly was here not just to stay but also to make plenty of runs – and centuries and make them handsomely. In the three matches, he had an amazing run of 109, 99 and 173 in successive innings, to add to his 147 in the Test prior to this series. He was the undoubted star of the series which, considering the fact that Tendulkar, Azharuddin, Dravid, Aravinda de Silva, Jayasuriya and Ranatunga were the other batsmen featured on the billboard, was a considerable achievement. It was not just the runs but the manner in which he made them that attracted considerable attention. The strokes were made with surgical precision and his off side play in particular had touched dizzy heights.

This form of Ganguly's spilled over to the one-day game as well. The month after the series against Sri Lanka, Ganguly played an innings that is still talked about. As a match winning knock, his 124 in the Independence Cup final against Pakistan at Dhaka in January 1998 has few peers. Pakistan led off with an imposing 314 for eight in 48 overs and India would have to come out with a world record effort to win the title. Tendulkar and Ganguly took up the challenge by belting 71 runs off 8.2 overs. Robin Singh promoted as a pinch hitter then played a cool and calculated knock but Ganguly just went for the bowling with gay abandon, hitting Aaqib Javed, Azhar Mahmood, Saqlain Mushtaq and Shahid Afridi wherever he pleased. Ganguly and Robin raised the 200 in 29.1 overs and pieced together a partnership of 179 runs that raised hopes of India pulling off the impossible. Ganguly's hundred, which anchored the Indian riposte and his stands with Tendulkar and Robin gave Hrishikesh Kanitkar the opportunity to hit the famous boundary off the penultimate ball of the match which heralded India's great triumph. Of course, Ganguly had already shown his expertise in the shorter version of the game by bagging the man of the series award for his stupendous all round feats in the Sahara Cup Series against Pakistan at the start of the season.

Through the crowded 1998-99 season, Ganguly maintained his reputation with a series of timely knocks in a crisis against Zimbabwe and Pakistan, an elegant unbeaten 101 against New Zealand and, of course, by his now trademark powerful yet elegant batting in the one-day games. This put him in the proper frame of mind for the World Cup in which he was expected to play a leading role in India's campaign. He started off well scoring 97 in the first game against South Africa. Playing in his 100th one-day international but first World Cup game, Ganguly put on 67 runs with Tendulkar for the first wicket and 130 runs with Dravid for the second wicket before being run out by a throw from Jonty Rhodes. Two failures followed and then came the magnum opus against Sri Lanka. Ganguly's 183 off 158 balls with 16 fours and seven sixes was the fourth highest score in one-day internationals and the second highest in the World Cup, just behind Gary Kirsten's 188. Ganguly reached his century off 119 balls and then went berserk, going to 183 in another 39 balls. No bowler escaped his buccaneering blade. Vaas and Upashanta went for eight an over, Jayawardene for seven, Muralitharan and Wickremasinghe for six, Jayasuriya for 12. Ganguly's 318-run partnership for the second wicket with Dravid, who also hit a century at almost a run a ball but was sedate by comparison, came up off 45 overs and was the highest in any one-day international. He followed this up with a man of the match winning performance of 40 and three for 27 against England and finished as the third highest run getter in the competition with a tally of 379.

Another busy season followed in 1999-2000 and for Ganguly, it marked a significant phase in his career. With centuries against New Zealand and South Africa in the one-day games, his newly won reputation as one of the leading batsmen in the world in instant cricket remained intact. He was still among the runs in the Test matches, proof of this being seen in his 125 against New Zealand at Ahmedabad when he added a record 281 runs for the fourth wicket with Tendulkar. Like many others, he too did not have a very successful tour of Australia but he was not a total failure. He finished third in the Test figures with 177 runs at 29.50, third in the tour figures with 301 runs at 33.44 and his tally of 356 with two centuries was the best by an Indian in a disastrous Carlton & United campaign. Most important, though, was his elevation from vice captain to the captaincy when Tendulkar stepped down. And as the new millennium unfolded the focus was more on his leadership qualities than his batting, not unexpectedly for he has proved to be not just a successful captain but also a very different one. Verily he has in the last five years changed the image of the Indian captain. But how much his success as a captain has affected his batting is one of the most debatable points in Indian cricket.

In the last year of the twentieth century Ganguly's Test average was around the fifty mark. In the first few years of the new millennium there was a steady fall and not unexpectedly the stories kept circulating thick and fast. And most alarm centered over his repeated failing against the short pitched delivery. Time and again he seemed to be a sitting duck for the short rising ball playing it awkwardly with his feet in no position at all to be caught off a skier. It was a serious enough problem for Ganguly to go back to the drawing board so to say and take some expert guidance. Gradually he overcame the palpable weakness, the first indication of this being a superbly struck unbeaten 98 with which he steered India to victory over Sri Lanka at Kandy in 2001. There were also some consistent scores in the series in the West Indies the next year. But it was on the tour of England in 2002 that he really shrugged off his failings against the short-pitched delivery. Successive scores of 68, 99, 128 and 51 provided clear proof as he negotiated the bowling of Caddick, Harmisson and Hoggard with aplomb. Somewhere in his sublime strokeplay were also shades of resoluteness. Ganguly seemed determined to shake off the bogey once and for all. But the charges returned to haunt him when he failed repeatedly in New Zealand towards the end of the year.

So it was back to the drawing board and a successful 2003 – three hundreds in the World Cup, a superbly crafted 144 against Australia at Brisbane – proved that he was slowly getting into the groove again.

By now, of course, he had relinquished the opening slot in the shorter version of the game to Sehwag who in turn struck up an exhilarating partnership with Tendulkar. But back in the middle order Ganguly has proved his worth – and not just in the World Cup. The point is that no one can really write off Ganguly, for every time the critics do so he comes up with a sterling performance or two. The simple truth is that Ganguly is too good a player to be kept down for too long. His aggressive instincts are all over him and anyone – captains, commentators or bowlers – who throws down the gauntlet does so at his own peril. He is yet only thirty-two and I venture to predict that his best – in both forms of the game – lies ahead. Let's not be too hasty in writing his epitaph. After all, one does not know when a tiger will pounce on his prey, right?

# 18

# Rahul Sharad **Dravid**

## The Ultimate Team Man

Rahul Sharad Dravid is arguably the most invaluable and selfless batsman in the history of Indian cricket. He was willing to open the batting – though he made it clear that he would rather not – in the interests of the team. He was ready to go in at number three or number six depending on the situation. He was willing to keep wickets to restore the team's balance in the shorter version of the game. He readily altered his approach so that even a supreme technician like him could prove to be invaluable in slam-bang cricket. Of course, his record is second to none – and that cliché is not lightly used here – in the number of times he has saved India from defeat or piloted them to victory. The facts and figures have been recorded for posterity and the statistics that have always meant something for Dravid underscore his exalted position in Indian cricket. While this book is about the top twenty Indian batsmen of all time, there are some who will figure in the list of top ten Indian batsmen. Where Dravid is concerned the figure can safely and predictably be narrowed down to five. Who the other four could be is open to question but there is no question about Dravid figuring in the top rank. Tendulkar and Dravid are the two current batsmen who will undoubtedly find a place in the all time Indian XI.

Indeed, what Indian cricket would do without Dravid is too frightening to contemplate. The perennial uncertainty at the top of the order, the stroke play of Ganguly, Tendulkar and Laxman and the fact that the tail is brittle has meant that it is imperative there has to be a batsman playing the anchor role in between. And that is what Dravid has been doing ever since his entry into international cricket at Lord's in 1996. I don't know how he got the sobriquet 'the wall' but it certainly fits his approach – simple, yet fully conveying the image of a man who does not sell his wicket cheaply. Left to him, he would not like to sell his wicket at all.

When the compactly built, neatly dressed figure of Dravid walks out to bat, you can rest assured that what will unfold at the crease for the next few hours is a most technically sound innings – an innings straight out of 'How to Play Cricket'. His stance is perfect, the most balanced and composed stance any student of the game can hope to see. And then, after he takes guard, the 22 yards between the stumps is Dravid's 'home'. He does not leave till he has completed his course in the Vijay Merchant school of cricket. And that school, according to what the principal himself said more than half a century ago teaches that 'batting is built around a specific science. The secret is timing and patience. For example, you do not play the hook shot till you are seeing the ball as big as a football. Eschew all risks. Get behind the line of every ball and play it on merit. If you stay at the crease, the runs will come.'

Dravid follows these rules like the Holy Gospel. And the results are well known. He is the rock on which the Indian innings is built. Dravid plans his innings like a mason, brick by brick, run by run. A deep thinker of the game, the stylist from Karnataka is able to read through any chance of strategy, any shift in tactics, that a bowler or captain makes. Nothing escapes his eagle eye or his sharp brain. He frustrates the bowler with his dead bat technique, his steady stream of strokes and his unflappable temperament till at last, in desperation and disgusted with life, as it were, the bowler turns to his captain with a gesture of helplessness as if to say, 'There is no use bowling to this bloke. He's never going to get out.' Indeed, Dravid does give the impression of batting all day and every day. He is unwavering in his concentration and determination but he never lets the bad ball go unpunished. Bowl him a half volley, a short ball or a full toss and as sure as night follows day, Dravid will hit the bowler for certain fours – and that holds good whether India's score is 200 for one or 30 for three, whether it is ten in the morning or four in the evening. He is the country's most totally organised batsman today, a product of the Merchant school of batting as I said – and he is a student who has passed out of that school with distinction plus.

The son of a food scientist, Dravid was born in Indore in 1973. He had his early cricketing education at St Joseph's High School in Bangalore and earned a name for coming good in a crisis even at the school level. The refrain among his schoolmates used to be: 'Rahul has just entered. Things will certainly change in our favour now.' The words are the same a decade and a half later, only the scene has changed from the school side to the national team. His coach Keki Tarapore was the first to unearth his talent and Dravid made good progress, benefitting from the BCCI Under-15 and Under-19 camps held at Bangalore. He made his first-class debut for Karnataka in the Ranji Trophy in 1990-91 and the next year, he captained the India juniors against New Zealand. A century by him in the Mumbai 'Test' was one of the highlights of that series which India won. By now, he had earned a name for himself as an obdurate batsman whose wicket had to be earned. That year, he headed the state batting figures with 380 runs at an average of 63.33 with two hundreds. The next season, he hit his first double century in first-class cricket on his way to figures of 670 runs at an average of 60.90 for the season. In 1993-94, he scored 846 runs at an average of 52.87 with two hundreds. The following season, he advanced to 1068 runs at an average of 59.33 with three hundreds, including a classy unbeaten 132 for Rest of India against Bombay in the Irani Trophy match. By now, he was already being termed in Karnataka as the torchbearer in the tradition of Viswanath and Brijesh Patel, as the side's best batsman and the next from the state who was destined to play for India. Indeed, he was hailed as a blend of Viswanath and Patel. Those who had not seen Dravid bat refused to accept such an exalted status being placed on an up and coming youngster. Even those who had seen him in action cautioned against such comparisons for they felt the lad would get spoiled. But Dravid was too level-headed even at this stage to get affected by such lofty titles.

In 1995-96, Dravid placed before the selectors a Ranji Trophy aggregate of 460 runs at an average of 57.50 with three hundreds in playing a major role in Karnataka's first title triumph in the national competition for thirteen years. A popular inclusion in the Indian team to tour England in 1996, Dravid did not take long in proving his credentials. He made light of the very different conditions in England thanks basically to his impeccable technique. Faring well in the tour games, Dravid forced his way into the Test side. Scoring 95 on his Test debut at Lord's, Dravid followed it up with 84 in the next. Very soon then, it was obvious that Dravid was a long term prospect, reflected by the figures for the tour which placed him third in the averages both in the Tests (62.33) and first-class matches (553 runs at 50.27 with one hundred and four fifties). Commendable though the figures were, it was the manner in which he made the runs – orthodox style, chiselled strokes, perfect defence, unruffled temperament – that attracted attention. For example, asked about coming so close to a century on debut and then missing out, Dravid said: 'It hurt. But I realised it would not do me any good to keep thinking about it.'

As Dravid returned from a highly successful tour, two questions remained unanswered. First, what was the ideal place for him in the batting order and secondly, whether his correct, straight bat technique could be successful in the slam-bang world of limited overs cricket. There were those who were firmly convinced that Dravid's game was good only for Test cricket. Aware of growing criticism against him being included in the one-day side, Dravid tackled it head on. He expressed the honest view that he had no problems absolutely in adopting to the two styles of cricket. 'But till I achieve a big score in these games, I do not want to discuss that aspect. However, I am very keen in proving my worth in the one-day games too,' he said. His forthright answer took care of one question. The selectors, however, took some time to decide on his position in the batting order, as there was already talk that perhaps Dravid was the answer to Indian cricket's perennial problem – the lack of a proper and reliable opening batsman.

In the two Tests in England, Dravid had gone in at number six. He stayed in that slot for the one off Test against Australia at the start of the 1996-97 season. In the three Tests which followed against South Africa, he went in at number three, was then pushed to the opening slot, before ending up at the number five position for the final Test.

Ever the perfectionist, Dravid did not like this 'yo yo' treatment but agreed for the sake of the team, even though he was aware that it might be counter productive for him in the long run. In the return series in South Africa, again Dravid was shuttled up and down the order. He started at number six, opened the innings with W.V. Raman in the second Test and then went in at number three in the third. By scoring 148 and 81 in the final Test, Dravid finally seemed to have found the right place. Of course, given his technique, temperament and style of play, that should have been the place for him all along. This key position was the ideal one for Dravid to play the sheet anchor role. And if any proof was needed that India had found the perfect one-drop batsman, it was provided in the West Indies in early 1997. He was one batsman to emerge with full credit and was consistency personified as scores of 43, 51 not out, 57, 78, 2, 37 not out and 92 illustrate. Just one failure in seven innings against the Caribbean pace barrage in a losing cause meant that Dravid, the boy of the hour at school was now the man of the hour for his country. He easily headed the Test figures with 360 runs at an average of 72.00.

As already mentioned, Dravid had expressed the view that while he did not envisage any problem in adjusting his style to be successful in one-day cricket, he added that till he achieved a big score, he would not like to discuss the subject. However, he had said that he was very keen on proving his worth in the one-day games too. Well, he did keep his word. In the face of an imposing Pakistan total of 327 for five in 50 overs in the Independence Cup match at Chennai in May, 1997, made possible by the world record score of 194 by Saeed Anwar, India had lost one wicket for nine when Dravid came in. It was almost entirely due to his efforts that the match did not have a tame finish, for India got to 292 before they were all out in the last over. Dravid got 107, attacking the bowling of Aaqib Javed, Azhar Mahmood, Saqlain Mushtaq and Shahid Afridi with dazzling, innovative strokes that almost made him look like the twin brother of Rahul Dravid, the Test cricketer. By this knock, he silenced his critics who said he was good for Test cricket but not for the one-day game. Of course, the criticism has been raised again over the years and every time Dravid has risen to the occasion with a timely riposte.

After a brief eclipse in the two Test series in Sri Lanka at the start of the 1997-98 season, in which he averaged only 29.00, Dravid was back to his usual ways in the return series at home. Successive scores of 34, 92, 93 and 85 gave him a tally of 304 runs at an average of 76.00 and second place in the averages. He maintained this form, when against the much stronger Australian attack a few months later, he aggregated 223 runs at an average of 44.60, including straight scores of 52, 56 and 86. By now, there was no doubt that he was lending the stabilising touch to a side brimming with stroke players in Sidhu, Ganguly, Tendulkar and Azharuddin. That did not mean that Dravid did not play his shots. Indeed, he never let the bad ball go unpunished.

At the start of the 1998-99 season Dravid had played 22 Test matches and had notched up only one hundred. He was consistency personified symbolised by his average of 48, but in keeping with his classy batsmanship, his twin powers of concentration and determination, his distinct ability to play a long innings, just one hundred in so many Tests had to be a disappointing proportion. Certainly Dravid would not have been satisfied but he was soon to set the record straight. In the one off Test against Zimbabwe at Harare at the start of the season he started off with scores of 118 and 44 (top score in both innings). The match itself was lost with none of his teammates taking a leaf from Dravid's book. He mixed a tight defence with stylish stroke play to score a determined century and put up a heroic fight in the second innings too. But it was at Hamilton in the first days of 1999 that Dravid reached his high water mark. In the face of a New Zealand total of 366, India had lost one wicket for 17 when Dravid entered. It was soon 17 for two. Dravid started the resurrection. First with Tendulkar, he added 109 runs for the third wicket. A middle order collapse then sent India crashing to 211 for seven. Dravid had just reached his hundred when Javagal Srinath joined him. The fast bowler, with some good old fashioned hitting, scored 76 and helped Dravid put on 144 runs for the eighth wicket. Then Venkatesh Prasad hung on determinedly for an hour and he and Dravid added a further 61 runs for the ninth wicket. Finally, Dravid, entrenched for more than eight hours for 190, during which he hit 31 fours, was out, playing a tired shot at Chris Cairns. His highest

Test score turned out to be a chanceless innings, marked by gloriously elegant shots. But he was not finished yet. Amidst a lot of expectations, he duly completed a second century in the match, remaining unbeaten with 103 as the Test meandered to a draw. Dravid thus joined Hazare and Gavaskar (who achieved the feat three times) as the third Indian to hit twin centuries in a Test match.

After moderate success in the two Tests against Pakistan and in the Asian Test Championship match against that country, Dravid returned to his century habit against Sri Lanka at Colombo. He scored 107 and added 232 runs for the second wicket with Ramesh. In the meantime, his tally of runs and centuries in one-day internationals had been making a steady upward mark and Dravid was confidence personified on the eve of the World Cup in England. And at the end of the competition, even the very few critics who were still not convinced of Dravid's credentials as far as limited overs cricket was concerned, turned over to his side.

Dravid started off with a splendid 54 against South Africa, putting on 130 runs for the second wicket with Ganguly. A rare failure against Zimbabwe followed, but in the next game against Kenya he got 104 not out and with Tendulkar was associated in an unbroken stand of 237 runs in 29 overs for the third wicket – the highest partnership in World Cup history, but as it turned out, the record stood only for three days. Dravid figured in this too for he and Ganguly put together their memorable stand of 318 runs in 45 overs which, of course, was the highest partnership in any one-day international. The stand ended when Dravid was run out for 145. He set the pace and reached his second successive century almost a run a ball. He followed this with an anchor like 53 off 82 balls against England, which proved to be invaluable in India's 63-run victory. In the Super Six stage, he again top scored with 61 against Pakistan and finished with 29 against New Zealand. Dravid's aggregate of 461 was the highest in the competition – Steve Waugh was second, 63 runs behind – and he and Saeed Anwar were the only batsmen to get two hundreds. There was much praise for Dravid, his modest and unassuming manner, his understated old-fashioned grace. He returned home a much feted hero, Kent offered him a contract for

2000 and Wisden hung his portrait as one of the five cricketers of the year. The shy, introverted Dravid took all this in his stride and concentrated on his main job for the 1999-2000 season – to make more runs.

- By now Dravid had got five hundreds in 29 Tests and his average had shot past the fifty mark. He started the season with his by now customary hundred – 144 to be precise in the first Test against New Zealand at Mohali. Four weeks later, he and Tendulkar again rewrote the one-day record books – this time with a partnership of 331 runs for the second wicket against New Zealand at Hyderabad. Tendulkar went on to make 186 not out, the highest score by an Indian in one-day internationals but Dravid was not far behind, scoring 153. It was, simply put, a phenomenal performance to which the Kiwis had no answer. But given his reputation, Dravid was perhaps the biggest disappointment in the three Test series in Australia. Nothing went right for him as he finished with the miserable average of 15.50 from an aggregate of 93 runs with a highest score of 35. Such figures against his name were unthinkable. In the Carlton & United series, he finished second to Ganguly with 268 runs with three half centuries but this did little to erase the failures in the Test series. Back home, he seemed to be still suffering from the hang over of 'Down Under' for in the two Tests against South Africa, he scored only 94 runs at an average of 23.50 with a highest score of 37. And after having cemented his preferred number three spot, he was again asked to open in the second Test in a desperate measure to try and solve the chronic opening problem. That was an absolutely needless tactical move, for after all Dravid was a leading batsman and not one to be used as a guinea pig. Why, even as late as November 2001 when he was vice captain and after he had played 46 Tests and scored nine hundreds – all in the middle order – he was still asked to open against South Africa as a temporary solution to the problem at the top of the order.

The travails of the 1999-2000 season meant that Dravid's average had fallen to 47. But he need not have worried for, as future events proved, this was the last time the figure would fall below the half-century mark. The 2000-2001 season, in fact, is one that Dravid and Indian cricket followers will long remember. Fresh from his successful stint with Kent in the county championship Dravid was a picture of poise and perfection. What else can one say when a batsman ends a two Test series with an out of this world average of 432? A run of 200 not out, 70 not out and 162 was the reason behind this phenomenal figure. At last Dravid was showing signs of playing up to his reputation. Big scores, long stays at the crease, intense concentration, fierce determination, technical excellence, impeccable defence, wide array of strokes – this was the Dravid one had come to admire and respect. This was followed by one of his most famous knocks. How he and V.V.S. Laxman turned sure defeat into a gloriously unexpected victory at the Eden Gardens at Kolkata in March 2001 is now firmly etched in Indian cricketing folklore. How the two combined to piece together a record fifth wicket partnership of 376 to frustrate the Australians. How Dravid stuck it out for 446 minutes to score 180. How for once he lost his cool and angrily waved his bat towards the press box on reaching his hundred after the experts had questioned his ability. Laxman in sublime form had temporarily displaced him at number three but it was only a matter of time before Dravid got back his rightful place in the order. By the end of the season he had scored nine hundreds in 43 Tests and his average spiralled to a shade below 54 – as I said never again to fall below the fifty mark.

In the last three years of course Dravid's batting has touched dizzy heights, and this is not just borne out by figures. Some judge batsmen by the number of runs made, others by the manner of their making. By either criterion Dravid ranks among the greatest. A cricketer who blends an old-world classicism with a new-age professionalism Dravid, very unusually for an Indian batsman, has a better average overseas. This figure is 64 compared to 50 at home while his career average is marginally ahead of Tendulkar's. During one purple phase in 2002 he had four centuries in successive innings, one short of Everton Weekes' famous record set in India in 1949. In the space of 15 Tests during 2002-2004 he scored four double hundreds. Impressive as the statistics are, they cannot represent the extent of his importance to the Indian batting or the beauty of his superbly crafted batsmanship. Two of the double hundreds helped shape notable triumphs at Adelaide and Rawalpindi.

In Australia he helped turn around an alarming situation into an improbable victory with a double of 233 and 72 not out figuring in a 303-run fifth wicket partnership with – who else but Laxman. And in Pakistan his epic 270 clinched a historic series victory, and saw his average creep past Tendulkar's. There seems to be no end to his insatiable appetite for runs and to pull off the rare feat judging by his hundred in each innings against Pakistan at Kolkata this year. Centuries number nineteen and twenty put him in elite company for he is only one among seven batsmen who have scored separate centuries in a Test on two occasions, Herbert Sutcliffe, George Headley, Clyde Walcott, Greg Chappell, Allan Border and Aravinda de Silva being the others. Sunil Gavaskar of course is the only batsman to have notched up the feat three times but it will not be surprising if Dravid joins him at the top in the next year or two. And like all great batsmen he takes the first-class game very seriously, something that is driven home by his average that places him in the top ten of all time.

With all his exalted stature in Indian cricket – nay, world cricket – Dravid is a picture of humility. To his embarrassment, fan clubs have sprang up and he remains a favourite among teenage girls, both for his batting and his impeccable behaviour. He is one of the most recognisable faces in the country thanks to the success of his TV commercials, and there are few cricketers who are held in higher regard than Dravid who has been adjudged the perfect role model for today's youth in more than one poll.

His amazing run of scores in the last few years has not by any means signalled a triumph of substance over style. Dravid, in fact, has more than enough of both. He is a classical strokemaker who plays every shot in the book and while his pulling and cover driving is especially breathtaking, he has every other shot in the book as well. He is both an artist and a craftsman, repeatedly constructing innings that stand out not merely for the beauty of their execution, but for the context in which they are played. Verily, the sky is the limit for Dravid and by the time he finishes, perhaps one should further narrow that figure spoken of at the beginning of this chapter to three – the other two being Gavaskar and Tendulkar.

# 19

## Vangipurapu Venkat Sai **Laxman**

### Touch Artist from Hyderabad

In a poll conducted on the CricInfo website last year, Vangipurapu Venkat Sai Laxman's 281 against Australia at Kolkata in March 2001 was adjudged the greatest innings ever played by an Indian in Test cricket. It was the final confirmation of something that had been acknowledged by cricket followers, experts and fellow players ever since the touch artist from Hyderabad crafted an unforgettable knock – a near triple century of epic proportions which turned a Test match around on its head so markedly that only for the third time in Test history a side that enforced the follow on crumbled to defeat.

Yes, sometimes one innings can turn a whole series around, besides changing a man's life. Just ask Laxman. Which way was the series against Australia in early 2001 going till he got that immortal 281? What was his stature in Indian cricket before that knock? Since then he has taken his rightful place in India's famed middle order, blending admirably with Dravid, Tendulkar and Ganguly to form a quartet that gives bowlers the shivers. And it is a tribute to Laxman's class, skill, technique, temperament and artistry that even in such a dazzling line up he has more than held his own, frequently coming to the team's rescue when the others have failed. As the 2004 edition of Wisden noted after Laxman elegantly pieced together two match-saving knocks against New Zealand at Mohali in October 2003: 'There are times when John Wright, India's Kiwi coach must be feeling like dropping to his knees and kissing the feet of VVS Laxman. It was Laxman after all who saved Wright's skin at Kolkata in 2001, his epic 281 setting the scene for one of Test cricket's most famous wins. And he was at it again at Mohali first compiling an unbeaten hundred as India fell just seven runs short of the follow on mark and then defying New Zealand for most of the final day to consign the second Test and the series to an honourable draw. Indian administrators are not known for their tolerance when their team loses at home and Wright would have been in the firing line had the side folded.'

Wright will not be alone in paying tribute to Laxman. His captain, teammates and the average cricket fan would be all too eager to adopt an obsequious approach towards Laxman. A stylist with a solid base, Laxman is very much a noble torchbearer of the rich Hyderabadi tradition of producing players who possess a silken elegance. Oriential artistry was seen in abundant measure in the batting of Jaisimha and Azharuddin. Laxman has carried on where Azhar left off. Wielding his bat as if it were a wand he just caresses the ball away from the reach of the fieldsmen playing shots that only he can. His drives are of the ethereal quality and the very personification of elegance and timing. Laxman is the one batsman who plays one of cricket's more difficult strokes – the on drive – with utmost fluency. Body balance, movement of the feet and adroit placing of the stroke has repeatedly seen the ball elude the fielder, bisect the gap between mid wicket and mid on and race to the fence. His cutting, both square and late are a joy to watch, and to old timers bring back happy memories of Viswanath. Like Azhar he plays the glance and the glide through slips so fine that it is impossible for any captain to set a field for him. With all his attacking instincts Laxman's defence is secure – assuredly so as his batting is based on an impeccable technique. At thirty, Laxman is the youngest member of the quartet and it can be said with much justification that his most prolific years are ahead of him.

Laxman wasn't a rookie who came good at Calcutta. He had been around for some time, earned a name for himself as one of the most prolific run getters around the domestic circuit and also won fame for his unforgettable 167 against Australia at Sydney in the early days of 2000. But then that 281 was something very different, in a league of its own, an out of the world performance – call it what you will, the adjective will still fall short. Perhaps Laxman was lucky that he had

Dravid for company and the two proceeded to bat through a whole day and more and shared a record partnership that turned the match – and as events proved, the series – on its head. But there is little doubt that Laxman took the initiative.

Laxman was born in Hyderabad in 1974 and made his first-class debut in the Ranji Trophy in 1992-93. The tall, slim right-hander had a steady, rather spectacular rise but there was something in him that held the attention of the spectators, the selectors and the media. It was quickly observed that he was another Hyderabadi stylist in the tradition of Jaisimha and Azharuddin. Could he go as far was the question Laxman had to answer?

In his first few Tests, Laxman did not fare badly, but did not exactly consolidate his position either. Against South Africa at home in 1996-97, his debut series he got 77 runs in four innings with a highest score of 51, batting at number six. He went on the tour of South Africa but was still feeling his way around. By this time, however, he had impressed enough for those in authority to try him out as an opening batsman in a bid to solve Indian cricket's perennial problem. In the West Indies in 1997, Laxman did fairly well in his new role, scoring 172 runs at 28.66 with two fifties. But he had nothing yet to cement his place in the side and, not unexpectedly, did not tour Sri Lanka or play against them in the return series at home. In the meantime, Laxman was having a run feast in the Ranji Trophy, the peak coming in the form of an unbeaten 301 against Bihar in the Super League stage. It was an amazing innings not because he batted 609 minutes, faced 434 balls and hit 28 fours but because the next best score was 35! Certainly this incredible marathon had something to do with his recall to the Test scene, for on the eve of the second Test against Australia at Calcutta in March 1998, he was not even in the first twelve. The selectors picked Laxman to open with Sidhu and the pairing was a total triumph. In just 40 overs, they put on 191 to lay the foundation for a big total and an innings victory. Laxman made a stroke filled 95 before he edged off spinner Gavin Robertson to Healy. It was his first commanding Test knock. Had he then found his place in the team as an opening batsman?

This was also the first of many seasons in a row that Laxman finished among the runs in a really big way around the domestic circuit. Figures in first-class cricket at home are generally taken with a pinch of salt considering the benign pitches and consequently the amiable bowling. But Laxman was in a different league altogether. That season he scored 611 runs at an average of 152.75 with two hundreds including that amazing triple hundred. In all first-class cricket, Laxman got 986 runs at an average of 89.63 with three centuries.

After being overlooked for the tours of Zimbabwe and New Zealand at the start of the 1998-99 season Laxman was back for the two Test series against Pakistan, with a new opening partner in Sadagopan Ramesh. They struck up a good understanding and in the Tests they had partnerships of 67 and 88. Laxman though was restricted to scores of 23, nought, 35 and eight. In the two matches of the Asian Test Championship, the two again came up with stands of 108 and 50 and Laxman did better with knocks of 67 and 25. Still, at this stage with a tally of 579 runs from 14 Tests at an average of 26.31 with five fifties, he had still not consolidated his position in the side and the debate continued whether he should be persisted with as an opener or would he be better off in the middle order. Even as the discussion continued, Laxman continued his run feast around the domestic circuit in which, of course, he batted down the order. In the Ranji Trophy, he scored 751 runs at an average of 83.44 with three hundreds and a highest score of 219. In all first-class cricket Laxman amassed 1017 runs at an average of 53.52. He was verily the 'dada' of the domestic circuit.

Laxman was not considered for the three Test series against New Zealand at the start of the 1999-2000 season with Devang Gandhi making his debut. But he was back for the tour of Australia. Considering his patchy record, not many expected him to succeed against McGrath and company on the fast and bouncy pitches 'Down Under'. The worst fears were confirmed with Laxman restricted to 54 runs in the first five innings. However, with nothing to lose and everything to gain, Laxman really went for broke in the final innings of the series. He simply stood there and hammered anything and everything that McGrath, Lee, Fleming and Warne could hurl at him. The transformation was amazing. Gone was the hesitant push and prod. In its place, the crowd saw full-blooded drives, rasping cuts and daring hooks and pulls. Out of a total of 261, Laxman hit 167 off just 198 balls with the next highest being Ganguly's 25. It was his maiden Test hundred in his 17th match and was thus memorable in more ways than one. In Steve Waugh's words, 'Laxman played a heroic lone hand, belting us all over the park while playing what might even have been the Test innings of the season.' The unbelievable onslaught, least expected, saw Laxman finish second to Tendulkar in the final figures, with a tally of 221 runs and an average of 36.83. On the tour, he did well, again finishing second to Tendulkar with 502 runs at an average of 41.83. But a double failure in the first Test against South Africa at Mumbai saw him out of the side again. So at the end of the season, he had still not made certain of a place in the team.

But even as he was still unsure of getting into the Indian side, Laxman was re-writing the record books around the domestic circuit. That season, he went into an orgy of run getting that, even with the proliferation of matches, will take some beating. In 14 innings in the Ranji Trophy, Laxman stroked his way to 1415 runs to set a new record for an aggregate in a season. Even more amazingly he got eight hundreds whereas the previous record had been only five. Included in this run feast was a score of 353 against Karnataka, making Laxman the only Indian to get two triple hundreds in the Ranji Trophy. More than any other single factor, it was Laxman's batting that enabled Hyderabad to make the title round, where they lost to Mumbai – despite the customary Laxman hundred.

And of course for Laxman, the 2000-2001 season revolved around his monumental Eden Gardens knock. In batting ten and a half hours during which he hit a record 44 fours he surpassed Sunil Gavaskar's long-standing score of 236 not out, the highest individual score by an Indian in Tests. As Laxman put it, 'It was really thrilling to break a record created by a legend in world cricket. The 237th run was the most important run of the innings. It overshadowed all the shots that I played.' Dravid was the first to pay compliments to Laxman on his knock. 'I saw the 167 that he scored at Sydney. This innings even beats that. It was a fantastic effort and it also inspired me to perform well,' said Dravid, who also ended his lean patch by getting 180 and sharing a record 376-run fifth wicket partnership with Laxman. By his knock, Laxman not only finally made his place in the team certain, but also took over the number three slot from Dravid.

Whatever happened to his career now, it would be almost impossible for Laxman to top the Eden Gardens act. That was a once in a lifetime performance, something straight out of fiction. His 281 – suddenly a very famous statistic in Indian cricket – turned Laxman into a national hero, a cricketer of international renown.

In an interview, shortly after the series ended – in the final series deciding Test at Chennai, he played two vital knocks of 65 and 66 to star again in the team's two wicket victory – Laxman said he was not complacent, and added 'the recent success of mine is only a base on which I have to build my career'. Admitting that batting at his natural number three position made all the difference, Laxman said, 'I was not very comfortable while opening the innings. I always had the feeling that I was trying to do something which I'm not really made for.'

His confidence boosted by his tremendous showing in the Test series, Laxman finally came good in one-day matches too. He scored prolifically in the five matches, finishing with 281 runs at an average of 56.20 and this included his maiden century in limited overs cricket. Prior to this, Laxman had struggled in the one-dayers scoring just 86 runs from 13 matches. It was the final transformation for Laxman from the King of the Domestic Circuit to Indian cricket's Mr Dependable.

In a way, though, Laxman with that 281 had built his own prison. From here on expectations would be sky high every time he walked out to bat. He would get a double hundred – or at least a hundred – every innings. He was an artistic stroke player capable of constructing miracles. Obviously this was not on but Laxman was trapped by his own brilliance! And when he did not get another hundred in the next nine Tests against Zimbabwe, England and South Africa – in fact there were only two scores over the half century mark – the pens were dipped in venom. Thirties and forties however beautifully compiled were good enough for lesser mortals not for Laxman. Moreover, he was back to shuttling between number three and number six. Not that it bothered Laxman one bit. All he – the total team man – wanted to do was to contribute to the team's cause substantially. The pressure, however, started to tell and Laxman temperamentally strong, responded in the only way he knew – with the wand that was his bat. On the tour of the West Indies in 2002 he finally broke free of the shackles of high expectations. In the five Tests he tallied 474 runs at an average of 79 per visit to the crease. He had a match winning role at Port of Spain with 69 not out and 74 and finally recovered his habit of getting the big score at St John's when while getting 130 he shared a record seventh wicket partnership of 217 with Ajay Ratra. On the tour of England that followed he started off well with 43 not out and 74 in a losing cause at Lord's but thereafter was not really required what with Dravid-Tendulkar-Ganguly triumvirate in sparkling form.

Still with only three hundreds from 35 Tests at this stage there were question marks over his ability to have extended stays at the crease. He seemed happy to be playing the beautifully compiled thirties and forties when bigger and better things should have been his objective. To be candid, Laxman himself was not very pleased at the way his career was shaping even though by now he was a certainty in the side and very much part of the most feared batting line up in the world. Hearteningly though the gap between the big scores was now starting to narrow. His hundred in the West Indies came 16 innings after the epic 281. His fourth Test hundred also against West Indies at home in 2002-2003 came after 11 innings. And it was a knock even Laxman could be proud of. India 139 runs in arrears lost four wickets for 87 midway through the fourth afternoon. But this match was being played at Kolkata and Laxman was next. The Eden Gardens is one of the great Test venues and Laxman was always the man for the big stage. He joined Tendulkar and even though there was precious little batting to come after this went straightaway for his strokes. For too long had he been satisfied with cameos. So much so some critics were calling for him to be dropped. Laxman met the challenge headlong. He built one more Kolkata monument. The pair were together at close, they were still together at lunch on the final day by which time of course the match had been saved. Tendulkar was out for 176 after sharing a record 214 runs in

70 overs. But Laxman relentlessly – and charmingly – carried on and remained unconquered on 154 after batting nine hours. The same critics who howled for him to be axed now wrote in glowing terms of how much a mistake it would be for the team to play without the Very Very Special cricketer.

It is said that no cricketer's career is complete till he has suffered the ignominy of a pair. Laxman became a 'complete' cricketer by failing to trouble the scorers in the first Test at Wellington on the tour of New Zealand in the last days of 2002. It was a disastrous tour for the team for none of the batsmen really could handle the whirling conditions in Kiwi Land. Laxman's misery was compounded by his failures in the one-day series and by now there was a strident cry that whatever his capabilities in Test cricket he was not cut out for the shorter version of the game. Ultimately, Dinesh Mongia edged out Laxman for the final place in the World Cup squad. It was an omission that hit Laxman hard and only served to make him more determined to make a comeback.

But before that there was Test hundred number five which incidentally came up only six innings after his rescue act at Kolkata. The opponents were New Zealand, the venue Mohali and the situation was precarious. New Zealand led off with 630 for six declared and India seemed to be going well at 330 for three midway through the fourth afternoon. Laxman and Tendulkar had figured in a fourth wicket stand of 112 runs but the latter's dismissal at this juncture led to palpitations in the hearts of Indian cricket followers. Vettori and Tuffey got among the wickets, there were a couple of run outs and suddenly India dismissed for 424 were following on. Laxman, however, could not be dismissed and remained unbeaten with 104. It was already the fifth morning but Tuffey in an inspired spell had India reeling at 18 for three. Defeat stared openly at the home team and there was already talk of New Zealand winning a series in India for the first time. But the Kiwis still had to get the better of Laxman. Back he came to the crease and despite the grim situation batted with all the elegance at his command. The strokes were unfolded without any pressure, the timing and placement was immaculate and very soon New Zealand's hopes had gone up in smoke. Akash Chopra gave him excellent support and the two added 110 runs to guide India to safety. At final draw of stumps Laxman was again unconquered on 67. What would India do without him? This was the signal for Wisden to come up with the tribute related at the beginning of this chapter.

There are certain quaint equations in Indian cricket. One that comes immediately to mind is Sunil Gavaskar + Queen's Park Oval = century. A more recent one would certainly be V.V.S. Laxman + Australia = success. A brilliant hundred in a losing cause at Sydney in 2000. An epic knock at Kolkata in 2001. What would he achieve in 'Down Under' in 2003? Expectations were naturally high as the Indian team landed in Australia for a four Test series – and Laxman exceeded these expectations! He just loves the Australian pitches – and the Aussie bowlers. Adam Gilchrist for one has hailed Laxman's record as extraordinary: 'He comes out against us and brings out these special innings, one after another. And then he goes away, and we hear that he is sometimes not in the team. We have never been able to figure that out.'

Laxman started the series at Brisbane with a modest score of 75 – modest by his standards against Australia, though he himself has rated this innings very highly. This was only a prelude to two bigger achievements. At Adelaide he and Dravid put on an encore of their Kolkata stand, a partnership of 303 runs for the fifth wicket that lifted a struggling India – 85 for four in reply to Australia's 556 – to such an extent that they ended up winning the game by four wickets. Laxman's 148 was second only to Dravid's 233 in terms of value. But in stroke production the two matched each other. And he was not finished yet. At Sydney, some twenty days later, he was at his artistic best again. Blending substance with style Laxman stroked his way to 178. Again the numerical value of his innings was second to that of Tendulkar's 241 with whom he added 353 runs for the fourth wicket. But in stroke production he probably stole a march over the maestro. As Tendulkar himself put it while being effusive in his praise: 'When he played all those shots in the morning, I decided it was best just to watch and enjoy his batting, rather than trying to do what he was doing.' Yes certainly there are certain strokes that only Laxman can produce. At this stage four of his seven hundreds were against Australia and the lowest among these was 148. He also became the only Indian to figure in three 300-plus partnerships – need it be said all against Australia.

How did he explain his phenomenal success against Australia asked an interviewer? Trust Laxman to come up with a typical reply. A shrug of the shoulders, a shy smile and an answer so very inimitably Laxman-like: 'I don't really know.' Having dedicated his 167 to his uncle, Laxman was asked who the glorious 178 was in honour of. 'My parents who have always been a source of inspiration to me and Steve Waugh who has also inspired me during my career.' The modesty and unassuming nature of this soft-spoken team man is almost unreal. But there is nothing modest about his record and that is thoroughly real. Like his batting he is all grace off the field too. Indian cricket is blessed by the pristine art of Laxman as well as his gracious behaviour.

# Virender **Sehwag**

### Swashbuckling Superstar

From a Tendulkar clone to a superstar in his own right. That in a nutshell sums up the phenomenal rise of Virender Sehwag. Indeed he has reached a point where he readily gets the kind of adulation that Tendulkar commands, he has reached a stage where spectators throng the stadium to watch him perform as much as they come to see Tendulkar bat. Going a step further it may not be inaccurate to say that the transition period has already commenced and it is only a matter of time before the Sehwag fans outnumber the Tendulkar fans. Certainly he is as recognisable a face on TV these days both for his commercial viability as much as for his swashbuckling stroke play.

Indeed, to see Sehwag bat is a revelation. He gets away with the boldest of shots, the most brazen of strokes. He might have started off as a Tendulkar clone in the manner of his aggressive batting, his gait and his stance. But the similarities between the two are getting lesser with each passing day. Tendulkar is basically an orthodox player whose batting is built on specific scientific skills. Because of his extraordinary gifts, he is able to make some innovative strokes. Moreover, in the last couple of years there has been a palpable change in Tendulkar's approach. Without exactly becoming defensive in his approach he is a bit more selective in his strokeplay and is a touch more solid.

Sehwag's approach on the contrary continues to defy the scientific aspects on which batting is based. There are flaws in his technique, his footwork is not exactly a connoisseur's delight, he plays away from the body. All these are invitations to disaster if one goes by the coaching manual. In the chapter on Mushtaq Ali I related the story of the coach who pulled up the boy for faulty footwork even as the ball he hit had raced to the fence. One is not sure whether Sehwag's coach in his early days pulled him up for something so impudent. But he certainly qualifies for the Neville Cardus essay on 'when arts triumphs over science' which I had mentioned in the chapter on Mushtaq Ali. For someone who is artistically – and destructively – gifted as Sehwag, the coaching manual is just a book full of theory and nothing else. Sehwag authors his own book on the field of play.

Indeed Sehwag is a throwback to the buccaneering days of Mushtaq Ali and Srikkanth. The same adjectives that were used to describe the swashbuckling batting style of these two cricketers – dazzler, conjurer, cricket's Errol Flynn – can well be applied to Sehwag. But there is one very important difference – the figures associated with this kind of rip-roaring batting approach. Mushtaq Ali averaged 32 from his eleven Tests. Srikkanth averaged a trifle under 30 over 43 Tests. These statistics are not unusual. There is always an element of risk in the devil-may-care approach. The stays at the crease are explosive, electrifying, enthralling – and short. Both Mushtaq and Srikkanth had just two centuries. But here we have Sehwag who averages 51 and has eight hundreds from 31 matches. One of them is a near double hundred (195). Another is a triple hundred (309). You certainly don't associate such figures with cavalier, stand and deliver batsmen. You don't associate such figures with batsmen whose technique is faulty, whose footwork is all awry, and someone who plays away from the body.

The Indiana Jones of Indian cricket was born in the capital in 1978 and very soon earned the sobriquet 'Nawab of Najafgarh' – the west Delhi suburb from where he hailed. By 1998 he was a member of the Indian team for the World Youth Cup. And as a hard-hitting middle order batsman and a capable off spinner, Sehwag was given his international break first against Pakistan at Mohali in the Pepsi Cup in 1999. It was a disastrous debut, for after scoring only a single he was hammered for 35 runs in the three overs that he bowled. He was then shortlisted among the 19 probables for the 1999 World Cup in England but did not make the final squad.

At the start of the 1999-2000 season he was still more of a chancy big hitter. The rough edges had yet to be sharpened. But during the season he came up with a couple of innings that proved that Sehwag was more than just a mere slogger. First he hit 187 for Delhi against Punjab in a crucial Ranji Trophy game. The runs were made in the face of a Punjab total of 530 for seven declared and one admired the manner in which Sehwag stuck to the task in taking Delhi to within four runs of taking the lead. That did not mean that Sehwag was dawdling along; the runs were hit off just 175 deliveries. A fortnight later came another knock that brought him back into national reckoning. Playing for North Zone against South Zone in the Duleep Trophy at Agartala, Sehwag stroked his way to 274. Again he concentrated on building an innings but never got bogged down. He scored his runs out of a record fifth wicket partnership of 381 with Rajiv Nayyar – enough evidence of his dominance. Further evidence is the fact that he got the runs off 327 balls with 36 fours and four sixes.

With all this Sehwag still had to shake off the image of being good only for the one-day game at the international level thanks chiefly to his hectic hitting. And while he was not considered for any of the Test matches during the 1999-2000 and 2000-2001 seasons, the selectors brought him back to play for India in the ODI's against Australia in early 2001. Sehwag wasted little time in displaying his ubiquitous talents. In the first match at Bangalore he helped himself to an electrifying 58 giving the innings the necessary impetus after the Indians were floundering at 122 for four. Then, just when the Aussies were in the midst of a strong reply, Sehwag sent them scurrying for safety with three wickets in the middle order. He had Matthew Hayden and Steve Waugh leg before, and Damien Martyn caught behind. The Australians slumped from 174 for three to 212 for six and their challenge was effectively over. Sehwag deservedly won the man of the match award in India's 60-run victory but was forced to miss the rest of the series with a fractured finger.

Later the same year came the innings that really caught everyone's fancy and transformed Sehwag into a star overnight. The Coca Cola Cup tri series involved India, New Zealand and hosts Sri Lanka. Tendulkar was absent due to injury and various combinations were being tried out at the top of the order. Promoted to open the batting Sehwag hammered a 70-ball ton, marked by clean hitting that brought back memories of the great man himself. In the face of a challenging target of 265, India were home in the 46th over for the loss of only three wickets thanks in the main to Sehwag who hit exactly 100 out of 170 doing pretty much what he liked with a bowling line up that included Tuffey, Mills, Vettori, Nash and Harris. Sehwag was overjoyed more so when he received a congratulatory message from Tendulkar who said he had enjoyed watching his innings.

After this he had to be given a chance in the Test squad and he took little time in showing that he was ready for the longer version of the game too. A century on debut in South Africa during which he dominated a 160-run partnership with his mentor was the royal way the 'Nawab of Najafgarh' announced his arrival on the big stage.

It was on the tour of England in 2002 that the team management got the bright idea of pushing Sehwag to the opening slot in a bid to solve Indian cricket's perennial problem at the top of the order. After all he was a success as an opening batsman in limited overs cricket and it only remained to be seen whether his stand and deliver methods would come off in the longer version of the game. There was no way Sehwag was going to change his game whatever his position in the batting order. It did seem a bit of a gamble but the team management reckoned that if he failed he could always go down the order again. If on the other hand he succeeded in the manner of Srikkanth it would give the team a big psychological advantage. After all there is nothing a fast bowler hates more than to be taken to the cleaners right from the start – new ball and all.

The gamble paid off in spades. Matthew Hoggard, Andrew Flintoff and Simon Jones were taken totally unawares by the ambush that Sehwag laid out for them. He just sailed into them in the first Test at Lord's and smashed 84 out of 128. He improved this to 106 out of 179 in the second Test at Trent Bridge. The moving ball, the seaming conditions and the red cherry all meant nothing to Sehwag who just stood there and hammered anything and everything that came his way.

So quickly then one half of Indian's opening problems had been solved – and in the most appetising way.

If he could get away with his bulldozing tactics in England it was always on the cards that he would be a whopping success in India. And so it proved. In the first Test against the West Indies in October 2002 before a wildly appreciative Wankhede stadium crowd Sehwag simply tore into Dillon, Collins and Cuffy in rattling up 147 from 206 balls with the help of 24 fours and three sixes. Some of his strokes simply took one's breath away as he dominated a 201-run first wicket partnership with Sanjay Bangar (55) who could have been one of the many thousand spectators. Given his approach there would inevitably be the half chances but this did not stop Sehwag from going for his strokes and playing with refreshing freedom. The same was the case with Sehwag during his 130 against New Zealand at Mohali a year later. Even in the face of an imposing total – 630 for six declared – he batted with gay abandon dominating a first wicket stand of 164 with Akash Chopra (60) before being third out at 218.

All the while Sehwag continued to display his pyrotechnics in the shorter version of the game. However well he had adopted the same buccaneering methods into Test cricket there was never any doubt that basically his game was Heaven sent for the one-day game. In clouting the ball high, hard and handsomely, in his ability to hit sixes at will, in his total annihilation of the bowling he was, along with Adam Gilchrist, the most destructive batsman in ODI's. With an overall strike rate of over 94 Sehwag's very presence at the crease has been intimidating and his equitable temperament has driven bowlers to despair. His expressionless face as he carved the bowlers and their figures out of shape said it all. After hitting a boundary or a six he would just fidget about in the crease impatient for the bowler to send down the next delivery that he hoped to again hit out of sight. Sure, there was a time last year when nothing seemed to go right for him but the way the team members backed him underlined the high regard they have for his unique capabilities to put any attack to the sword. Heading the Sehwag fan club would be Sourav Ganguly. The Indian captain is known to back Sehwag to the hilt knowing fully well that he has a match winner on his hands.

While his lean patch is only a passing phase and it is only a matter of time before he resumes his piratical deeds Sehwag has not let his substandard form affect his batting in Tests. In fact, he has gone from strength to strength without sacrificing his swashbuckling style. His average has rocketted from the early forties to the early fifties. In the last year, in fact, he has struck a purple patch with a number of three figure knocks that have attracted international attention, made TV viewers run up to their sets to watch him bat and increase his fan clubs many times over.

First came his 195 at Melbourne. Not unexpectedly, he started off by dominating a first wicket partnership of 141 runs with Chopra (48), pushed Dravid (49) into the background during their second wicket stand of 137 before depositing an innocuous full toss from the occasional left arm wrist spin of Simon Katich to deep mid wicket. This was shortly before draw of stumps, he was five short of his double hundred but it never occurred for Sehwag to play for time. He was fourth out at 311 and his 233-ball knock included 25 fours and five sixes. Brett Lee and company were sure glad to see his back.

It was in December 2003 that Sehwag played that innings which constituted the highest number of runs made by an Indian in a day. And yet just three months later Sehwag broke his own record by stretching the figure to 228. The only difference was that he was still not dismissed. Yes, on the opening day of the first Test against Pakistan at Multan he simply went berserk. Shoaib Akhtar, Mohammed Sami, Shabbir Ahmed, Saqlain Mushtaq and Abdul Razzaq were all treated with absolute contempt and disdain. Long before the day was over they had raised the white flag of surrender. Only they did not know that Sehwag had not finished with them as yet. The next morning he simply carried on from where he had left off passing Sunil Gavaskar's 236 not out, then V.V.S. Laxman's 281 and then reaching his triple hundred – the first Indian to cross the landmark. Whoever would have thought that Sehwag with his adventurous style would have this distinction? Anything is possible with Sehwag around and he reached both the hundred and the triple hundred with sixes, the first off Akhtar and the second off Saqlain. Starting off by dominating a first wicket partnership of 160 with

Chopra (42) Sehwag then proceeded to share a 336-run third wicket partnership with Tendulkar. Perhaps 'shared' is not exactly the right word. Tendulkar outclassed by Sehwag's brilliance contributed only 130 to the stand, before the record wrecker was third out for 309 with the total 509. The 375-ball knock included 39 fours and six sixes – truly remarkable statistics. Tendulkar who seemed content to play a secondary role was full of praise for Sehwag's knock terming it as 'a fabulous innings'. Asked about the advice he gave him, Tendulkar laughingly said, 'He hears me but I don't know if he always listens to me. I told him it was a great opportunity for him to get a really big one. Very few guys in the world can manage with that sort of stroke play. I am just glad he plays for our team. He can be a nightmare to play against.'

At Lahore, Sehwag got a 90 in a losing cause and by the end of the tour there was little doubt that he was the most talked about Indian cricketer. For once even Tendulkar almost willingly took a back seat. Certainly Sehwag could not have picked a better time to tie the knot!

Anything after this could only be anticlimactic but not for Sehwag. He continued his merrymaking ways through 2004 and for audacity of stroke play his 155 against Australia at Chennai and his 164 against South Africa at Kanpur could hardly be bettered. At Chennai, he handled the formidable Aussie quartet of McGrath, Gillespie, Kasprowicz and Warne with panache. Figures are the best way to illustrate Sehwag's dominance and his 155 was hit out of 233 before he was sixth out. Twenty-one fours in an arc from third man to square leg marked the knock that enabled India to gain a handsome 141-run lead. At Kanpur he did pretty much what he liked with the bowling of Pollock and Ntini. He shared a 218-run first wicket stand with Gautam Gambhir – the second highest partnership for India after the world record 413 runs that Vinoo Mankad and Pankaj Roy put on against New Zealand at Madras in January 1956. Sehwag was second out at 294. For good measure he got an electrifying 88 in the second Test at Kolkata and proved that consistency and cavalier batsmanship can go hand in hand.

For all his brilliance Sehwag is still a primal talent but whose rough edges make him all the more appealing. He is a batsman after one's own heart for he produces match winning, crowd-pleasing knocks. A nonconformist, Sehwag is perhaps the most confounding batsman of his generation. He continues to bewilder bowlers and bewitch spectators. How on earth is a batsman who appears to be so fallible so consistent? The figures against his name certainly defy conventional logic. He is able to pull off the most incredible shots with a perpendicular bat in the manner of classical stroke players. In a way his approach may be outrageous but can one argue with success? And Sehwag and spectacular success have gone together for some time now. In his own way he has carved out some method in his marauding ways and one senses that underneath that cavalier spirit, that apparent casualness is steel and purpose, ambition and a hunger for success. The most encouraging aspect from the spectators' and the Indian viewpoint – if not exactly the bowlers' – is that the entertainment and the fireworks might have just begun.

# STATISTICAL SURVEY

| BATSMAN | TEST CAREER | | | |
|---|---|---|---|---|
| | Matches | Runs | Average | Centuries |
| C.K. Nayudu | 7 | 350 | 25.00 | – |
| Lala Amarnath | 24 | 878 | 24.38 | 1 |
| Vijay Merchant | 10 | 859 | 47.72 | 3 |
| Mushtaq Ali | 11 | 612 | 32.21 | 2 |
| Vijay Hazare | 30 | 2192 | 47.65 | 7 |
| Polly Umrigar | 59 | 3631 | 42.22 | 12 |
| Vijay Manjrekar | 55 | 3209 | 39.13 | 7 |
| Chandu Borde | 55 | 3061 | 35.59 | 5 |
| M.A.K. Pataudi | 46 | 2793 | 34.91 | 6 |
| G.R. Viswanath | 91 | 6080 | 41.93 | 14 |
| Mohinder Amarnath | 69 | 4378 | 42.50 | 11 |
| Sunil Gavaskar | 125 | 10,122 | 51.12 | 34 |
| Dilip Vengsarkar | 116 | 6868 | 42.13 | 17 |
| Navjot Singh Sidhu | 51 | 3202 | 42.13 | 9 |
| Mohammed Azharuddin | 99 | 6215 | 45.03 | 22 |
| Sachin Tendulkar | 123 | 10,134 | 57.25 | 34 |
| Sourav Ganguly | 82 | 4949 | 40.90 | 11 |
| Rahul Dravid | 89 | 7696 | 57.86 | 20 |
| V.V.S. Laxman | 64 | 3961 | 43.05 | 7 |
| Virender Sehwag | 34 | 3079 | 55.98 | 10 |

| BATSMAN | FIRST-CLASS CAREER | | |
|---|---|---|---|
| | Runs | Average | Centuries |
| C.K. Nayudu | 11,825 | 35.94 | 26 |
| Lala Amarnath | 10,426 | 41.38 | 31 |
| Vijay Merchant | 13,248 | 71.22 | 44 |
| Mushtaq Ali | 13,213 | 35.90 | 30 |
| Vijay Hazare | 18,621 | 58.19 | 60 |
| Polly Umrigar | 16,154 | 52.27 | 49 |
| Vijay Manjrekar | 12,832 | 49.92 | 38 |
| Chandu Borde | 12,805 | 40.91 | 30 |
| M.A.K. Pataudi | 15,425 | 33.67 | 33 |
| G.R. Viswanath | 17,970 | 40.93 | 44 |
| Mohinder Amarnath | 13,747 | 43.22 | 30 |
| Sunil Gavaskar | 25,834 | 51.46 | 81 |
| Dilip Vengsarkar | 17,868 | 52.86 | 55 |
| Navjot Singh Sidhu | 9571 | 44.31 | 27 |
| Mohammed Azharuddin | 15,855 | 51.98 | 54 |
| Sachin Tendulkar | 18,537 | 60.97 | 58 |
| Sourav Ganguly | 11,106 | 43.38 | 21 |
| Rahul Dravid | 16,219 | 57.31 | 45 |
| V.V.S. Laxman | 12,430 | 54.51 | 37 |
| Virender Sehwag | 7153 | 54.18 | 23 |